ISBN 978-1-330-35685-2
PIBN 10039193

Similar Books Are Available from
www.forgottenbooks.com

THE OLD SCHOOLMASTER

OR

FORTY-FIVE YEARS

WITH THE

GIRLS AND BOYS

BY

WILLIAM SMITH KNOWLTON

AUGUSTA, MAINE
BURLEIGH & FLYNT, Printers
1905

TO MY BEST BELOVED PUPIL,

MY DEAR WIFE,

WHO,

FOR TWO-SCORE YEARS HAS BEEN

THE PARTNER OF MY JOYS AND SORROWS,

THIS VOLUME

IS AFFECTIONATELY DEDICATED.

PREFACE

For a year or two I have had in mind to write a book something like the following pages, but no definite plan presented itself until last summer. I then sent circulars to many former pupils regarding the matter. The replies received set me to work. I thought when I commenced the work I could devote my whole time to it, but conditions compelled me to teach; hence the story of my experiences has been written nights after teaching school for six hours. A radical change in the material used has also been made. The conception first entertained was to make the book consist mostly of biographical sketches of former pupils. I made this idea known to my pupils, and the almost universal voice of all called for a change. The demand was for more about the "Old Master" and less about the boys. I yielded to the request though still thinking the change was a mistake. I wish to thank, with tears of gratitude filling my eyes, the "Boys and Girls" who have helped me in this labor and kindly encouraged me.

Foxcroft, May 1.

CONTENTS

Birthplace East Sangerville.

THE OLD SCHOOLMASTER

CHAPTER I.

CHILDHOOD.

I was born at East Sangerville, Maine, October 21st, 1839. My earliest recollection is an old clock that stood in the corner of the room where I slept in a trundle-bed. This bed was rolled out at night and served for a sleeping place for my brother and myself. In the morning it was pushed under the bed where father and mother slept. That trundle-bed had a history. There were fourteen children in all, and, although the house was large, with an ell on either side, yet it was always crowded, as my father boarded the men who worked in his mills.

The bed was about four feet long. Two boys always occupied that bed till their feet began to stick out over the footboard; then they graduated to a real bed in a large room where there were three beds. Sometimes the boy had to leave the trundle-bed before his feet touched the footboard; since the graduate from the cradle was obliged to make a place for the last new comer.

That bed now lies neglected in the attic. It finally fell into the hands of my brother Kendall. My brother and wife belong to the new century, and believe in allowing the foreigner to fill the schoolhouses and swell the Census Reports. So that poor old rheumatic trundle-bed was relegated to the darkness of the attic, where it grows old more gracefully than its former occupants do.

That old clock was very intimately connected with my child-hood days. I could see it as my mother bent over me to give the good-night kiss. It stands, as I write, in the hall, constantly reminding me of that dear mother with whom it was so long associated, though its hands, like hers, are folded at twelve and its voice, like her dear lips, is silent. The clock belonged to my maternal grandfather. It was an eight day clock, was very stately and dignified, always on time, like my mother. It reached from the floor to the ceiling. It once had a sort of head-dress or crown on its head, but this had been removed when once it stood in a low room. This gone, it had, as I thought, a kind of bald-headed look. In the other room was another tall clock that belonged to my paternal grandfather. This one had to be wound up every day. This was typical of my father. He wound himself up every morning for a busy day of hurry and bustle.

There was also a cupboard I could see from the bed. There were two doors. Behind one, I knew, were those precious china dishes that were used only when distinguished company came to tea. The other door enclosed a family medicine chest. I real-ized, as I gazed with a shudder, just what that door concealed from view. There was that nauseous castor oil; that detestable rhubard; those abominable salts; some peppermint and camphor. There were herbs there also; burdock leaves for the feet, when a cold had been contracted. I have often wondered since if that burdock plant did not illustrate pretty well some of our moral and physical antidotes of today. That plant was cultivated in those days for its curative properties. Today almost every farmer spends hours in trying to extirpate an obnoxious, useless weed.

Perhaps some of our social fads, so highly recommended by our professional quacks and learned theorists, may, in the future, stick simply because of their burrs, and not because of any real value.

When we had a cold in the head mother put burdock leaves on our feet, so some of these modern old ladies apply the "medicine of their advice" to points in the mental body politic farthest from the real trouble.

I could also see from my bed a small fireplace, and a cranky one too it was, and always smoked when the wind was in the northwest and, as that was the prevailing tendency of the wind, the smoking habit of that fireplace became chronic. I have since discovered that the smoking habit, once assumed, is a life-time habit. I suppose that chimney smoked to cure the effect of the cold north wind, and continued to try the medicine through length of days. So men, with the pertinacity of a senseless chimney, persist in a treatment of some imaginary trouble, hoping that before old age comes on, a complete cure can be accomplished.

Not long ago I slept in that same room. The clock is gone but the cupboard is there; the fireplace still smokes, but the trundle-bed is in the attic.

From the back windows of that room I could see a grove of lofty pines where afterwards my woody temple of worship was. My father's house was situated in the middle of a large plain, which was nearly encircled by a high ridge or horseback. The mill stream and pond subtended the arc on the other side. The house was a large, story and a half one with ells and there were long sheds and a big barn. The chimney of that house was four feet square and stands today a monument of the faithfulness of the artisan of ninety years ago.

Back of the house, at a distance of a quarter of a mile, there was a deep ravine between two parallel horsebacks. Through that valley flowed a small stream. On both sides of the ridges grew some lofty pines. Opposite the pines was a waterfall of some fifteen feet. I remember now the many happy hours I spent, sitting near that waterfall, hearing the noisy waters dash against the rocks, while the wind soughed through the branches of the somber pines.

There were a few tall spruce trees near by whose contralto tones coalesced with the high treble of the sharp toned birches and maples. The rhythm was complete. It was Nature's orchestra, attuned to my appreciative soul.

I had read about Niagara; but that cataract was to me a paper waterfall. Here was a real one that eclipsed Niagara a thousand fold. That torrent seemed so majestic; that defile so marvelous; those pine tops so near Heaven. I loved to go there and read the simple rhymes that delighted a rather precocious childhood.

This was my Paradise. Adam had his, but it was never more real to him than mine was to me. In my childhood days, my mind took on a religious and poetical coloring that seems now rather remarkable. I worshipped here and saw and heard God, speaking to me. The doxology of the majestic, solemn pines, the cooing of the pigeons which filled the tree-tops, the noisy chatter of the fearless squirrels, the reverberating notes of the waterfall, the happy voices of the many colored birds; all seemed to inspire me to lift up my voice in joyousness and praise. There was a cluster of violets close by and a few bunches of arbutus. In those flowers I saw God, a being so pure, so kind, so sweet and attractive that I could but worship him. And my God talked and walked with me, as with Adam, and sweet was that companionship, and many lessons sank deep into the soul in that, my Paradise. I resolved to be like the God I saw in my beloved Shekinah.

Those flowers were sacred, those squirrels God's choristers, those pines his temple. And I thought it would last; never dreamed the scene would change, or that I should; thought life would be one grand meandering through pleasant scenes, or sauntering through flowery meadows that ever were in bloom.

After I graduated from college I visited that well-remembered Eden, and did not recover my spirits for a month. Black berry bushes had overgrown the old familiar path, the ruthless hand of man had laid low those sacred pines, vandals had shot the squirrels, the pigeons had long since departed; the very brook had nearly dried up; the water, as it trickled over the well-worn rocks, seemed to lament its departed glory. I was saddened, discomforted, shocked. I could not worship there, could not dreamily muse and talk with my old friends, could realize one fact only—that my Eden was gone forever.

I have since learned, in revisiting the scenes of former activities, something sharper than briars have obstructed my pathway; that the temples of friendship, cemented for eternity, have crumbled to dust; that selfishness has slain every impulse to even remember.

There were also mills,—a shingle-mill, sawmill, and grist-mill. In those mills I learned to exercise and develop my muscle. There was no football in those days.

My father's name was Isaiah, and my mother's Lydia Pollard, Knowlton. The Captain Knowlton who fortified Charlestown Neck and fought so bravely at Bunker Hill was one of our ancestors. The first man killed in that battle was Luke Pollard, a great, great uncle of my mother.

The Pollard family was good stock, but have nearly all disappeared from this part of the State. W. T. Pollard, the efficient game warden, is a cousin. My father had many brothers and sisters, most of them settling in Sangerville, hence about a quarter of the people of the town are relatives. The Knowlton people in Sangerville were and are good folks. They are industrious, peaceable citizens, and are favorably regarded. There have been several teachers in the family—my nephews and nieces. George H. Knowlton was for many years a prominent superintendent of schools in Massachusetts.

There were fourteen children in my father's family. Nine of whom survive.

Whether or not any of my ancestors came over in the May flower I do not know. If they did, I must confess that many of their descendants have sadly departed from their theological views. The name has never been prominent in history. Some have, however, occupied eminent positions. The Rev. Ebenezer Knowlton was, at one time, a Congressman, and the Hon. Hosea Knowlton was an eminent Attorney-General of Massachusetts. No one has ever been hung, and none, to my knowledge, have served the State at Thomaston. My father was Captain in the Militia, and came near covering himself with glory, in the Aroostook War. Before he got there that famous command had been given:

"Run, Strickland, run! Fire, Stover, fire!"

He was Justice of the Peace and hence known far and near as "Squire." It was an office of some repute in those days. His father, Isaiah, and his mother, Jemima Johnson Knowlton, came to Sangerville from Framingham, Mass., when my father was seventeen years old. He felled the trees and cleared the farm on which he lived till he was nearly eighty years old. There was, on the falls of the Black Stream, a small grist-mill, when he came. This mill was run by a man by the name of Phineus Ames generally known as "King Ames." It was a very accommodating mill. It took care of itself mostly. Mr. Ames would pour into the hopper two bushels of corn and hoist the gate and go away to his farm. At noon he would put in another two bushels, which sufficed till night. At night he would put in four bushels, and that rickety old mill would rattle and bang and wheeze, and faithfully grind away till morning.

Father lived, for some time, in a log house. In 1815 he built the house in which I was born. He afterwards built and rebuilt shingle, saw and grist mills.

Sangerville was settled by five distinct classes. East Sangerville was mostly settled by Massachusetts people. They were a thrifty, hardworking people, who cleared up their farms, lived on them till their deaths and left them to their children. There are few spots in Maine where so many farms in one community have remained in the same unbroken line of possession. The Oakes, the Ponds, the Lanes, the Adams, the Watermans, who were the early settlers whose descendants are prominent citizens at this time.

East Sangerville has always been noted for the sobriety and progressiveness of the people, and the interest taken in education. General Jackson was never more firmly established in the principles of democracy than are those untrammeled voters.

Toward Dover came the Buckfield clan, consisting principally of Thompsons, with a few other families sandwiched in. Three Thompson brothers settled on the same road, on adjoining farms and lived there many years. This family became a prominent one in town and county. One of the farms still remains in the Thompson family, F. D. Thompson occupying the farm his father cleared.

The southern part of Sangerville was settled by people from New Hampshire. This was the religious part of the town. Hon. J. F. Sprague was born here. Sangerville Village grew up, like Topsy, with no particular parentage. There were some very characteristic men, however, among the early settlers.

The Carleton family was somewhat noted. Old Elder Oakes, the grandfather of Wm. P. Oakes, of Foxcroft, was a noted preacher and when he spoke in stentorian tones "Words of sequipedalian length and thundering sound" came forth and routed all the hosts of sin. His son William, known as "Colonel," was the father of a large family of boys, all of whom were men of more than ordinary ability. Elder Clark occupied a prominent position in the town. His son, William, died at middle age, but left a large family of boys and one girl. The boys nearly all became lawyers and each one distinguished himself.

Four served in the army during the Civil War. Two were Colonels and the others held positions of responsibility. They are nearly all dead now. Col. Charles A. Clark lives in Cedar Rapids, Mich., and is well known in the West and in Maine as of sterling worth and eminent ability.

The Hussey family was well known. I personally knew one of them. I slept with him one night after he had eaten a quarter of a custard pie, two boiled eggs, three poached eggs and a fried egg or two. He groaned, squirmed, and groaned and "gritted his teeth" all night long. He said, the next morning, that he had the nightmare and dreamed that he was Sinbad the Sailor, and had eaten a roc's egg.

The Carr family later became well known. One of the original settlers is still living, Moses Carr, over ninety years of age. He has always been a very busy man and has accumulated a large property. He helped build a church a few years ago and is a constant attendant.

Sangerville Village is now a large and flourishing one; has modern factories and other industries. The history of Sangerville is, on the whole, an interesting one. It is the best farming town in the county and has sent forth into the world some very bright men. "Brockway's Mills" was, in my boyhood, an enterprising place. There was a hotel, store, and blacksmith shop there and some lumber mills. Nearby the mills lived a very peculiar man by the name of Maxim. He was an undeveloped genius. He invented a machine which would turn out an oblong bowl, but some other reaped the reward. Mr. Maxim used to come to my father's mill to have his grain ground, and often Hiram would come with his father. I remember he was full of fun and a great boy to laugh. He is now Sir Hiram and lives in England but occasionally revisits the scenes of his boyhood. His history is so interesting that I have appended to this paper a more extended narrative.

Another boy whom I knew was born near by. His career is a noted one. With but a limited education, he started out in life to make his own way. He became a trader, and later, a speculator in real estate. But this did not satisfy him. He determined to educate himself by an extensive course of reading, with the result that he has become a master of classical English and has published books. Mr. S. has been thrice in the legislature and prominent in the political world. In the meantime he was admitted to the bar and has a lucrative practice. He is a member of the Maine Historical Society and is Notary Public and is now Referee in Bankruptcy.

He is well known to the political world as the Hon. J. F. Sprague. Should Mr. Sprague devote his whole time to literary matters, he would do honor to his native town.

The Thompson family was a prominent one. I have spoken of them before. Dr. E. A. Thompson, of Dover, is the son of James Thompson, one of the early settlers. The doctor is one of Dover's most prominent citizens. He has had an extensive practice and is still in practice as a consulting physician of wide reputation. Dr. Thompson has been one of the Council, and occupied other prominent political positions, is President of the Board of Trustees of Foxcroft Academy. Four years ago, he gave ten thousand dollars to found the Thompson Free Library. I know of no way in which a man can embalm his memory more certainly in the souls of men than by furnishing them with good books. Bacon says: "Reading makes a full man." No man can be an all-round educated person without extensive reading. The especial reason why one person is a ready speaker, a good conversationalist, a sound adviser and deep reasoner, lies in the one fact, he has read much and read good books.

But it is all important to know just what books to put into the hands of the young. I know of no better way of judging the influence of a book than for a teacher to read the book and then sit and think it over; call up the characters one by one and discover where his sympathy lies; to picture to himself the whole career of the chief characters and discover if the character is one that leaves an impression on the mind of the reader that sin is rewarded. Is vice made attractive, and virtue neglected? Does the book leave an impression that tells for purity, honesty, and a useful life?

No one would be so stupid as to take a child to an abattoir to teach refinement. Certainly we would shield the young from brutal sights and associations in actual life; so should the child be kept from brutal mental visions which degrade. But, it is urged, the young do see all these things in real life, then why not in books? In real life the moral goes with the deed that is objectionable. In books too often the sequel is not as well known. The suggestive is often worse than the blunt statement of facts. There are books that, on a casual reading appear all right; yet a careful perusal locates them among the objectionable.

There are but few objectionable words in "Don Juan," but the whole poem is fit for the fire only. A superintendent once objected to my pupils reading "Jane Eyre." I can see no objection to the book. A young lady reads the book and learns that wickedness is terribly punished; that virtue and decency can only bring peace and happiness. The reading of that book, in my opinion, would make every one better, and none the worse.

"The Scarlet Letter" is another book under ban with many teachers. I would put it into the hands of every young lady. The literary style of the book is worth everything. The book is interesting, and will compel a complete reading. It gives an admirable description of the social and religious conditions of those stern times.

Lastly—the moral impression left upon the mind is that sin, —however secret,—will be proclaimed from the housetop; that every deviation from moral rectitude engenders a punishment that is the more terrible as the crime is more repulsive. The book is full of the most minute details in every part that appertains to events of life, and especially in describing mental anguish and pain, but the crime is just alluded to. It is the specific details in questionable books that give offence.

I do not believe in giving to the young nothing but "namby-pamby" books. "The Bonny Brier Bush" will do nicely for the goody boy or girl who dies young. Feed their intellect on such breakfast food as that book for a year; the result would be debilitating in the extreme. The age does not demand young men who are good simply because they have not activity enough to lead them in devious pathways.

Many teachers object to Dickens. They think him coarse, rough, and vulgar; and advise their pupils to refrain from reading his books. I take issue immediately with such critics and advocate reading Dickens' works by all means. The first and obvious reason is that Dickens' characters are so interwoven into literature that a knowledge of his writings becomes indispensable to an accurate appreciation of other books. "Barkis is willing" will never cease to be quoted; "Like Oliver Twist" will be a simile for many years to come. A page of description and denunciation of brutality can portray no such appreciation as the simple name of "Squiers." I hesitate not to venture the statement that many an incipient Pecksniff has been driven shamefacedly from a chosen course in Pecksniffism by reading the portrayal of that airy impostor. Observation of any man shows very clearly that the man who would win the ladies' affection does as fresh and green things as the man in small-clothes did when he threw cucumbers over the wall to Mrs. Nickleby. How would the aspirant for political honors know how to close a letter to his constituents, if he did not have "Micawber" for a guide? Lots of men and women have been made better by becoming acquainted with Varden and wife, and Dolly—the charming, true-hearted, good-natured Dolly—every girl ought to know her.

Someone called Dickens' description of "Little Nell" and her death "bathos." Nothing can be farther from the truth. If that is bathos, then much of the writings of Washington Irving is unworthy of perusal. It seems to me that every word in that almost inspired description expresses the real emotion that a man with a human soul in his breast would feel in seeing and recording his emotions.

The description of the death of Paul Dombey is unrivaled, No writer has ever even approached the delineation of a character like Dombey's wife. Esther will never fade from human appreciation. I have seen the Cheeryble Brothers in actual life. Mr. Carker lives in every village. No writer ever described a repulsive murder with less unsightly exhibitions of the horrid as did Dickens in the death of Nancy. Mark Tapley has been a source of great enjoyment to me, and not only that, but many a dark hour when the tired brain and discouraged heart was almost ready to lay down the burden, the jolly Tapley has driven away the "blues" and brought back a fresh determination to still strive and hope. Sweet "Little Dorrit"—who does not love her and in loving become better? Tom, loving, trusting, Tom Finch. Every town needs just such a man and, if he cannot be found in actual life, then it is something to find the character delineated in books. Nor is Tom Finch an impossible character. I have met just such men. I could not wish all men to be such as he was, neither would the world be very comfortable if everybody was like Martin Chuzzlewit.

But books are as different as men. One man leads by his association to a higher and better life; while another injures everyone with whom he comes in contact. So with books—One moulds the taste in the right direction, gives true views of life, stimulates the ambition, and furnishes the mind with an immense fund of knowledge. Another book ruins the taste, vitiates the morals, and gives wrong conceptions of the duties of life. It is my opinion, formed by careful observation of young people, that there need be no cheap or bad book read. I fully believe, if a requisite amount of good reading be placed in the hands of the boy or girl while young, that a taste would be formed that would make it impossible for them to read a bad book.

I am aware there is a great diversity of opinion concerning books and what I might call a good book another might call bad. I lay down this rule that no book should be read that does not refine the taste. No one can afford to be made coarser than he is by nature.

There must be a good literary style about a book; or it should not be read, however much of good thought and fact there may be expressed within the covers. Every book should teach something, or it is not worth reading. I have been told that the author of "The God of Things" remarked that no definite aim actuated her in writing that book. But still, I can read between the lines, I think, a half-hidden advocacy of a certain condition.

There are books just to amuse. That is a necessary book for the tired brain-worker. The book may not contain an idea worth remembering, but still, it had an object and had accomplished it.

I have no doubt but that, should every woman in the land read "Great Expectations" there would be less termagants in the home. When a person sees a delineation of themselves in print and recognizes the likeness, it leads to reform and a change of life. Even an habitual scold would be disgusted with the performances of "Mrs. Joe."

There have been a few books written that should never become antiquated. "The Vicar of Wakefield" left an impression upon the literature of that day that still lives. The same is true of Dickens' works. Most books die young. All do which do not present to the reader a distinctive character. There is nothing in "David Harum" which will immortalize it except the one point—the presentation of an unique character, coarse though it be.

My boyhood was so uneventful that but little comment need be made. I know I was a quiet boy, and very shy. I liked some kinds of fun and sports and became an expert wrestler.

There was a maiden lady living on one corner of our farm who used to lecture us boys a good deal, and we liked to teaze her. One day we threw snow-balls down her chimney. She told father, and he said he would whip all four of us, in the morning. I remember lying awake a long time that night, wondering how he would do it: whether he would stand us all up in a row and go up and down the line and switch each as he passed by; or whether he would take one at a time, while the rest looked on and pitied the one in "actual commission;" or if he would use a shingle; and then I wondered if one shingle would last through; again I pictured the condition of each after the operation was completed. I felt sure I should cry the loudest.

But the shingle-mill broke down that morning, and father had to go to Bangor for repairs, and forgot all about it. I have ever felt grateful to the unknown workman who manufactured that defective saw. Wish I could feel that my misdeeds lead to such happy results to somebody.

I can remember that once, and once only, did I swear. Then I was chasing the sheep. I feel sure that no one ought to swear. But, if the Recording Angel does ever, with a tear, blot out the record of an oath, he will be especially gracious to a boy chasing sheep, or trying to make a calf drink milk. My mother heard me swear, and I was very much ashamed. To evade her I went to bed supperless that night; and received a severe punishment, alone with my conscience.

My uncle lived just across the mill stream. There were three girls in the family. One of these girls was a little younger than I. I used to go to school with those girls. That is, I ran along ahead of them, or capered along behind them as boys generally do. I used to be desperately in love with Emily, but was very careful not to let her know it. In those days there were large farm houses in which was one room without a carpet. The young people of East Sangerville would, in the winter time, meet at our house one week and dance till twelve; next week at Mr Pond's, and so on. All my brothers learned to dance. I never tried to do so. I guess, if my mother had danced I should have learned; but no desire, however strong, could have made me face a girl on the floor. I rather enjoyed sitting in the corner and watching them. I wonder if I was the last boy created who acted that way?

CHAPTER II.

When I was three years and seven months old I attended school for the first time. The schoolhouse was nearly a mile from my home. To get there we had to pass through a dark cedar swamp, full of death-dealing monsters, as I thought. My older brother and I started on that eventful morning for that old schoolhouse. We came, at last, to a post on which were two boards; on one was painted Dover, on the other Deacon D. I had never seen Dover, did not know whether it was a man or some other animal, or a house. Another board pointed up a road that had much grass in it, with wheel tracks on each side. That board told us that Deacon D. lived up that way.

I knew the Deacon. He once caught me sliding on Sunday and told me I would go to perdition if I didn't stop that. The Deacon was a nice old gentleman but he had some peculiar notions about how to preach the Gospel of Peace.

At one time there was a drought and my father's mill was the only one in the county that could grind wheat. As all the people raised the wheat that produced their flour, it is plain to see that the mill had to be kept going day and night and Sundays too. The good Deacon was passing by the mill one Sunday, on his way to church and heard the sound of the grinding. It vexed his righteous soul. He felt it his duty to remonstrate. He remembered that, in ancient times, the Sabbath-breaker was stoned. Just beyond the mill was a steep hill. The Deacon was withal a man of considerable discretion in executing rather rash resolves. So, unlike the strippling David, he selected a large stone and, having ascended the hill a little, he hurled it with mighty force against the mill.

It struck the mill upon the left flank and knocked off some shingles. Those shingles have never been replaced. The old mill shows today the disastrous effect of the Deacon's attempt to enforce muscular Christianity.

The Deacon was sectarian to a remarkable degree in his religious associations. The Congregationalist church held meetings in the Union Meeting house, when I was a small boy. When my maternal grandmother died, the funeral services were observed in that house and a Baptist clergyman officiated. On the following Sunday, as I stood near the door I noticed that the good Deacon hesitated a little and when Deacon F. asked him if he was not going in, he snarled out: "That house must be purified by brimstone before I want to enter it." I didn't know what he meant till mother told me that night.

It must be difficult for a young person of today to realize that such bigotry could have existed. But it did. The prejudices existing in the soul of people of one denomination against those of another were the most intense and undying possible; and the world wondered. But, if the world had carefully considered the conditions, it would have seen that "Such things must needs be."

If a man should act that way now, he would be thought insane. But the conditions are all changed now. At the present time as each one travels his own chosen road to Heaven he recognizes the fact that there are many other roads, more or less parallel to his, all tending toward the New Jerusalem and that they all finally converge into a common highway at the end of the "Covered Bridge." This makes us tolerant of each other's opinions. We think our road is the best and rather pity the other fellow, stumbling along through by-paths, while we tread the well-paved boulevard of an established thoroughfare, but we expect to find him by the storm-lashed Jordan's bank, and that we shall stand beside him by the still waters of the "Jasper Sea."

In the old days each one was sure he alone was right. This was almost imperative from the condition of things. There were so many that not only did not believe but were active in opposition; so whoever did believe in Christianity had to fight his way all along. Infidels had to be met and answered, unbelievers met and confounded, and scoffers put to shame. And as a man who comes home at night after a day's contest in the political or business world is poorly fitted to receive advice from his wife in those matters, so the old theologians, fresh from a fierce fight with Appolyon had little patience with an ally who used a different carbine and a longer sword. Christian truth was not so well established as now. It was comparatively new. Fifty years is quite a fraction of the 1900 years comprising the Christian Era.

I once heard a man preach who was one hundred years old. Nineteen men like that would carry the line back to that wonderful Preacher whom the world had awaited for four thousand years. Christianity has done wondrous things, notwithstanding the many errors it has committed. What it can do for the world has only been intimated. The Sermon on the Mount today furnishes the text for all pulpits and even deacons have yielded to the marvelous eloquence of that sublime sermon.

It was said, a few lines back, that the effect of that stone, thrown by the hand of the over-zealous Deacon, could be seen on the side of the mill at the present time. That was more than half a century ago, yet the effect is discernible, and sure am I that that indiscreet act of a rash advocate left impressions on human hearts that will live when that mill has crumbled to dust. One of the most telling proofs of the truths of Christianity is that it has survived the advocacy of some of its friends.

The schoolhouse where I learned my A B C's was a low, unpainted, ramshackle of a house. It was built on a small mound rising a little out of a frog pond, in the edge of a cedar swamp. I do not know why it was built there but suppose it was done on ethical and perhaps financial grounds. The town did not raise money to pay a music teacher, but the committee were bound to have music anyway, and have it they did. On every dark or rainy day at three o'clock those frogs would commence to sing sub-bass in such solemn and profound tones that the bad boy ceased sticking pins in the other fellow and stared in awe-struck wonder. Then the little frogs began to pipe up on the high notes which made the nervous little girl jump.

The discord was increased by the shrill voice of the teacher and the low mutterings of the bashful boys.

Nearby was a little brook where we got a supply of rather muddy water for laving and drinking purposes.

I attended school at that house for several terms. Every year the old building leaked worse and worse, and, at length, took a lurch toward the road and plainly showed that its usefulness was over. By a vote of the district a new house was to be built farther away from our house. Three years later a "Little Red Schoolhouse" was built and the old one turned into a sheep pen.

That old house is now gone. Thistles and burdocks now cover the spot. The wide-mouthed descendants of that outside choir still sing and that little brook still lazily passes along. The boys and the girls, where are they? Many are sleeping on the hillside a mile away; a few still live in the town, while many are in all parts of the land.

Nearly opposite the schoolhouse was a farm-house. The farmer was also a shoemaker. Here all the boys went to get their boots made and mended. The father of the shoemaker lived with him. The old fellow believed in witches and devils. I was there one day in winter when the old man was churning. The cream was cold and the butter would not come. The aged patriarch declared in solemn tones: "The Devil is in it." He heated the tongs red-hot and thrust them into the cream. "Hear him hiss" said the old Puritan. The butter came very soon, and the old man was confirmed in his superstition.

The Devil seems to be a kind of "scape goat" for a great many people. Some claim he tempts them when even his satanic majesty would hardly feel complimented by the least association with them. We also often blame him for the results which follow a lack of care on our part. It is much easier to blame an absent party than to face a visible one. It seems to me if a pair of red-hot tongs would drive the Devil out of men as well as cream that every town should have a pair of proper officers to apply them to those who are possessed with such spirits.

The position selected for the new house was as peculiar as the other. It was in one corner of as bleak a sheep pasture as the town of Sangerville possessed. The snow always drifted to the corner of the house on the south side, and higher still on the other sides. Across the road was a cow pasture, descending in precipitous abruptness; half-way down the hill was a spring from which an aqueduct ran. We used, in summer time, to eat our dinner here and sometimes put bread crumbs in the aqueduct, just to see if they would come out at the other end. This did not cause Mr. Thompson to love little boys very much.

A tall elm tree that looked very much as I have seen politicians after election, groaned and wailed every time the wind blew, stood a little east of the house; and close by the lugubrious elm grew a pugnacious maple tree. Every branch of that tree seemed to be in battle array. They did not, like most limbs, point gracefully upward, but proceeded right out straight, like pikes or bayonets. There were a few dead branches, from which the bark had fallen, bristling like spears.

Nearby the schoolhouse was a large orchard, owned by Mr. W. G. Thompson. Of course, we small boys visited that orchard every day and partook freely of the forbidden fruit, with the usual results. The first reader, sour apples, the colic, and essence of peppermint all were factors in my experience of those days.

In this new schoolhouse I enjoyed the ministrations of some very good, and a few very poor teachers. One incident of those days is indelibly stamped upon my memory, and from which a moral can be drawn. For some misdemeanor, I presume, the teacher, a grim, hollow-eyed woman, compelled me to sit beside the wall on an invisible stool, which, indeed, had no physical existence. I sat in that position for half an hour, suffering all the tortures of the ancient martyrs, while the class in grammar was reciting. Inseparably with the recitation of grammar were associated the horrors of that excruciating punishment. Whenever a teacher suggested to me that I ought to begin the study of Grammar, my legs would begin to ache with the most intense pain, from simple recollection. Whatever halting my reader discovers in the grammatical fluency of this book I beg will be ascribed to that unfortunate associating of grammar and aching muscles in the calf of the leg. So, for two years, I refused to study grammar.

The moral I draw is that there are many men and women in the world who like or dislike sentiments, propositions and relations—not because of anything inherent in them, but because of early associations. There is in my mind, at this late day, a teacher associated with almost every study I pursued when a boy.

A sour-faced Miss Green attempted to teach me long division. I disliked the teacher and hated long division. One day she kept me at that battle-scarred pine blackboard for a full hour, "bringing down," substracting, multiplying, putting next figure in the quotient,—till I cried for mercy, and was told that the teacher could do the same at ten with perfect ease.

I remember with great pleasure the first real teacher I ever had. For that venerable lady I have, to this day, the greatest respect and love. She taught me geography and history in such charming ways that I have ever had her pleasant smile before me whenever attempting to teach those lessons. I wish to express, at this time and in this book, a recognition of the deep obligation under which I have ever been to that teacher who first inspired within my soul a desire to become a scholar and teacher. It was so easy to study when she assigned the lessons. It seemed nice to become a teacher, if she could be imitated. To Mrs. Sarah Carter-Vaughan I owe more than to any one teacher, nay, than to all my early ones. Very few persons ever so perfectly satisfied every demand made by their positions in life and society as has Mrs. Vaughan. As a teacher, none was her superior,—as a business woman, no one is more implicitly trusted. Kind of heart, sympathetic in affection, interested in all things and persons around her, she does not grow old like most women. Every year seems to me to add some new grace to that dear teacher I loved so well more than fifty years ago. *"Redeat serus in coelum."*

That schoolhouse had a blackboard fastened to the wall by small ropes. That little seven by nine blackboard had a history which illustrates the difficulties every teacher meets who seeks to adopt new and better methods. Blackboards were unknown in the town, but one day, a new teacher was engaged, who wanted a blackboard. Everybody in the district laughed at the idea; every old lady said it was ridiculous and every old man objected to such extravagance. The committee opposed the idea and the agent derided, but the teacher, at length, prevailed and a carpenter was employed to build a blackboard. The teacher's plan was discarded. The carpenter thought he knew best how to build a blackboard, as he had built barns all his life, so he matched two wide pine boards and painted them with oil and lampblack. One board had a big knot in one corner, surrounded by streaks of pitch pine. When the room became hot that corner of the board would sweat, the same as we did. The carpenter, contrary to orders, persisted in varnishing that board. Vain were the protests of teacher. "I have painted floors all my days," said he, "and I always varnish them." Varnish it he did. The chalk would slide over that board and leave no more impression than the appeal of a tearful teacher to a mean, sullen scholar. Sandpaper had to be used every day. That Carpenter has been dead for forty years, but it took many sheets of sandpaper to rectify his mistake.

How many times have I had experiences similar to that in attempts to improve the schools where I have been employed. There is always, in every town, somebody ready to immortalize himself as a nuisance. The laws of the State of Maine recognize certain things as public nuisances; now, if that law could be so amended as to include educational obstructions in the garb of committee men and superintendents of schools a great benefit would be conferred upon the course of education. I have found men and women who once were efficient in those positions, but the position has progressed; they have not, and are hinderances, stumbling-blocks, active and passive in every attempt to promote progress. I have been asked to teach as I once taught, forty years ago. I have been criticized for methods of teaching the most approved by all educators simply because the critics had been so long dead in educational matters that any resurrection could not be even hoped for. Men there are who, because they had planned a very convenient carriage house or barn think they know all about the needs of a schoolhouse; because they know that potatoes are first planted, then hoed, then dug,—think they are fully qualified to invent a course of study for the development of the mind of a child; because they can run an engine, or make a martinhouse, with unpardonable pomposity assert that every part of the machinery appertaining to educational progress is fully understood by them.

That old red schoolhouse still stands on that bleak hillside. The paint has grown somewhat dim, the chimneys show the decrepitude of an old man in his weakness, the blackboard, cleft in twain, hangs from the wall by one end; the seat where I carved my initials in straggling hieroglyphics, shows the effect of forty years of service and the worse results of ten years of idleness. The groaning elm still moans disconsolately when the wind blows, and the unsightly maple thrusts its dead limbs threateningly toward every passerby; but no boys slide there now, no urchin steals Mr. Thompson's apples, no bread crumbs disturb the aqueduct. The red schoolhouse *fuit*. *Nos discipuli fuimus.* Where forty scholars once slid, played, and fought, the ungainly sheep now run and bleat, and the educa tional mudcart conveys the half-dozen juveniles, seeking knowledge, to another district.

When I was about thirteen, we were set off into the Corner District.

I attended that school for two or three years, and occasionally went two or three miles to attend some district school while our school was not in session. In fact, I never lost an opportunity to attend school. It must have been almost a craze with me. —Almost every night my mother had to send me to bed. That love for study has never left me, and I hope it never will. No pleasure has ever pleased me as those derived from intellectual pursuits, and I can discern no diminution whatever in this matter. I was, in my younger days, rather prococious in some studies, and just fair in others; always had a liking for mathe matics and rhetoric.

I was a very bashful boy and never appeared in public if I could help it. I have never quite overcome my reluctance to public services. I do not think one ever does. I have often envied the men who seemed to enjoy occupying public positions and exhibiting themselves on the stage. I have never been a fluent conversationalist, have always preferred to listen rather than speak. Perhaps some of my pupils will question the last statement.

I had become by this time a fair scholar in grammar and mathematics and began to think about attending Foxcroft Academy. I desired much to go but dreaded to commence. I have never met a more bashful boy than I was. Nothing but an irresistible desire for an education led me to present myself at that school.

CHAPTER III.

When a small boy the newspaper became my constant companion. I read it completely, advertisements and all, and thought the editor wrote it completely and must be a most extraordinary man. The Piscataquis Observer was the family paper. When ten years old I decided to become an editor.

We lived about three miles from Dover and Foxcroft villages. Those towns personified, in my youthful mind, the sum total of all that was typical of the great, bustling world. One day my father took me to the town to see th sights. I can recall, at this hour, the marvelous things I saw, the individuals I met and the impressions received. The first place we visited was the printing office. Father hauled a load of wood to pay for the Observer. Then, for the first time, I saw a real, living editor. The reverential awe that stole over me as I gazed upon the solemn features of G. V. Edes completely paralyzed my tongue, and caused me to whisper in low tones, as I enquired about the paraphernalia of the office. Mr. Edes was a tall, spare man, somewhat deaf, and spoke in loud tones. He was busily pulling a long lever backward and forward, and I discovered that it seemed hard work. That operation took away some of my desire to become an editor. The dingy little office did not seem just what was expected, and when I saw a compositor pull ing bits of unwashed metal from the mouth that had become, by association of the same color as the type, my desire grew fainter still, and when Mr. Edes informed my father that the

My F ther's Mills.

occupation was not a healthful one, the last desire vanished, and all the glorious achievements of Horace Greeley, that had so stimulated my soul, passed by like the Pharisee, on the other side.

The memory of G. V. Edes should not pass lightly from the remembrance of the citizens of Piscataquis county. He was not a learned man, but a thoroughly honest one. He faithfully did his duty and made his paper the best possible. With him the publishing of a paper was not simply a business enterprise. He felt that the editor of a paper occupied the position of a moral reformer, and that he ought always to be found on the right side of every social controversy. No doubtful advertisements appeared in his paper.—He never kept silent because silence paid. His influence upon the moral and political world around him was always good, and will never die. I suppose we must grant as true in general terms the statement I heard an editor make that men engaged in newspaper work just as in any other enterprise, for money making only, but the public do not so regard it, and certainly there must be a duty resting upon the editor that he cannot, in honor, escape.

My father also pointed out to me Deacon Mayo and Deacon Parsons of the Congregationalist church. They were both tall, spare men. I was not then well posted on deacons, so, in my childish mind, I drew the conclusion that a deacon in that church must be tall, very thin and stern-looking.

Father also informed me that a big, fat man, with a smile that enveloped his whole face, was Deacon Leonard Robinson, of the Baptist church; hence I became fully satisfied that all Baptist deacons were fat, and jolly, with a nasal twang in the voice. This conclusion was verified in a few moments when Mr. Buck, another Baptist deacon, came along and passed a joke or two with father.

By the way I came to know Deacon Buck very well when I taught at Foxcroft, and enjoyed his paternal advice very much.

There was in his makeup a keen appreciation of the finer attri
butes of the soul. I have always thought of him as the con
necting link between the past and the present. There was in
his soul the old puritanical conception of duty, rigid adherence
to recognized dogmas, and yet, the odors of a kindlier interpretation distilled from every exhortation he gave, and showed the
prophetic dawning of a Christian era more glorious, because
more Christ-like.

Afterward I became acquainted wth his family. Alfred,
late minister to Japan, was a dear friend to me and
"steered" me into the DKE fraternity at college. Addison and
I were friends to his death. I always enjoyed meeting a man
like him who had a kindly word and a warm hand for a fellow
mortal. There is lots of good blood in the Buck family.

I remember also that we, father and I, went into Sawyer
and Woodbury's store. Mr. Woodbury sold us some nails.
I thought Mr. Woodbury the politest man I had ever seen.
He said some nice things to me, and, in fact, the first kinds words
a stranger had ever before said. Boys of ten or twelve are not
the recipients of many lauditory remarks, as a rule.

I learned to love Mr. Woodbury when a grown-up boy, I
saw him very frequently. He did many kind things for me
when I was teaching at Dover and Froxcroft. I always felt
that a visit to Dover was never complete without a half hour's
chat with C. A. B. Woodbury. The last time I preached at
Dover, Mr. Woodbury came to hear me, and said some very
kind things about the sermon. Dover has never been the same
since that kindly, lovable man passed to his reward.

In every town there are two especial treasure houses where
are recorded the facts that men have lived and died. The one
is the living memory of immortal souls; the other is a costly cen-
tograph, covered with snow half of the year, and moss the rest,
vainly seeking to make the dying, the perishable, immortal, and
forever honored.

I also saw Squire Holmes on that trip to Dover. He was the first lawyer I ever saw. His hair and whiskers were very long and white; so the conclusion was reached that lawyers were never barefaced. I have seen many legal gentlemen since, and the bare-faced cheek of some was rather striking.

Father called to see "Old Cat" Chamberlain to get him to repair the mill. Mr. Chamberlain was a distinctive character. He spoke with a nasal drawl that no one could imitate, and emphasized every remark with a sort of prod of his long, stiff, middle finger, which he waved to and fro, sweeping away all adverse argument. His face, as I remember it, was wrinkled to a remarkable degree; his eyes were rather deep-set and twinkled just a bit when he said some sarcastic things about the peculiarities of other men. I never saw him smile. Once in a while, the wrinkles on each side of his eyes would begin to curl up a bit at the outer ends, promising a smile, but immediately a counter current would set in, and every line would disappear, just as waves do on the lake when winds blow crosswise. Then the old wrinkles would reappear, and the eyes would twinkle anew with the same critical scrutiny.

The peculiar sayings of this old-time philosopher were many and original. He occasionally practiced law in a small way, in a manner peculiarly his own. On one occasion a lot of sheep disappeared, and their heads were found in a flour barrel in the barn of a certain man. The man was arrested and tried for larceny. Lawyer Holmes, in conducting the defense, said the sheep were not stolen, but had strayed away, as was common in the spring. Mr. Chamberlain in reply said: "Yes, I know sheep dew stray this time of year but they don't usually leave their heads in flour barrels in the haymow."

He went to Guilford to settle a case with the selectmen, but failed and gave this report: "Mr. A. will do nothing wrong, if he knows it; Mr. B. will do nothing at all, if he knows it; and Mr. C. will do nothing right, if he knows it."

On one occasion when the waiter at the table did not refill his cup as quickly as he wished, he threw it into the fire-place, remarking, "I have no further use for you."

It is only pioneer life that develops eccentric characters. They disappear as the attrition of the daily contact with a bustling world rounds off the sharp corners.—They are still found in newer places, and have a distinct individuality.

CHAPTER IV.

I commenced to attend Foxcroft Academy in 1857, and continued till the spring of sixty. Mr. Davis was the first teacher, and S. C. Belcher the last. In those days the country boy had to get "acquainted" with the village boy before he could enjoy life. The first week was not a Millenium dawn to me, and when Friday night came, I had nearly decided to resign, but when Monday morning came a new idea struck me. I resolved to assume the offensive. The change of base was a success. Within fifteen minutes I had humbled the minister's hopeful son, nearly broken the neck of the lawyer's boy and walked into the good graces of the school at a two-minute gait.

Mr. Belcher was a very stern, exacting teacher; but if Maine ever had a better teacher of Latin and Greek, I have never seen him. Every lesson must be thoroughly mastered and readily recited. When I left Foxcroft Academy, I could commence with the first paragraph in Andrew & Stoddard's Latin Grammar and recite it to the finis, exceptions and all. I always fall back upon that old grammar, if in doubt about any peculiar construction. Every word in the text was parsed and rules given. It is the only way to teach Latin. There is no "short course" in Latin; it is only a part of a course. "Caesar Read in Six Weeks" is the title of a book in my library. The idea is ridiculous, and the experiment a sad failure.

I wish to explain here the manner in which Latin should be taught. The first book used should be one of the modern

Latin books arranged for the first year. Collier's is a good one.
There is only one objection worthy of note. The daily vocabu-
laries are too long. There should be about six or seven new
words learned each day. At the end of the first year, the student should have a complete knowledge of all declensions of
nouns and pronouns, conjugation of verbs, and the general rules
of syntax.

Caesar and the regulation grammar should occupy the attention of the pupil the second year. The whole attention of pupil
and teacher should be devoted to the solving of the construction
of the Latin language. If the forms are not familiar, they
should be made so at once, then the syntax ought to be most
rigidly scrutinized, and finally, every phase of the subjunctive
should be understood. I do not think that the literary merit
of the text should receive much attention. Many text books
and teachers make a mistake in this matter. The whole attention should be given to construction, forms, and rules. If the
attention is diverted to other matters, good work will not be
done where it should be.

The last half of the spring term may, with profit, be devoted
to Ovid, as a substitute for Caesar. When the pupil has completed the course indicated, he will be prepared to read Cicero
with profit and pleasure. Now is the time to study the literature of the Latin language. The metaphors, similes, compari-
sons and other beauties of the language should be noted and
enjoyed. The same idea should prevail in the reading of Virgil,
but still a few moments each day should be given to syntax and
the discussion of poetic construction, but the Latin language as
a whole should be taught.

Of course, prose composition should be taught all through
the four years, and at the close of the course, three or four weeks
should be devoted to composition alone. This should be done
in a systematic way, but should be very general, and continued
until the student is able to write any statement in Latin with
accuracy and readiness.

There should be a very thorough training of every student in Latin who proposes to enter college; because the amount of time devoted to Latin in college is short. If a boy enters col lege with an inadequate knowledge of Latin, he will certainly come out with imperfect knowledge of it. He certainly will not be fitted to teach it, and I hold this to be true that the teacher who has not the proper knowledge of Latin, is a sinner for whom no repentance is recognized. And if that student does not design to teach, he has lost the benefits resulting from a knowledge of the language, because he never can appreciate the beauty of the literature of the language, and the discipline the study engenders has never been received.

I am every day expecting to read in some paper that Latin will be dropped and some milk and water affair substituted. I hope not, but would rather, if Greek is to entirely disappear, that more time should be devoted to the Latin.

Greek is passing out, and it seems to me that the deathknell that tolls the passing of that sublime language, rings in a culture as far inferior to that as is a French novel to the unsurpassed poems of Homer. A people who invented the most beautiful architecture that ever existed, whose lines of beauty are unsurpassed, whose literature has been recognized for more than two thousand years as the model of all that can charm, instruct and adorn, should not in this age of progress be discarded without the concensus of opinion of those qualified to judge.

If the Greek scholars of this country in convention should, after due deliberation, decide to discard Greek, because it is no longer conducive to scholarship and culture, then will be the proper time to substitute French for Greek. The pupils should never dictate a college curriculum. That college that cannot live without catering to the claims of those whose judgments are too immature to be of value, had better write *hic jacit* on the campus gate. If a knowledge of Greek literature does not refine the literary taste, does not cultivate the sublimest imagination, does not give a style obtainable in no other way, does not infuse into the very soul the living fire that burned on the altar of Minerva, then let Greek be dropped. But if it is to be excluded because it is too hard for the carpet-knight pupil of these days, because it takes the time that practical studies need, then let classical colleges be converted into schools of technology at once. French can never be of any practical use to the ordinary college graduate. If Greek is to be dropped, better leave the space once devoted to Greek in the catalogue, a complete blank adorned with an ancient urn closed and sealed. Let not the ashes of Homer be rudely violated by the chattering of any unpoetic modern.

As long as the Christian religion remains in the world as the only power or influence that can lift humanity from the slough of ignorance and barbarism that today engulfs all non-Christian people, so long should Greek be read and taught, it seems to me. I can never disconnect the Greek from the religion of Christ. The rise and development of the Greek language was, I believe, a part of the new dispensation. There was a people of the same general parentage of all Europe. No historian can classify the influences that developed those simple men into the most refined people of the world. I have no doubt whatever but those people were as much commissioned to become factors in propagating the coming religion as Abraham was when God sent him forth to Paran's wilds.

God inspired this people to love the beautiful, the symmetrical, the good, and the true. When the mind had been thus trained, it began to express itself in language fitted to the object that had absorbed that mind; and thus came forth the Greek language. By means of that language, the most accurate one ever spoken, were recorded the words and acts of the most beautiful character ever on earth. No language could do that perfectly except a God-ordained one.

When those words and deeds of Christ and the disciples had been once recorded, then it came to pass that the Greeks ceased to become a peculiar people. They fell back among the nations, to their natural level and began to speak a language in keeping with their mental and moral condition. These people ceased to speak the ancient Greek. That became a "dead language," and in that statement lies an important fact. A dead language never changes, never deteriorates. Hence that record mentioned can never become corrupted.

This consideration makes the language a sacred one to me. Now from this point of view, and from that before mentioned, a conclusion comes that the world cannot afford to lose the influence of the Greek language.

Many think that a further knowledge of the Latin will compensate for the loss of Greek. This idea is erroneous. "From the Greeks, and not from the Romans, we derive all that is beautiful in architecture." The Roman personality gives its own influence, a grand one; but Rome can teach its own lesson alone. But still there would be something lacking, an indispensable something that nothing else but Greek can supply. Macaulay was right when he declared that the influence of Athens would be in its immortal youth when London had passed to nameless ruin.

Among the pupils at Foxcroft were several who are before the public at the present time. There was a slim, tallish girl, attending who wore in her hat a small flag with Fremont's name on it. She was quite young, but active in all public matters; would talk politics, temperance or religion with the older ones, and was a great favorite with the young men. She lived in a pretty house a mile or so out of the village, surrounded by pines and other trees. We knew her as Marilla Ames, and millions know her today, in America and Europe, as Mrs. L. M. N. Stevens. I have had the pleasure of meeting Mrs. Stevens several times within the past few years, and have listened to her eloquence with great pleasure. Se is not only a fine speaker, but a keen business woman; and is doing a grand work for humanity.

There can be no question about the influence exerted by the organization she represents. Many a young man and innumerable young women have received the first impulse to become useful from the ministrations of the leaders in that order. Mrs. Stevens certainly shows that a woman can, with no adventitious aid, accomplish a great work among men. The doors through which females may pass to fields of usefulness and independence are wide open today. No young lady need feel obliged to marry who has a particle of independence. Of course, there are many who can never excel; but even this ought not to discourage them, for only a small per cent of men succeed. The rest must be content to occupy unknown places in the world. Many women do become prominent, and these are not the exceptions. They strike the average attained by men and ought to be satisfied with that.

Uriah and C. C. Lee were among the first boys I came to know. C. C. Lee has been a teacher for many years. Lyman K. Lee, late principal of Foxcroft Academy, is his son.

H. O. Pratt and Evans S. Pillsbury were among the students who showed that they possessed more than common abil ity. Mr. Pratt was for two terms representative to Congress from Iowa; and Mr. Pillsbury is district judge in California. J. F. Robinson of Bangor, was a sure prophet, even then, of what he has since become. S. O. Brown was the best declaimer in the school and a fine all-round scholar. Mr. Brown should have been a literary man. He would have been eminent, I am certain. He has been a success as a business man, but he might have been more than that. It would be but natural for a man of my habits and pursuits to put a premium on intellectual achievements. Recognizing that only one man in a score or more has the natural ability adequate to guarantee success in purely intellectual lines, I feel that the world has lost something when business absorbs the attention of one who possesses that ability.

Col. Charles Clark was a fine scholar and showed in those days, some rare fighting qualities. I remember a very pretty girl whose name was Annie Kimball. She had her lessons perfectly prepared and was very smart, but she did like to teaze Mr. Belcher and sometimes adorned the front seat at his suggestion. Sarah Bailey, perhaps the most intellectual young lady I ever met, was a student of Foxcroft Academy at that time. L. H. Whittier of Guilford, recalls himself to my memory as a quiet, industrious student attending strictly to business. I remember a very pretty girl in the Latin class by the name of Lydia Brown. She attracted my attention very much. I suppose it was on account of the fact that my mother's name was Lydia. Higgins, all the old boys will remember as the janitor, who rang the bell and built the fires.

One day Mr. Belcher said: "Higgins, increase the caloric." Higgins stood up and looked wildly around the room. Mr. Belcher repeated the request. Higgins scratched his head and rolled up his eyes, and said: "Sir?" twice. Mr. B. then said: "Replenish the fire." Higgins' face became a panorama of swift moving pictures for the next moment, at length, grasping the situation he rushed to the stove and put in some wood.

One day the boys, at recess, tied Higgins to the bell rope and went in and left him. Mr. Belcher went out at last, and rescued the boy. Higgins would not tell who did it, and we did not volunteer any information.

We use to play football but after a fashion of our own. Two boys chose sides and then the captains stood out in front, facing each other; then the ball was tossed into the air and the fun commenced, one side kicking the ball in one direction, the rest in the opposite direction. No one was allowed to touch the ball with the hand after the first rush. One day Mr. Belcher was the captain opposed to me and, as I was rushing the ball along toward our goal, he got on my back to stop me; I felt a slight incumbrance detaining me, but kept right on and kicked the ball home. I weighed one hundred and seventy and he about a hundred and ten. The boys called me "Atlas" for a time, as I had carried a world (of knowledge) on my shoulders.

Elijah Pond, Frank Parsons and I hired a room and boarded ourselves, and attended school. I remember the difficulty I had, the first morning, to make the sheets fit the bedstead; after several attempts I discovered that I had got them on cross-wise. Frank settled the coffee with half a pound of codfish skin. I made some toast by stewing some soft bread in milk for half an hour. We improved later on.

W. T. Stubbs was a very busy student and always had his lessons. He was also a good debater. I am sure Mr. Stubbs would have made a successful literary or professional man had he thus devoted himself. He has been one of the trustees of Foxcroft Academy for some years. Mr. Stubbs was a very successful teacher in the West for many years. It was a loss to the educational world when he retired from the schoolroom.

Alonzo Bunker was a very brilliant student. He graduated at Waterville College and became a missionary in India. Dr. Bunker is now in America. He was very effective in his work and is highly esteemed by a host of friends. I had the pleasure of eating turkey in his room at college when I was a freshman. His wicked chum, I suppose, furnished the turkey.

J. H. Wing was a very breezy young man who was a great beau among the ladies. He took Horace Greeley's advice and went West. The Averill young ladies were very fine scholars. Miss Annie Averill has written poetry that places her among the inspired. Miss Mary Averill has been connected with schools for many years.

I visited her school, when supervisor, and found the school a model. The quiet, lady-like ways of the teacher, the scientific methods of instruction; the thoroughness of the work, all made the schoolroom into a home where all were happy. I do not wonder that scholars sometimes do not like to attend school.

But a boy or girl that would loiter on his way to Miss Averill's school must be callous to all good influence.

The school had among its students, one A. B. Stickney—a tall, active young man who took great delight in theatricals. Mr. Stickney is now a very wealthy railroad president out West, and the husband of an admirable wife who once lived in Dexter, and was a pupil of mine.

Among the sweet faces of the young ladies I thought Miss Mary J. Thompson's was the sweetest. I was not then acquainted with her, but admired from a distance. Among the other young ladies was one Louise Campbell, a beautiful girl with glorious eyes. She became, later on, an active worker in the field of temperance and an advocate of Woman's Rights. She was much older than I, but I thought her sublime, wonderful, almost angelic. One night, after Lyceum, she asked me if she could ride home with me. I had to drive nearly four miles, the road passing by her father's house. Of course I consented, with stammering tongue and blushing cheeks. I never expected to attain to such happiness. I did not dare to help her into the wagon, but held the horse by the bits while she nimbly stepped into the carriage.

We started. She was very gracious, but the bare thought that I was seated beside that beautiful, talented woman so paralyzed me that my "right hand forgot its cunning" and could hardly guide the horse, and my "tongue cleaved to the roof of my mouth." I remember today every rod of that drive; what she said going up the Hines' Hill; how she talked about Venus, slowly descending in the west; what she said about Mr. Spaulding's dooryard; and her impressions of Mr. Hill,—how slowly I drove that last mile, and when we arrived at her home, I got out of the wagon and helped her down and drove the horse the rest of the way with the other hand. That woman never knew that she, that night, "Raised a mortal to the skies;" but I felt sure my old horse "drew an angel" home. As I looked upon

Venus last night I again could see the glorious eyes of that rare young lady.

Among the pupils was a black-eyed miss hailing from Brownville. Her name was Lizzie Nason. She became a teacher and taught for many years in Brownville. I suppose there is not a man forty years of age in Brownville today who cannot remember receiving at least one flogging administered by the vigorous hand of Lizzie.

I visited her school several times and always found the strictest discipline. Her methods of teaching were good and progressive. Miss Nason now lives in the West.

There was also a young lady from Brownville who had shot a bear and hence became a heroine among the boys but I noticed that she could throw a baseball no better than a village maiden. Some of the timid boys who lived on the street where she boarded used to walk home with her to be sure of a safe escort.

From Sebec came a black-eyed boy whom I much enjoyed. His name was Cushing, Wainwright Cushing. He was a gentleman when a boy and has become one of our best known and highly respected citizens.

CHAPTER V.

FIRST SCHOOL.

My first teaching occurred in the town of Sangerville. It was in my own district. The schoolhouse was old, cold, and small. The floor slanted upward towards the back seats, where the big boys and girls sat. The aisles were always slippery When the scholars came in at recess and passed up the aisles one or two were sure to slip down, precipitating several more into a common mass, from which heads, arms, and feet protruded. This caused some confusion at first but soon it seemed a part of the program, and ceased to cause any merriment.

There were sixty pupils crowded into a space where thirty would have been sufficient. In one corner of the room there was a kind of box stall or throne, somewhat elevated from the common floor. Here the teacher sat in all his glory when he was "monarch of all he surveyed," and it became his place of refuge when storms lowered around him. That desk was rather sacred even to the bad boy. In it usually were the teacher's books, some pieces of white chalk just as they came from the earth; some bottles of ink, pens, writing books and sometimes a ferule and withe. This desk also became a prison house for roguish boys and giggling girls.

The stove and funnel were divorced once a week regularly. The door was a marvel. There were four panels. No one of these was like any other. One was taken from a blue door, one from a yellow one, and another from a red one, and the last one put in was green. It seemed that almost every old house in the district had contributed some part of itself to patch up that old schoolhouse.

There was a long back seat in the rear, on which sat a lot of large girls. I was very bashful, and the roguish girls liked to tease me. They would ask me to assist them in arithmetic, and when I sat down, they would sit up close beside me just to make me blush.

I suffered much that winter in this way, but toward the close of school began to realize "blessed are the martyrs."

There was a board running across the house, separating the boys from the girls; on one side, perpendicular to the board, was a seat occupied by a girl, and on the opposite side sat a boy. One day I caught my brother kissing a girl across that board. My first thought was to punish him severely, but when I considered that he was much larger than I, discretion suggested that no precipitate act should transpire. It is strange how our moral perceptions are biased by conditions. I also took into account the temptation. She was very pretty and those laughing eyes always seemed to dare one to do desperate things. Those lips I had often thought were just made to kiss. The more I looked at her that afternoon the less wicked my brother seemed, and by the time school closed, I did not think him a bad boy at all, and so let him off with a mild reproof. Teachers, remember he was larger than I, and she was pretty.

The agent's name was Edward Oakes. There were agents in those days. Perhaps the present system is better, but, in one respect it seems to fail. No one agent could have so many relations as three committeemen and a superintendent.

Mr. Oakes was one of those very useful men in any community. He never married. He used to beau the girls of his own age around till they got married, then he dropped back to the next product and did his duty to those. When these passed on, he was still in the field. By this time he was recognized as a confirmed bachelor, and hence was always sought after, so life became to him an every-day picnic. He never seemed old, and was everybody's friend.

Dr. Simeon Mudgett was supervisor. I have his certificate before me. It says that "William S. Knowlton is a young man of good moral character, fitted by disposition to govern, and capable of teaching the branches taught in common schools, especially Arithmetic, Geography, Grammar, Reading and Spelling." It does not mention writing.

I received seventeen dollars per month and boarded myself. The school was fifteen weeks long. Several of the scholars were older than I. There were higher algebra, the national arithmetic, and almost every study in vogue in that school. I never worked harder in the schoolroom. I think the school was fairly profitable, as schools then went. That old house is gone and two houses have been built since.

I can see, in memory's reproducing mirror, just how those scholars looked, and how I taught. The small girls all stood up in a row in the floor, toeing a large crack which runs completely across the room. The girls all wore short dresses, and pantalettes with frills round the bottom. The frills were starched stiff and projected downward at an angle of ninety degrees, and reached down to the tops of the boots.

Some of the older girls wore hoops. Those were made of the same material as baskets were—brown ash—and sewed into the skirt. Crinoline had not made its appearance yet. A young lady then occupied a large portion of space, and when two happened to meet in the narrow aisle there was always trouble to discover who had the right of way.

My second school was in Dover, on the road to Dexter. It was a small, ungraded school. More than half of the pupils bore the name of Mitchell and Stanchfield. The Mitchell children were all very bright and industrious. There was one little boy in school who especially attracted my attention. He had a way of spelling every word with a rising inflection, thus: d-o-G, and he has been a rising man ever since he started in business.

4

His business powers are wonderful. He can make the wildest Western bronco into the mildest family horse in two hours—on paper. He is one of Caribou's town fathers now.

While teaching that school, I saw the great comet of '58, for the first time while riding one night with my oldest pupil. We discussed it together. It made a deep impresson upon my mind. I never think of that comet without remembering that girl. Ah, well! the comet came and went, and never returned to my gaze, and so did the girl. It seems the orbit of both were parabolic.

There was a cat where I boarded that weighed fourteen pounds, and ate cheese. These were the chief events of that term of school, as I remember them. It was an uneventful term and most of the pupils have joined "the silent majority." The schoolhouse is still there, but only one man lives in the district that did in those days.

I remember I took turns with the boys, building fires. I also remember there was a schoolhouse minister in the district who used to preach occasionally. He would stand in the floor and, with his long right hand, paddle himself round and round, so that he was back to the audience about half the time. He had a way of ending up every sentence with an "ur." One night he said "I have lived forty years on the Lord's sidur." The good old man tried to do his duty, but I think he could handle a plough better than he could the Scripture.

I suppose it is a grave question whether or not a censor should be put upon the pulpit, as well as upon the press. Perhaps, since there are all kinds of hearers, there should be all kinds of preachers, but it appears, in a casual survey of the situation that, if a druggist has to study four years to learn how to supplement the knowledge of a doctor, who has studied four years, and a lawyer must study four or five years just to learn how to manage our financial affairs, that a clergyman who has the highest concerns of the human soul committed to his care, should devote himself to an equal educational preparation.

My next school was in Abbot. This was a large graded school. War now threatened to destroy the peace of the coun try. No young person in these days can understand the condi tion of things in those days. Old friends became bitterest enemies; brothers ceased to recognize their mother's sons; societies were severed, and even churches dissolved. I boarded by chance with an intense Democrat. The Republicans of the village insisted that I should change my boarding place. This I refused to do without cause, and for a few days, there was much excitement. At length the excitement began to flag, and finally ceased altogether.

There were some fine scholars in that school. I remember a girl about thirteen or fourteen years old. Every lesson was perfect, and her reasoning faculty remarkable. In later life, she became just what she promised to be. As the mind reflects upon the pupils in that single term of school, emotions of joy and sorrow arise in surging waves. That girl, Albina, who can estimate the good influence she has produced in the family cir- cle, in temperance work, in every cause calculated to lift up, ennoble and energize human thought. Another young lady afterwards became the wife of a college mate of mine,—a clergy- man of great ability, whose early death caused many eyes to weep. She was a lady of great capability and usefulness.

There was a teacher who attended school a little while. She later married a Western man and went to his home soon after. More than twenty years after, it chanced I preached in the town of Abbot one Sunday, and was to receive for my "stipend" the whole contribution. The people were not many, the financial condition depressed, and that gaping hat disclosed, after it had painfully made the circuit of the house, just thirty- seven cents. Among the audience was the above mentioned teacher and her husband, who were visiting her brother. He had no money in his pocket on that occasion, but the next day he sent me a dollar. Think of it, my clerical readers! What think ye of a man who would, unsolicited, a stranger, send a contribution to a preacher under such circumstances? That dollar will ever remain one of the most precious treasures I ever possessed, always suggesting more optimistic views of the human soul. May perpetual fortune and happiness be the abiding guests of that Western home.

One studious boy enlisted soon after school closed, and not long after slept beneath the flag he had died to defend. Everett Delano was the first pupil of mine to thus consecrate his young life to the preservation of the government of his native land. A fine scholar, a good boy, a patriot. My kindly remembrance of him will never fade.

The measles closed that school in a summary manner.

CHAPTER VI.

In August, 1860, I united myself with the Baptist Church of Dover and Foxcroft. Rev. C. M. Herring was the pastor. I have never regretted that step. I firmly believe that it was the proper thing to do, and that great help has come to me therefrom.

I have never been able to discover why anyone should hesitate in this matter. It seems to me that religion, or rather, Christianity, has made our civilization what it is, and, if it can help men in the mass, I cannot see why it may not individually.

Further, the subject presents itself as a duty. If a duty, then neglect implies a loss. The subject has never seemed to me the mysterious, indefinite something that some people believe in. To strive to live according to the Sermon on the Mount, and practically be what Christ declared we may and ought to be, is a very sensible course of life. That created man should revere his Creator is honest, proper, and obligatory.

When I was a student at the Academy at Foxcroft, I became quite well acquainted with A. G. Lebroke. He was always interested in every boy attending school who was striving to make the most of his opportunities. He himself wasted no time and had no patience with the idle or listless student.

He, one day, called me into his office and talked to me for a full hour.

I wish it were possible for any one to fully describe the characteristics of Augustus G. Lebroke. It never has been and never will be. I shall only try to give the impressions I received when

a boy of eighteen.   His earnestness and sincerity first impressed.
His physique was the indispensable outward form for an orator.
He made but few gestures in speaking, but when some especially
brilliant thought was flashing from his mental consciousness
through the medium of the brain and the tongue, the eye would
light up with an electric glow, the whole face became illumi-
nated, his words somehow breathed forth pathos, truth, conviction, and when that marvelous burst of eloquence had ceased,
and the supercharged mind of the hearer had begun to recover a
little; a gentler strain took him over the same ground, and
showed less astute reasoning and things easier to understand;
when all was fully comprehended, then occurred another flight of
eloquence, loftier than the other, followed by more complete
analysis and illustration.

Mr. Lebroke's mind was so comprehensive in its grasp that
every detail received recognition, and each part of the subject
discussed was made to become an important factor, necessary
to the whole.

He attacked every position in front and on either flank at
once, and enveloped the position by facts arranged in double
columns with such impetuosity that unconditioned surrender
quickly followed.   His mind had such a tremendous grasp of
facts which he could instantly group into logical order that his
resources never failed.   Many of those facts would seem trivial
presented by any other man, but when he presented them in
proper grouping, each one appeared an indispensable link for the
complete chain of evidence.   The "mole-hill" did become a
"mountain," when he had sunk every surrounding argument to
a sea-level.   He did not, like many speakers, fight his way along
point by point with a vigorous opponent, but sought to confound
him at first by impetuosity of the attack, and the overwhelming
array of superior forces, and each separate spear and lance were
one by one hurled at the prostrate foe no longer capable of
vigorous resistance.

His words were remarkably well chosen, and though many, none seemed superfluous. His memory was remarkable. That enabled him to marshal his forces and leave no places or corners unprotected. His quotations were plentiful, and always served as a clinching stroke to the argument. In an arson case when a man was tried for burning a house in the night, when he had dwelt at length upon the enormity of the offense, the endangering the lives of seven innocent women and children and exposing them to terrible torture and death, till the eyes of the jurymen fairly began to flash fire, he turned suddenly more directly to the jury and said, "Shall that fiend of revenge, darkness and death, stalk at midnight around our unprotected dwellings, crying, 'Sleep no more to all the house. Macbeth hath murdered sleep, Glamis hath murdered sleep.' Sleep no more, ye innocent babes in tired mother's arms. Sleep no more, wearied, laboring man! Macbeth hath murdered sleep. The prisoner at the bar has living in his heart the lurid fires of hell that robs the eyes of sleep and banishes every thought of security."

I recall that scene as vividlv as though an event of yesterday.

Mr. Lebroke had many remarkable qualities. Among them was the happy faculty of being pathetic without descending to bathos. Few men can do this. How often have I heard speakers, seeking to move a heart to tears, instead provoke him to smiles. Mr. Lebroke never did this. He never descended to commonplace when lofty heights had been occupied. If the end found him there on the mountain top he stood and said the last word. Metaphor and simile were favorite weapons with him, and he used them judicially and forcibly. He was never coarse or common in his public address. His style could not be called strictly classical. There were no isolated exhibitions of eloquence for the sake of eloquence, but it was all eloquent. His style was most like that of Cicero in the second oration against Catiline. Had Mr. Lebroke received a thorough classical education, he would have been, in my opinion, the greatest orator Maine ever produced.

One day he showed the grasp of his mind to me in an hour's talk upon the Bible as the foundation of all law. He discussed the Levitical Law, the Judges, the prophets, the new Dispensation, Paul's expositions of law and Peter's thesis. He grouped all these together in such manner as was marvelous to me. He closed his remarks by saying that every law student should spend many months in Bible study before he opened Blackstone. His sympathies were for all, but he most liked to assist the boy who had his own way to make in the world. He would spend hours talking to such, and rarely refused his council. His sense of humor was keen, and he could tell a commonplace story in such a manner that it seemed new and striking. Of course no one will think that I have attempted to write a memorial of A. G. Lebroke, or even to approach it. I have simply talked about a marvelous man that I knew when a boy as I remember him. His public career is too well known to be noticed in a reminiscence of this kind. The world knows that he was a very successful lawyer, an astute politician and a safe legislator. He would nave made an excellent judge. His capabilities would have put him in the United States Senate.

CHAPTER VII.

COLLEGE.

At the close of the spring term of Foxcroft Academy, I decided to enter college. I spent most of the summer reviewing my studies. At Commencement time, S. T. Pullen and I started for Waterville with a sort of compromise team. I furnished my father's horse, and he, his father's carriage. We stopped at Pittsfield for dinner, arriving at Waterville at six o'clock. We were examined the next day when Mr. Pullen, two others and myself were admitted without conditions. The rest of the class had assignments to be made up later. I have always been very glad that I decided to secure a college education. That education has not only been a means of livelihood, but has afforded me most exquisite pleasure. But on that momentous occasion, when I sat in that gloomy recitation room, I had quite a mind to withdraw and go home. Had I failed to pass, I am sure I would never have tried again. I remember now just what my examination was. I can repeat the Greek poem which Prof. Foster asked me to read. He requested me to scan a line of Virgil. Now it is well known that there are six feet in every line of Virgil, but I felt generous on that occasion and gave the astonished Professor seven feet. It was a mistake on my part. He said six was enough. Prof. was always a little fussy.

By kind permission of Herbert C. Libby, I quote an article here that some years ago I wrote for "Colby Stories."

TOM AND SMITH.

"One day in July, 1860, a carriage passed slowly down College street drawn by a dusty black horse, and containing two very anxious looking boys. The cause of their anxiety was two-fold,—examination next day, and a desire to find a blacksmith shop. The shop was soon discovered and a shoe set on the said horse. And when the financier of the duet demurred at the price, fifty cents, the begrimed son of Vulcan informed them that it was 'Commencement Week,' and horseshoeing was on the *cornua taurorum.* '*Dies irae*' occurred the next day in the Plutonean abodes of the old Chapel, concerning which *animus meminisse horret.*

"By the way, the platform in that underground room became decayed and a motherly-looking toad had a home there, and she came out every day to hear Waldron's essay in the rhetoric class. One summer the wicked boys put ten toads under the platform and waited for the Prof. to come. All were quiet enough till Brackett began to read Latin. They couldn't stand that anyhow, so out they came and hopped for the door at full speed. 'The effect was electrical.' There were few X's that term.

"On Commencement Day those two adventuresome youths were allowed to follow at a respectful distance the awe-inspiring Sophs down to the church. The boys discovered some very original characters among them. During the halt of the procession, one of the Sophs stepped back and asked Smith in a very peremptory manner, 'How did you get that hump on your back?' Fresh replied that the Almighty had put it there. The Soph seemed to be astonished that it should have been done without his consent. He then demanded of Tom—'Why in thunder do you wear glasses?' Tom said he was near-sighted. The Soph was still dissatisfied, and said so. There used to be a tradition around the college that the habit of inquisitiveness commenced very young with him. His first inquiry was, why he didn't have two mouths as well as two eyes, and his next sentence criticised his father for not wearing more clothes on the top of his head.

"Soon another Soph stepped back and seemed anxious to know where they had left their 'horns' when they came to college. Smith timidly asked what he meant, and received for an answer that 'cattle' from the country always had horns. Smith replied that he was a 'buffalo' and didn't have horns, and later on showed said Soph that he was a vigorous kicker if he couldn't hook.

"Another small, back-eyed, blaick-haired, pretty little Soph attracted their attention. He said nothing to them but every hair on his aristocratic head seemed to say, *procul, procul, este, ye* Freshmen! He is a great man now and occupies a high position.

"The two Freshmen looked down the line ahead and noticed in the Junior class a dark-haired man, tall, rather good looking, and modest. Smith afterward learned that the name of that Junior was Isaiah Record. Later he roomed opposite him in North College; he further learned that Mr. Record was the noblest man he ever knew. Conscience in him was the ruling power. Nor was he a cad.

"On one occasion when the faculty, disregarding the wise counsels of the students, employed an unregenerate man to cut the grass on the campus, the boys sent Somnus to the ivory gate and helped the faculty out by cutting the grass themselves by moonlight. Every boy practiced in that star-pictured gym, that night, Record and Barker excepted. Barker unfortunately slept over, and Record stayed in his room and interviewed conscience. He reproved no one in the matter, and it was all talked over before him with perfect freedom. There was no Pharisaical spirit in him. In after years Smith sat by his bedside, with tears coursing down his face, received his last farewells, and has found less on earth to enjoy ever since.

"A strange circumstance was connected with Mr. Record's funeral. At one commencement, Annie Louise Carey sang. In the gallery sat Isaiah Record, Rev. A. C. Herrick, Paymaster Barton, U. S. N., and Smith. At the close of the concert, the four adjourned to the hotel and talked till two o'clock. They were to separate next morning. One was going to Japan, one to California, Record to Houlton, and Smith to Massachusetts. As they parted that night Mr. Record said, 'When shall we four meet again?' One dark day later, the body of Isaiah Record lay at rest in a casket, in the vestibule of the church at Houlton. Gazing sadly down upon those noble features, stood Smith, when upon the right and left stepped simultaneously Mr. Barton and Mr. Herrick, and as they mutely and tearfully clasped hands, they felt they had all met again. (W. S. Knowlton is now the only survivor.)

"The peculiar laugh of a Soph attracted the boys' attention next. He had a perfect Grecian face and a smile that was exhilarating. Some one called him Thomas. He was a fine fellow and liked a joke. One day the president called him up on review in Butler's Analogy and told him to pass on to the 'Future Life.' Thomas promptly responded, 'Not prepared, sir.'

"Gazing further down the line Smith saw what seemed a human head seated on top of a tall pole, but a rift in the crowd showed that it was a human form divine, but not 'divinely fair.' He heard 'Mac' declaim later on in the Chapel when he, with his head *ad astras*, in a sort of piping, grunting voice, said,—'It is strange how little some people know about the stars.'

"Had 'Mac' lived in Job's days he could have sung with the 'Morning Stars.'

"While waiting at the church Smith took a good look at his classmates. Near him stood Seeley,—a harmless little fellow. He had a brother in the Sophomore class who was a genius. He went up into Aroostook county to farm and preach. He was a far better farmer than preacher. He made a failure of farming. One day he was ploughing on the side of a steep hill with a pair of steers. The cattle were untrained and he didn't know how to drive. The steers would 'turn the yoke,' thus half the time they faced the plow. To prevent this movement he tied their tails together, and at noon unyoked them thus united *a tergo*. One started east, the other west. For a time action and reaction were equal; at last one fell down, the other hauled him down the mountain by the adhesive force of the caudal vertebræ.

"The sight was inspiring. The *bos* on *pedes, ferens caput altum cornibus,* snorting victory with every wild leap; the *bos* on *dorsum,* roaring with disgust and marking the dust with his horns like Hector's spear.

"Brother Seeley gazed calmly on the scene and gently whispered, '*Descensus Averno facile est,*' and next Sabbath took for his text—'Be not unequally yoked together.'

"Next to Seeley stood a tall, finely proportioned man who to-day wears the insignia of a Major General, U. S. A.,—H. C. Merriam. He and Smith were great friends later on; Merriam liked a joke and so did Smith. In those days the Junior class doled out an original declamation in the Chapel every spring. The other classes must attend or be fined ten cents. The whole thing was a bore. The night before '63 spoke, Merriam and Smith went down town and 'borrowed' from Mr. Merryfield's back shop a huge cloth sign.

"The heraldic emblem on said cloth was a life-size picture of an elephant. The boys added a legend, reading, 'Elephant Show—$.10 admission,' and nailed the advertisement high above the Chapel door. The third-year men were not pleased a whit, but the Profs thought it a grand good joke. You see, they were not in it.

"The General fixed this all up with Mr. Merriam last Commencement. The General was a good scholar and wrote poetry sometimes. There were two or three more poets in the class. They belonged to different schools of poetry. David said if he got the rhyme all right, he didn't care for the metre. Harry said if he got the metre all right, he didn't care for the rhyme. And Smith also wrote one poetic translation of Horace. It was Ode XVI, and here is a specimen of it:

> "O! bewitching filia,
> Handsomer than your mamma!
> How could I such an onus prove
> To write Iambics 'bout my love!
> Burn those verses, every speck;
> Dump them in the Kennebec.
> When Prometheus made my head,
> Softer than a loaf of bread,
> In my bosom he put this:
> *Vim insani leonis.*

"Smith bet the peanuts he would read it in the class. Prof. Foster was rash enough to call him up on the advance and Smith read the whole thing through.

" 'Sit down, young man!'

"Result—Ten minus the one.

"Smith never wrote poetry afterwards.

"Nearby stood Mayo. He was a very rigid man in morals. One night when 'town and gown' were discussing how hard a blow it required to paralyze the brain, Mayo received a severe shock from a club in the hands of a 'yager.' He brought up reinforcements and threw said 'yager' into a muddy pool. The 'yager' naturally swore. Mayo remarked, 'Look here, this is a Baptist institution and swearing is not allowed. Chuck him in again, boys!' And in he went until the profanity was all washed out of him.

"A little behind stood Young of Calais. He had a witty way of putting things. When Weston's name appeared in the catalogue with a † before it, Young said, 'Weston must be a mighty good man; he bears his cross daily.'

"Just behind Tom stood a girlish-looking boy. His name was Littlefield. Studious, talented, he carried off most of the honors. He was very absent minded. A club of twelve once boarded with a lady who frequently reminded them that she had seen better days. Before the term was over the boys thought *they* had. Now there boarded at the place a very prim lady whose age had never been accurately ascertained. Littlefield sat beside her. One day in the heat of argument he placed his arm on the back of her chair. She sat up a little primly; he became a little excited and proceeded to put his arm around her, and soon was emphasizing every remark by an unmistakable hug, all unconscious that he was disregarding proprieties. Smith will never forget the expression on that woman's face. Glorious Littlefield! The daisies adorn his grave to-day.

"'Green be the turf above thee, friend of my better days.'

"Just here the procession moved on; the two boys were lost in the crowd and Smith has never emerged therefrom."

There were thirty-five in our class. Most of them were young men of good ability and studious in habit. In those days there were some conditions that seem very strange in these days. No preparation in Geometry was required, and the class were forced over six books in twelve weeks. That class recited at six o'clock in the morning. Think of it! Six o'clock! We had to learn the lesson the night before, hence we were very sleepy in the morning. Many a time I have been in bed when the bell ceased to toll. Out of bed we jumped, pulled on our pants and boots, wrapped a long shawl around the shoulders, and minus stockings, coat and vest, raced for the chapel, where the Prex. read a chapter and offered prayer. Perhaps that was a profitable service, but it was rather difficult to concentrate the whole soul upon religious lines with the sword of Damocles in the form of Davies Legendre hanging over one. After reciting we went to the rooms and dressed for breakfast. The amount eaten was proportionate to the result of the attempt to recite in Geometry. If a boy took but one egg we knew there had been some trouble in readily quoting from the text book. If he took no egg at all, a dead flunk had predestinated the condition, we knew.

There were some very fine boys in the class. When the spring term was nearly finished the boys began to enlist in the army. The faculty was patriotic, but did not like to lose the students. Nearly half of our class enlisted. The President finally sent us all home without examination. Those that did not enlist came back for the spring term, but the class was small and at graduation we were only eight. As far as I know, only four survive. N. C. Breckett was one of my chums. He was for many years president of a college for colored people in Virginia, and is enjoying his *otium cum dignitate* in his native town.

Freeman, who fancied he resembled Daniel Webster in looks, was in Oregon to the last of my knowledge.

The irrepressible Waldron, the much engaged man, was living in Ohio a few years ago.

S. T. Pullen, my room-mate the first term, is living in Portland. Mr. Pullen has occupied prominent places in the political and commercial world.

Gen. H. C. Merriam was a member of the class. He was a fine mathematician and a poet withal. I suppose we look upon him as the big man of the class, whose glory will redeem it from oblivion.

A. H. Keezer was the best dressed man, and a great beau among the ladies.

E. C. Littlefield was, in my opinion, the most intellectual boy in the class or college. He died a year after graduation with brain fever.

Cushing was a grand good fellow, and so was H. M. Pratt, but they left us long ago.

I was class poet at the time of graduation, and Littlefield was orator. I had just recovered from typhoid fever at Commencement, and Littlefield's brother was killed in battle at that time, so the class day exercises were omitted.

One circumstance connected with that fever I have never forgotten. Dr. Boutelle attended me for seven weeks, day and night, and furnished me some medicine and presented me with a bill for nineteen dollars. I hope the Doctor knows in heaven how much benefit that kind act of his did me. I shall ever have a green spot in my soul for Dr. Boutelle.

I remember another event of that sickness. Waldron was to be my nurse one night, and promised to come at ten o'clock. My mother went to bed in a remote part of the house at a quarter of ten. Ten o'clock came but no Waldron; eleven slowly passed by, then twelve and so on until morning. I lived many years during that night. The explanation was this: Waldron went to see his girl and became so absorbed that he entirely forgot me, and that absorption was so complete that even when he had torn himself away and said good-night for the twentieth time, he went in a sort of ecstatic condition to college and never thought of the poor fellow in the delirium of fever. That girl never looked pretty to me after that.

The class has never received any honors from the college. There have been several D. D. and LL. D. given members of classes graduating since. I do not know under just what conditions those honors are given, and hence ought not to discuss it. I have always thought, however, they struck as lightning does. Lightning sometimes strikes a tall oak and sometimes a puny alder.

The D. K. E. society did me the honor of inviting me to join it. I did so and have never regretted the act. I fully believe in college societies, and regard college life as incomplete unassociated with a society. It may not be easy to define the reasons for this conclusion, but every member of the society fully appreciates the benefits. If the society is a proper one, it is a safe guard, a home, a shrine, and in some cases, the college. I have never lost interest in our society, and enjoy beyond measure meeting the old and new boys whenever I can. I have prepared quite a large number of boys for college, most of whom have

5

shown in practical life that no mistake was made when they went to college. I have had boys in Bowdoin, Amherst, Colby, Bates, Harvard and University of Maine. I still believe in a college education when the pupil has the capital to commence with. It is a foolish thing for a young man to attempt to attend a college who has no mental capacity. Study never produces, but simply trains and sharpens what God created.

As I review college life, how many things seem callow, presumptuous and almost silly, but they did not then. All our presumption and zeal was a part of the conditions of things of our ages, and the accumulation of a high self estimate. It naturally follows that when one or two hundred boys meet together, each one possessing just a small per cent of conceit, that the percentage will run up quite far. Well, suppose it does? Who is injured? Let the boys still enjoy their world with all its freshness. It would not be college without it. Let them feel that the illimitable universe is every day regulated by their desire and needs. We had our day. We swaggered and fought our battles of more importance than Waterloo or Sedan, reveled in veal and enjoyed it. So say I, let the college boy of to-day have his fling. Veal will become beef in due time. I enjoy the boys as they are.

At last Commencement, after the public services were over, I met some of the boys at the Chapter House and spent two or three hours with them and enjoyed the occasion very much. As we sat around that fireplace, I saw fields of usefulness, positions of importance, sacred trust awaiting those young men in the great world beyond college walls. If ever I offered an earnest, heartfelt prayer to the Master, it was when I retired that night, that they might be kept from sin, that the high ambition animating their souls might find its highest fulfillment in a life of usefulness, honor and success. I shall probably never meet many of those young men again, but feel sure the world will honor them when the writer of these lines "shall sleep in cold oblivion." Then we say, let them go to college and be a college boy while there and then go for work for joy and sorrow as the Father wills.

I look back to my college life with pleasure, on the whole. There were dark spots which I still remember but care not to recall them. My health was the chief drawback, and sometimes a lack of funds did not cast a roseate light upon the pathway. But, on the whole, I enjoyed college life very much. I always enjoyed studying. I was a good average scholar, excelling in Mathematics and Rhetoric. I did then just what I should recommend a student to do now.

I suggest that he be a first-class scholar and simply that; then spend what time he can spare from athletics, in reading, reading, reading. In advising this course, I mean reading of the old English classics, poetry, history, essays and lectures. But more than this, he should read some modern books as a sort of pastime. There are a few modern books worth reading and these should be read; but in reading many of them there is no profit. Those one does read should be selected with care and read with a deliberate purpose. What I mean is this: If a pupil reads Addison the purpose should be to enjoy the style. Read with such a purpose, the essays will insensibly steal into the perception and refine the style of the student. Macaulay should be read with the same purpose in mind, but when a person reads David Harum he should do so simply for mental rest and diversion, and that fixed purpose should be ever before him, then the reading will do no harm; but the book should be forgotten as soon as possible. A constant reading of such books would lead to intellectual imbecility.

I was obliged to be out of college, teaching, nearly half the time, and made up those terms. Most of the professors I liked very much. There was an individuality about each that I recall distinctly. Professor Hamlin pleased me the most. He had a personal interest in every student, and was not afraid to show it. I remember he called me to the desk one day and asked about my health and suggested some treatment. Stern and exacting in the recitation room though he was, we all felt that he was just and kind, and that all received the same treatment.

Dr. Champlin was never a favorite with the boys, but I rather liked him.

The Doctor had a grim sense of humor which showed itself occasionally, and he appreciated a joke, even at his own expense. One day he gave us a very long lesson in Butler's Analogy— one paragraph in the lesson said that a man would try with all his might to do a thing, though the chances were ten to one against him. I recited that paragraph when the Doctor said: "Give a practical illustration." I replied: "For a student to try to get such an outrageous lesson as this." The old Doctor at first frowned, then drew his face down several inches and a grim smile began slowly to jump from wrinkle to wrinkle, and he said: "It seems you did succeed." I had the great pleasure of entertaining Dr. Champlin at my house for a week once, and never enjoyed a man more. I shall never forget a scene on the campus, right before the old chapel. Gen. Martel, the janitor, one day became very much intoxicated and wanted to leave. Dr. C. did not want him to go in that condition, so would not pay him. The General, who weighed two hundred and fifty pounds, walked up to Dr. Champlin, who weighed over two hundred pounds, and, shaking his fist in the Doctor's face, said: "Dr. Shamplain, you pay me or I spile your face!" The boys got around the General and led him away. The bets among the boys were about equal.

The President had a funny way of selecting Scripture for the morning lesson. One day, when some of the boys left town to avoid too intimate acquaintance with the Constable, the Doctor read: "The wicked flee when no man pursueth." Another time he read: "They that were drunken are drunken in the night." That morning two young men had been suspended for indulging in the flowing bowl. When a large freshman class came in he read: "How are they increased that trouble me!"

I have had the pleasure of knowing every President who has presided at Colby since 1860. I thought Dr. Robbins a man of the best intentions. I never listened to a more interesting man than Dr. Small. Every sentence he uttered was a Grecian model; not one word not the best, every sentence in perfect logical order, and every thought following some suggested idea. Dr. Small is a great man, and is so regarded by men better qualified to judge than I.

One might, perhaps, reverence Dr. Small more than love him. Of Dr. Butler I have the pleasantest recollection. I admired the man for his kindly sympathy, his keen intellect and logical mind.

Dr. Whitman was a good friend of mine and I dearly loved him. A man of superior intellect, of great heart, of rare eloquence, he left impressions wherever he went that were lasting for good. I shall not attempt to describe Dr. Pepper. I shall say but a word, simply quoting from the Book of Job,—"Canst thou loose the bands of Orion," etc. I shall attempt neither impossible task. I know 'Dr. White quite well, and enjoy the man, respect the clergyman, and admire the scholar. The Doctor is a rare speaker and impresses his audience with the sincerity of his convictions and the soundness of his logic.

Of course, I know nothing about the administrations of these presidents. I knew them simply as I met them in public places and at my home; and certainly I can assert that they were men of noble character, large ability and earnest piety.

CHAPTER VIII.

ATKINSON.

I next became the teacher of the graded school at Atkinson. The town had no village. There was a Corner, and the Mills, situated about two miles further south. I never could discover certainly why a collection of houses and people is called a village in one town and a larger collection in another town, is simply dubbed a "Corner."

It seems to be a fact worth remembering that one's estimation of himself is always higher than others are willing to grant. Just as long as the people at a Corner call it a Corner, so long will other people call it so. But let the people living where several roads meet begin to call the dozen or twenty houses there a Village, all the world will dignify it by that title.

I have noticed, also, that just as soon as a Corner becomes a Village, great changes begin to take place, within the houses, and in the newly-born Village. Lace curtains replace the paper ones, front yards become lawns and fresh paint is in evidence; and a Meeting House springs up,—another blacksmith shop sends up its black smoke and silk hats appear. All these things would not have been had not some ambitious man or woman, with prophetic inspiration called that collection of houses, a Village. Shakespeare asks "What's in a name," Why,—a good deal, sometimes everything!

I taught at Atkinson Corner and Richard C. Shannon taught at the Mills. We boarded together at a half-way house. Mr. Shannon was a Senior and I a Freshman at Waterville College and he was a man of note at that time. He was the best athlete in college, took first prize in Junior Exhibition, and was honored with a Junior part. He was an excellent reader and the central star in the reading circle that winter. He used to read Dean Swift to me evenings, much to my edification.

That was his first experience in country life and some things struck him as peculiar. He went out into the barn one day, and noticed how the cattle were fastened to the stanchion, and came in and indignantly protested against chaining cattle up by the neck.

It was also his first attempt at teaching. The scholars thought some of his methods a little too original. He had a pair of parallel bars built and trained the boys after school in gym nastics. His farm constituency wanted the boys to chop wood and milk the cows, so that apparatus disappeared one night, and Brother Shannon was very much disgusted. He would have been much more so had he seen it, as I did next summer, serving ignominiously as a hen roost.

In the following spring Mr. Shannon enlisted in the army and served during the war, with distinction, becoming Colonel. He afterwards travelled extensively in South America, and held important offices in Brazil. After spending some time in Europe, he came to New York and commenced the practice of the law, and was elected to Congress and held the position for four years and was on important committees, and ranks high among his fellow members. Six years ago he gave fifteen thousand dollars to build the Shannon Observatory at Colby. Mr. S. was a member of the D. K. E. fraternity and took much interest in the welfare of the society and has ever been a stout supporter of his Alma Mater. Mr. Shannon is a man of superior ability and kindly spirit and a gentleman of pronounced type. He has amassed a large fortune and has a home where every refinement adorns.

The school at Atkinson was a good one, and was enjoyed by the teacher. Among the pupils was a bright-eyed girl of ten, whom I especially remember. No lesson seemed too hard for her. That sweet smile still remains in memory's grasp and the innocence of that fine face was that of the Madonna. Sweet Mamie Ford! How I missed that girl when she happened to be absent. In fact, in the whole development of the human face there is none that can compare with the face of a girl of ten or eleven years of age. Younger, there is too much of the child in the face; at an older age, too much of the world appears to mar the picture I am trying to paint. The first bud of girlhood is getting ready to unfold. There is all the sweet programme that afterwards is spread abroad to the world, infolded in the soul, closely hidden there. Purity, love, sweetness, innocence, every attribute that Heaven can lend to mortals in harmonious commingling, beautify, spiritualize and glorify the face of the sweet girl of this period of life.

If I ever felt like becoming an idolator, it has been when I have seen girls like this. They seem nearer to the Divine than any created object. I do not say a girl of that age is the most fascinating of all, but do claim that she is more adorable than at any other. Happy is she if she has a mother who keeps her thus as long as possible. Would that every mother could understand that there is an angel in the household while her sweet child is standing "where the brook and river meet," and that, like Asturia, that angel disappears when "knowledge comes and wisdom lingers." Not all girls would be recognized by my description. Many are premature in knowledge; some are stupid; some hereditarily depraved, and others are characterless. But many there are who ought to be recognized as special gifts from God.

Dickens, with all his marvelous genius, never wrote as well as in describing the life and death of Little Nell.

There was another girl in school, somewhat older, with the brightest black eyes. Her name was Alice, a sweet name. I expected her to be nice, having that name, and she was. I never could quite disassociate a name from an ideal which I have associated with the name and have been terribly shocked sometimes to find that some coarse, loud, violent girl had been christened "Gertrude," or "Mary," or "Lucy." They should have been called "Joan," or "Martha," or "Belinda."

There was a small boy in the school that justified my concep tion. His name was Fremont, and he had all the aggressiveness of that restless campaigner. He was informed one day that his place was in the floor. He allowed that he would not go, and it became necessary for me to show him that superior force could overcome inferior resistance; and he came out. I don't know the after history of that boy, but feel sure that, unless his discretion has increased, he will find his journey through life somewhat thorny.

There was another Mary, sixteen years old, who was very bright and deserved the name. Louise has always seemed a charming name, and as almost every girl by that name that attended school was a blonde, so the Louise of that school was very fair and exceedingly talented. She would have made a college professor. Hittie looked so much like her sister Alice that I could not distinguish one from the other. Hittie was generally in mischief, and when I called out sharply, "Alice!" by mistake, the painful surprise on Alice's face used to haunt me nights.

A slender, pale-faced boy of thirteen showed many of the traits that have made him a success in life. He was very studious and obedient. His chief point was mathematics. He became a physician of extensive practice, and can sing a song or take off an arm, with equal grace. His avoirdupois shows that he has never lacked for good living.

Dr. Ford is now one of the associate physicians in the Sanatorium at Moosehead Lake. The Doctor is very popular in his profession. "May his shadow never grow less!"

One day there appeared in the schoolroom a very tall, black-haired young man of striking appearance. He desired to study Latin. I can see that young man now, as he appeared on that occasion. His hair was cut short, and every spear stood straight up, pointing skyward. There was an individuality about his hair that marked the man. His absorbing power was marvelous. Whole pages of Latin Grammar seemed but to whet his appetite for more, until the length of the lesson had to be adjusted to the time the teacher could allot to him. His reasoning faculties were equally good. He was what we sometimes call "a natural scholar." He would have made an excellent college president, but then the State would have lost an admirable librarian. This same boy appeared to me later in another school, where he changed his devotion from Mars to Venus. I shall speak of him again.

Mr. Carver had a mind decidedly logical. There was method in all that he did. His use of the right word in recitation seemed the result of intuition rather than of training. That careful attention to detail which has made him such an admirable librarian was very marked.

With that school disappeared many of the names that had been familiar. Hitherto the politics and religious preference of the parents could be ascertained by many of the names of the scholars;—John Fairfield, A. K. P. Paris, Bion Bradbury, Andrew Jackson, Thomas Jefferson; all told that the father voted the Democratic ticket. Winfield Scott and Zachary Taylor informed the world that the parent belonged to the forlorn Whig party. I was sure that John Wesley belonged to a Methodist family and that John Calvin's father was a follower of that stern Reformer. The George Washingtons, alas! disappeared. Whether or not there has been less truthfulness in school I cannot tell.

By the way, I object to the shattering of my youthful idol by those remorseless vandals who magnify every trait and habit of Washington that would detract from his ideal life. What good can come from proclaiming the fact, if it be a fact, that Washington did sometimes swear, under great provocation? Thousands of boys have been kept from swearing by being told that Washington never swore.

Every nation has some patron saint, a character that boys may imitate. What better one than Washington?

A story was published, a few years ago, by the author of "The Honorable Peter Stirling," that perfectly disgusted me in an attempt to glorify Washington by claiming for him many objectionable characteristics.

Let the boy still believe in the hatchet story,—that Washington could jump twenty feet,—and that he never swore.

And some "Gadgrind" idiots would destroy every ideal of childhood and banish Santa Claus to the barbaric ages of King Thor. The attempt is positively wicked. Santa Claus is the first supernatural existence appealing to the child's mind. His faith in Santa Claus is implicit. His moral conduct is regulated by Santa's wishes. The boy, through him, learns, for the first time, to have faith in a semi-spiritual agency. Why destroy all the fond fantasies of a thousand years? And just to please a few fanatical philosophers who would take all the poetry out of life, destroy every air-castle, and repress every flight of the imagination.

There is no attribute of the human mind that conserves greater and grander purposes and results than arise from the proper use of the imagination. It should never be repressed, but should be directed, cultivated, refined and combined with other mental faculties.

Of course, if the imagination is allowed to run loose, it will run riot and lead to mendacity and story telling. But such condition need never exist. The person who fatally is lacking in imaginative power will never rise above the veriest commonplace. This world becomes a very small planet to such. Even the stars are only bright spots in the sky if we see in them only stars.

The war changed the political standing of many parents. New issues arose and gradually the old custom of naming a boy after somebody ceased. I am sorry the habit of perpetuating a family Christian name no longer prevails. Isaiah led off in our family for several generations, but finally the mantle fell upon the bachelor brother, and a prophet no longer appears in the family.

I am sorrv that young ladies feel called upon to abbreviate their names. Gertrude is euphonious, Gertie is harsh; Margaret is a sweet name, Maggie is flat; and so on, through the whole list.

The old, ungainly names are mostly gone. It is well they should pass out. I once had a pupil by the name of Nehemiah. He was a short, dumpy sort of a boy, and had a piping, shrill voice. When I called the roll in the morning, I did not blame the pupils for smiling when that little chit answered to that ponderous name.

A young lady, in another school, rejoiced in the name of Mehitable Marjorie Matilda. She was small and squint-eyed, and round-shouldered—and no wonder. Zachary Tavlor, in another school, had to fight many a Buena Vista, like his illustrious predecessor.

I've no doubt there are boys in prison who are made quarrelsome by the teasing they received from the other boys on account of their names. Parents are more careful nowadays about the matter.

I made some very pleasant acquaintances in the town. The Snows, the Ramsdells, the Lyfords and the Hammonds were very kind, and made my stay in town pleasant. The cold Friday of 1861 found me walking a mile, facing the north, and wading through snowdrifts three feet deep, trying in vain to protect my unfortunate nose from the wind, forcing the air against it at the rate of sixty miles an hour, which had been cooled down to 30° below zero. That nose, the next day, was beyond classification.

I collected the pupils, that day, around the stove in the schoolroom and taught them till three, and sent them home. That night the Colonel and I read from Milton's "Paradise Lost," and almost envied Satan's new quarters. The young stock froze, that night, in several barns in town; many poor people suffered severely, and two persons perished in the road, not far away.

The Colonel and I slept in a small bed-room in the north-west corner of the house. We had family prayers and I remember I got so near the stove that I burned a hole in my coat. Our boarding mistress was a lovely woman, blessed by a kindly smile and a sweet voice.

Atkinson is still a "Corner." There has been but little change. The old families are nearly all gone, however.

CHAPTER IX.

MILO.

Milo next engaged my services. There were three grades in the school. The High School was under my instruction. The school was a large one and pretty well advanced. Milo was, at that time, quite an enterprising village. There were some very prominent citizens and some very peculiar characters.

There were some very pretty, very smart girls in school, who had a lot of fun with me the first week. I was never more perplexed than in deciding what to do with them. They were the daughters of some of the best families, and simply wanted to have some fun with the schoolmaster. They were too big to whip and too good-looking to keep after school. And they learned their lessons first-class.

The "innocent surprise" that would show itself in their pretty eyes when I reproved them for any misbehavior would have made Maud Muller seem bold. "I am sure," said Sarah, "I never intend to be out of order," and so said they all. One day all four commenced to chew gum. I suggested that rumination was not in order. "We are sorry," said one, "we have always chewed gum in school and didn't know it was wrong. We are sorry." Ten minutes after each had a very long striped pencil stuck over the ear, protruding six inches before the face; and thus on through the day. For every act, they were sorry and did not intend to be out of order, they said.

It is somewhat marvelous what an immense power for mischief a pretty girl has when she is inclined that way. I suppose this fact is but the exhibition of a law of nature that whatever is capable of producing great good is equally capable of producing great evil. Caloric, in the form of what we call fire, is, perhaps, our best natural friend, but remorseless and terrible when on mischief bent. The better anything is, the worse it becomes when turned to evil. It took an Archangel, according to Milton, to make a mischief-making Satan.

The thunderbolt, that for many ages hurled death and destruction among so many people, ought to have taught the world long ago that there was an inestimable good wrapped up somewhere in those bolts of Jove. It seems strange that philosophers, reasoning from effect to cause, had not earlier sought and found the good. No one did for ages,—Franklin simply sought to escape the evil or turn it aside. The philosopher should have considered the proposition: "Here is a mighty force doing much harm in the world. God never made it for that purpose. It must have been created for good." When, in these later days, scientific men began to investigate with that idea in mind, the result became apparent at once.

Why not account for the appearance of sin in the world on the same hypothesis; that all sin is perverted good; that God never created sin, or anything sinful, but that all things were good and made for good and that they became evil when improperly used. Corn is a blessing when made into bread and an evil when changed into whiskey. The conclusion we reach is that all things were created for good only,—including girls.

In speaking of mischievous girls, the question arises: Who can do the most harm in the world—a wicked man or a bad, malicious, wicked woman? In a discussion of this nature there should be taken into account the whole influence exerted upon the world, young and old; which one affects the future the most, which has the most influence to tear down the social fabric Christianity is endeavoring to erect; which destroys public conscience the more, and exposes abstract goodness and virtue to greater dangers. Does a bad man do harm in the same way that a wicked woman does? Certainly not. An abandoned man seems to possess a personality that a wicked woman does not. She seems to stand for the sex. He passes as an exception.

She represents a class. Let a man from Siam come to town and show himself a villain; the people will not judge that all men from Siam are equally depraved. But let the first immigrant from Siam be an abandoned woman, then the conclusion is reached at once that all Siamese women are bad. It is unmistakably true that heredity taints more surely follow the sins of the mother than those of the father. It is equally true that the persuasive powers of woman are far greater than man's, for good or evil.

But there is one grand distinction between a thoroughly bad man and a depraved woman. She may lead her victims farther in some particular direction than a man could, but yet she never quite forgets her mission in all directions. She may murder her rival, but would weep over the sorrow of her aged mother, bemoaning her murdered daughter.

Well, I studied those girls carefully for two days, and spent most of the nights meditating, and finally decided what to do. The decision was a happy one. It led to a very harmonious state of things. What was it? If I should ever write a sequel to these papers, I will reveal the whole affair, and give my comments on it.

One of the girls afterwards married my college chum, and made a most exemplary wife. I had one boy who never smiled or said a pleasant word. When I asked him how he was getting along his answer invariably was "Well enough." I hope that man never married. Just think of a pleasant-faced woman sitting a whole evening through with a man like that! Two of the boys became doctors. One bore the distinguished name of Hannibal Hamlin. It took him quite a long time to cross the Alps, but he succeeded at last and sunny Italy appeared to him in the classical town of Orono, where he now very successfully practices.

Another boy became a lawyer and settled in the West. Winfield Scott, true to his name, became a great conqueror of—female hearts, and Zachary Taylor fought adverse fortune like a hero.

Four of my pupils afterwards entered the Union Army. Many of the girls married very well and are living in Milo and adjoining towns. The school was the best I had taught and I am sure it was so regarded by the pupils and parents, since, the next spring, four pupils went to Monson to attend Monson Academy, where I taught.

Milo sent a larger percentage of her citizens to the war than any other town in the county except Monson. Most of those came home, and several of them attended school at Monson.

There were two churches in Milo. In one a very rough, uneducated man hurled all the terrors of the Law at his attentive congregation. The house was always full. The other clergyman was an educated man who preached very well prepared and interesting sermons to a very small congregation. I asked one of the people how this happened. He said: "Oh, he gives us brimstone, and we deserve it and like it."

The people of Milo were very kind to the schoolmaster,—that was what we were then—and I have always enjoyed visiting the town.

The Leonards and Macombers and Goulds were very nice to me, and so were the Kimballs and Ramsdells, and others. Dr. Kimball was a most excellent man. Three children attended school. They were all very nice and bright. Only one survives. She is now the wife of Bert Ramsdell, a prosperous farmer. Bert was always a good boy and I liked him every day. Mr. Gould had a daughter, Della, in school, whom I remember as near perfection.

Mrs. Abbie Owen Stubbs taught the lower grade in the same building. She was a fine teacher and a nice young lady. I boarded at her father's, and she and I, that winter, settled many points in theology and ethics that other people have failed to do.

6

If Brother Stubbs listens as attentively to his wife as I did that winter, he will never go wrong.

Will Owen, her brother, I shall never forget. His son was Senator from Piscataquis County last winter. The youngest Leonard boy was Representative.

Milo is, at this time, a very prosperous town, and has brighter prospects for the future.

I remember one very peculiar man in town. He knew a great many small facts in history, most of them unimportant. I have known several men like him; men who have a naturally retentive memory, but have not intelligence enough to comprehend any historical fact of importance. These men become the most interminable bores in existence. They will corner some really well-informed man and fire at him a cannon charge of historical questions of the most trivial nature and annoy him beyond endurance.

This man of Milo had made the lives of my predecessors miserable. I had heard of him, and was prepared for him. One day he met me in the Post Office and approached me and said, "I suppose, Mr. Knowlton, you are conversant with the facts of history?" "No, sir," I replied, "I am totally ignorant of the history of any nation or people." With surprise written on every line of his moon-shaped face, he exclaimed, "Why, ain't you a college graduate?" "O, yes," I said, "but it is a lamentable fact that I don't know history." He gave me a look of supreme disgust, and left me. He afterwards criticized the school committee for hiring a man to teach school who didn't know history.

One day each one of the boys in the army from Milo wrote him a letter. In those days when the mail came in and had been sorted, the Postmaster, with a bundle of letters in his hand, would call aloud the names of the fortunate receivers, and pass the letters to those who responded "Here." When those army letters arrived there was fun in that office. The Postmaster would call out "C. A. Abbee," "Wm. Owen," "C. A. Abbee,"

"Wm. Gould," "C. A. Abbee," and so on till the end. When the historian went home, he had to borrow a small basket, in which to carry his letters. He came down town one day, and said that there was a new General commanding the fleet in the Mississippi River that was destroying the rebel fleet, "General Rise."

The paper had said, the day before, that "a general rise of the river had damaged the rebel fleet." He told me, one day, that he did not believe the story in the Bible about the "Sea-pulcre." "The idea of a person's being buried in a 'Sea-pulcre!' I don't know how big a 'Pulcre' is, but I don't believe it is big enough to bury a man in."

How many men there are very much like him, who, with a little smattering of knowledge in one thing, presume to possess what they never could attain with life-long effort!

I have a theory that every idiot could be educated in one particular direction. Had I the training of such a person, I would discover in what line there was the most promising outlook, and direct every effort in that one line. Scholars there are who can simply learn to spell; others to write; and others in some other direction.

I boarded with Wm. Owen, a very fine man, blessed with an excellent wife. My room was a small chamber, looking out upon the street. I had become addicted to the use of tobacco, but had reformed, and had concluded that, if I was to board at a deacon's, I must be very good. The first few days found my resolution unshaken, but on the fourth day my stove began to smoke, and this fact was seized upon and made use of. My reasoning was, if the deacon's stove smoked, why should not I? So the stove and I had our social smoke occasionally, during the winter. How many men and women there are to-day justifying their conduct by arguments as trivial as that! Very few are willing to admit that their depravity is really a determined con-clusion to do just what they want to do the most.

Thousands of drones are pleading many reasons why they are not as other men, when the truth is, there was just one cause,—simply laziness. Many, in describing the prosperity of others, say:

"O, he had a pull, had some one to help him start." That may be true, but I have noticed that the fortunate man always pulls himself. "They all began to make excuses." The fact is, no one is quite honest with himself. "Hamlet" should be engraved upon the tombstones of thousands of men; men who knew their duty; wanted to do that duty, but, somehow, never did it; and, oftentimes no one can assign the real reason why life is a failure in their case.

With some lack of physical force seems to paralyze energy, ambitions, aspiration. It is difficult for a person to start out on some enterprise requiring great mental effort, and be obliged to execute great undertakings while the feeble body is all the time demanding rest and nursing. Some men can do this, but life generally soon wears out and the end comes as a relief. Another lacks faith in his ability to perform the duty fate assigns him. The mountain seems too steep to climb; but there is an earnest desire to be upon the height. That desire never dies: He is not content to remain in the valley, nor has he courage to try the ascent. So there he stands all his life long, desiring, fearing, finally dying with life's work all undone. Such men are to be pitied rather than censured. The difficulty is generally a constitutional one, and is rarely overcome. Those men are not utter failures,—many a dreamer has thought out ways and means that men of less brains but more executive ability have presented to the world, and wrought out marvelous results.

The father of Hiram Maxim was a dreamer, but he conceived the idea of the famous Maxim gun long before the boy had thought of such an invention. Neglected and unknown graves, all over the land, hide from human gaze, many forms in which once dwelt the brightest sparks of divine intelligence, while the marble mausoleum flaunts to the world that the remains of the

Great repose in the tomb. The lamented Great was but the executor of the real genius. Some one has said that every genius was inspired, that such a person was the recipient of a divine influence, only given in rare instances. Granted, then must follow the conclusion that such devine power, operating upon the human, so overmasters the human as to partially paralyze the common worldly faculties, and renders the man a simple spiritual force, acting almost solelv in mental lines. Such a man can invent, can speculate, can conceive of almost divine schemes, and possibilities; but it must be left to the common worluiy mortal to put in force that which his inspired brother has received from the great source of all knowledge.

CHAPTER X.

MONSON.

I went directly from Milo to Monson. The school at that place had been a failure. A gentleman of that town had once been County Commissioner, and so had Mr. Macomber, of Milo; Mr. Chapin wrote to Mr. Macomber, inquiring about a teacher. Mr. Macomber called me into his office and informed me that a teacher was wanted at Monson. I accepted the position, and went. That Hegira produced as much influence upon my life as it ever did to any good Mahometan.

The seemingly trivial circumstance of the acquaintance of those two men, living thirty miles apart, produced a crisis time in my life and predestinated much of my career. I presume the same is true in the life of most men and women. Little things, almost unnoticed events, seeming accidents, have played controlling parts, not only in the lives of individuals, but events that shaped the destinies of nations. A slight shower rendered Napoleon's artillery ineffectual at Waterloo and probably decided the battle; a dinner party, prolonged till midnight, prevented the War Secretary of England from sending orders to Clinton to join Burgoyne at Saratoga, and sounded the knell that was consummated at Yorktown. The poet says: "A pebble, in the current dropped, has turned the course of many a river." The history of the world illustrates the same fact.

These events are crisis times. Though a person live his allotted three score and ten, a retrospect of the past shows that he has experienced only two or three real crises periods, that those events were really his life. All the years, labors, and trials simply led up to the crisis time that predestined many years to come.

When a young man seriously decides what course in life he will pursue; when he stands, for the nrst time, with a glass of wine in his hand; when a profession is decided upon; when he is aware that he is doing his first deliberate wrong; all these moments are living agents ever acting upon the trivial events of his life which fill up the interim till the next crisis.

Happy is the man who takes advantage of the tide that leads on to fortune—hopelessly does he battle against the ebb that can only hurry him on to the death-dealing shallows. That man must wait till the tide turns; all he can do is to keep off the rocks and look out for hidden reefs. He must keep his oars in hand, ready for any current helping him out of danger.

Monson was, at that time, a small village, nestled away among mountains, lakes and valleys. Half of the township was donated by the Legislature of Massachusetts to Monson Academy and half was also given to Hebron Academy. Monson, Mass. Academy sold its land to settlers from that part of the State, and Hebron did likewise. Each exercised great care in the selection of settlers and the result was that no town could boast a more reliable band of pioneers. Nearly all the pioneers were church members, and soon two churches were formed; a Baptist and a Congregationalist. A school was organized in the very beginning of the settlement. This was taught first in a private house. An old settler informed me that in his part of the town the first school-house had a peculiar origin. The bears troubled the flocks of the settlers so persistently that they gathered together one day and built a strong log house, some ten feet square. In one side they cut a door large enough for a bear to pass. In the door they set a "dead-fall" to which was attached an apparatus so arranged that when the bear went in and began to eat the bait laid out for him, the trap would let fall the door, and bruin would be imprisoned. When bears became scarce and children plenty, the neighbors met again, put a roof on the log pen, laid a floor, put in a window and lo! a school-house appeared. The first word the scholars learned to spell was b-e-a-r.

The town was decidedly puritanic for many years. There is quite a large lake in the center of the town, and also good hunting near the village; but, during the first years of my teaching there, I never saw a boat on the lake, or a fisherman, with his rod, or sportsman with his gun, on Sunday. Everybody went to church, and very many were members of the churches. There was also a very active literary sentiment among the people,— among the early settlers were some well educated ladies and a few men. These gave a tone to society that was transmitted and increased as more advantages presented themselves.

There was, in those days, a great interest in education. This had been shown years before in a practical way. In 1847 the people resolved that there should be an Academy in Monson. They called a meeting and appointed committees, and, having obtained aid from the State, by means of private money and contributed labor, erected a building in 1848. This structure was burned twelve years later, but another was built in 1861, which is still used as a school building.

The slate quarries had not then been opened. Farming, lumbering, and trading absorbed the attention of the people. There was no railroad to Moosehead Lake, hence all the travel to that place went through Monson. The only riotous times in those days were when the river-drivers went through the town, and when an old Militia Major ran amuck.

Card playing was tabooed and dancing was thought a heinous sin, and Masonry was not regarded as conducive to righteousness. There was not a large amount of wealth, but quite an even distribution.

None were very rich, and few very poor. On the whole, there was a high moral tone among the people, who were contented with their lot and wanted nothing better. If there was just a trifle of the spirit of the man in the synagogue cropping out occasionally a little, it could readily be pardoned.

The crisis before mentioned came to me in the most agreeable manner. Among the pupils there was a young lady who, afterwards, became my wife, and I have ever had cause to bless the circumstance that induced me to go to Monson. That lady was an only child; this circumstance kept me at Monson many years. I passed, in all, some twenty-five years in that town and saw many changes there. In 1871 slate was discovered and a quarry opened, the railroad to Moosehead Lake was built, and the lumbering interest began to flag. A new class of people came in; new conditions began to appear; new societies arose, and a new standard of propriety seemed to be raised up.

The history of the development of the slate quarries has never been written and never will be fully till the Recording Angel renders up his final account. Companies rose and fell, fortunes were made and larger ones lost, in alternate rapid succession. Men came to town for a month, and went away, to give place to more new comers; new quarries were opened and old ones abandoned; new companies were formed upon the debris of shattered predecessors, till, at last, the business settled down upon a solid basis and seems now to be profitable to owners and workmen.

There were many pathetic events connected with the history of those days. I went to bed one night, feeling sure that my name would one day sound very much like Vanderbilt's, but waked in the morning to discover that it would sound better beside that of Lazarus. Wealthy men became poor, and poor men wealthy. Quarries were found everywhere. Every ledge of rock promised its owner a fortune, and every house-lot invited a mansion.

One circumstance in the upheaval resulted very fortunately for the recipient. An aged clergyman, who had been pastor for some twenty years in town, had just resigned. His worldly possessions consisted of a small house and a few acres of land.

In the cellar of that house real slate was discovered. A speculator bought the premises and thus the good old man was made comfortable in his declining years. He moved away, but the influence for grace he had exerted still lingers, with sacred memory, in the character of many whose lives he influenced.

An old pasture that was nearly worthless, belonging to my wife's folks, sold for twenty-five hundred dollars.

That "Wall Street" financiering in Monson produced some Napoleons of finance. Some of them are still active agents and promoters in the booming business, and are wealthy; while others met their Waterloo in the first skirmish and had never a St. Helena for refuge. At that time I realized that lack of knowledge is a serious deficiency. Many a day had I sat upon the protruding rock in that old pasture with never a thought there was value in it. I believe there is an old proverb about Heaven lying at our feet, if we can only see it.

Great changes have taken place in the slate business. The motive force that lifted the rock out of the first quarry was a sad-eyed, long-eared donkey; to-day several sixty-horse power engines are always at work. The water was removed by one of Uncle James' wooden pumps,—now the steam pump hisses day and night. Roofing slate only was at first manufactured; now almost every conceivable household and mechanical convenience is subserved by finely wrought slate implements; and when one dies, he can sleep his last sleep encased in a highly polished sarcophagus of slate.

It seems to be a granted fact that Monson slate is the best in the world. It withstands the attacks of acids, and alkalies, better than any other. The business of quarrying and manufacturing slate has become the all-absorbing interest of the people of the town.

I cannot see just how slate should be connected with the gun and fishing rod, but somehow, on some alluring Sunday mornings, gun and rod have, in later years, occasionally appeared.

Perhaps I may be pardoned if, right here, I discuss the mental, moral and physical aspects of fishing and hunting. The man that really enjoys fishing is a fortunate being. He ought to congratulate himself. Of course, I do not mean those men who fish just to get something to eat. There is no more good coming to such men from a day's fishing on lake or brook than there would be to him engaged in any other kind of labor. But to the man who loves nature, solitude, the breezy lake, the sparkling brook, who can see a thousand beauties beaming upon him from beech, maple and pine; whose tired nerves are soothed to rest by every wave, beating music upon rock and shore, the rod is a magical wand that opens up more treasures than Sinbad ever dreamed of.

CHAPTER XI.

FISHING.

It may be that an attenuated drop of the blood of the old Druids circulates in my veins, prompting a love for trees. There is something sacred about an ancient tree that seems, almost, to call for worship. Bryant says: "The groves were God's first temples." Wordsworth declares:

> "One impulse from the vernal wood
> Will teach you more of man,
> Of moral evil and of good,
> Than all the Sages can."

Nature is a wonderful teacher; but she requires an attentive pupil. The student must be in harmony with nature. Her voice can only be heard and her language understood when teacher and scholar speak the same language. To listen to her voices there must be the attentive ear and absorbed attention.

To the hunter, with gun on shoulder, with slaughter in mind as he, with Indian-like tread, steals through the forest, nature offers no Paradise, sings no songs, lulls to no repose. I am making no attacks upon hunters or hunting, but simply wish to note the ethical effect of the one and the other recreation.

Take a trip with me, wearied preacher, discouraged teacher, sleepless man of law, as in retrospection I seek rest, comfort and inspiration from never unwilling nature. The road winds gently away from the thoroughfare and, as the sleepy horse plods dreamily along, through the rifts in the mist veil, more beautiful than princess ever wore, hanging in air, occasional flashes of sunlight come, making weird forms and shapes dance upon the lazy waves of the lake, just awakened from profound repose; anon the veil would roll itself up into folds made bright and gorgeous, blushing red as the sun god kisses the mythical Lady of the Lake; at length island and farther shore begin to appear, and loon and wild duck, gracefully sporting in the water, assure us that the marvelous panorama upon which we have been gazing, is a real lake of physical existence.

Its beauty invites us, its repose allures us, its dreamy calmness soothes us, but more charming music the soul requires to-day, more sublime solitude must breathe into the soul its mysterious repose. Then on we go, with umbrageous accompaniment on either side, over little streams, some laughing, some complaining in plaintive murmurs, till the deeper forest is reached; where the hoary trees, in sober garments dressed, begin to infuse into the soul a gladsome feeling of repose. They are so much wiser than the short-lived human passing by. They have seen so much. Beneath their branches the lordly moose mayhap has taken refuge; the sad-eyed deer ruminated careless of hunter or wolf; the foot of the red man has, it may be, trodden the leaves at their base,—defiant of storm and lightning flash for ages, have they stood in majestic solitude!

A slight curve in the road brings the stern, bald head of Boarstone in view. There are no sharp corners in the road, switching off one's dreamy contemplation by violent abruptness to other scenes, but just gentle windings, so that every new view is interblended with the last, as colors of the rainbow blend. Thus the "gentle musing" is uninterrupted, and soon takes possession of the whole soul.

At length the forest path is reached, winding in gentle curves through tangled shrubbery and over gently rising knolls, moss-covered, reaching the tiny lake at a point where the view is most picturesque.

A gem of a lake lies embossed among circling hills. On the north ridge rises above ridge, till a lofty summit is attained, crowned with evergreen trees; on the east there is forest, circling down to the water's edge; on the west precipitous rocks rise abruptly out of the water and tower aloft into the air, fringed with mosses, lichens, and trailing arbutus. Every step in the panorama is beautiful, artistic, symmetrical. The alternate ridges, rising with perfect demarcation one above another, with alternate growth of deciduous and evergreen trees, the circling shores, the lofty headlands, the dense forest; all form a natural poem, which the poet, the lover of nature, the aesthetic, can read, feel and assimilate.

With rod and line we seat ourselves in the boat and gently paddle out from shore. We cast the hook into the water and await results. The fish are not plentiful. We lie back in the stern of the boat and let nature talk to us. Forgotten are cares, enemies, if we have them, everything not in keeping with the almost supernatural repose. We still have the rod in hand, which seems to be the connecting link between purely spiritual enjoyment and earthly pleasure. Should a venturesome trout disturb the bait and rouse us from our meditation, we, for a moment, come back to an earthly existence; gently lay it in the boat and admire its graceful outline, its ever beautiful livery, and rejoice that it is in keeping with the artistic beauty all around it. Then we fall back again to our meditative state and the mental faculties begin to show their supremacy. Deep questions in philosophy are solved, moral perplexities fade away, theological solutions are now easy. If some congenial friend occupies the boat with us, an occasional word is spoken, usually in subdued tones.

But under no conditions are friends so near together, so true, so dearly appreciated.

And so the day passes away and the evening shadows come, all too quickly, and the nervous, pessimistic man of the morning lays his head upon the pillow that night, feeling that he has received a recipe from the Great Physician, and this world, after all, is a glorious one.

Recreation should develop the physical, stimulate the mental, and improve the moral. It should never brutalize or render less refined the sensibilities. There is nothing in a day's fishing calculated to do this. There is no scene that would offend the sensibilities of the most delicate lady,—and great moral lessons may be learned. We discover that if we catch men, lead them to higher and better life, we must not lash the waters of the social world in frenzied fervor; nor shout our convictions as though the world was deaf, but with argument suited to the occasion, cast and wait, ever willing to accept what conditions have offered.

I spent a day last year on a beautiful little lake where every condition was conducive to repose, to ethical thought, to poetic conception. My companion was a gentleman from New York, a lawyer of extensive practice and successful in every undertaking. But I feel very sure, though the bar would have lost much, that the college would have gained more, had he become a teacher instead of lawyer. We fished, talked, admired, meditated, and spent an ideal day. We discussed many weighty subjects, decided, to our own satisfaction, at what age students should enter college, what constitutes an education, compared a liberal education with the practical superficiality of the day, and many others.

I afterwards tried to reproduce that conversation. It was impossible. The setting was lacking. The genial, inspiring influence of my companion was absent, and that absence was fatal. No substitute could fill that place. He was just the man, with his overmastering genius, that called out the best in me. The lake and the forest had driven away all common thought and cares, and left the mind free to receive impressions of a higher and better nature. Those came from the keen analysis of thought emanating from the brain of my companionable fellow fisherman. His words inspired me, the unspoken sentiments of his soul, by the undefined channel of spiritual influence, inspired my soul, and the unrestrained abandonment of my whole being to every influence around put my mind into a condition capable of the highest intellectual and spiritual efforts. Only occasionally can every condition be so completely met.

The unseen, self-acting influence of mind upon mind is a common theme for discussion in these days, and much may be said upon the subject, but still the theory is little understood. The phenomenon is still a theory. There are daily exhibitions of what we recognize as simply action of mind upon mind, without any physical movement whatever. These instances are not theories, but facts; but what is needed is to discover under just what conditions this influence will always operate.

That there is an indescribable influence which emanates from one mind to another cannot be denied. But that influence will sometimes be an active force, and sometimes not. When it does manifest itself, it is the most potent that can be brought to bear upon the human soul. Men have been led by this indescribable influence to do that which no argument or persuasion, expressed in words could cause them to do. And under no other condition can this spiritual influence be felt as in the temples not made with hands and casting shadows upon the placid waters.

CHAPTER XII.

MONSON ACADEMY.

I found the school at Monson in complete confusion. There were no very bad scholars, but the school had been an utter failure on the part of the teacher to control the scholars. There were about twenty-five large boys and girls out of a total of sixty-five. Some of these are prominent people in Monson at the present time. Among them was D. P. Bailey of Everett, Massachusetts. Mr. Bailey was a very excellent scholar, and showed at that early age the promise that later reached fulfillment in a very prominent career as a lawyer, financier and statesman. I remember that in one term the whole twelve books of Virgil were read. There were six in the class and each read two books apiece and no two the same.

The schoolroom was rather dark so I sat a red-headed boy in the dark corner to illuminate that vicinity. That same boy was once out fishing through the ice. Vice-President Hamlin was there, having some live bait. My pupil had none but wanted some so he approached the Vice-President holding out at arm's length a big old-fashioned cent and said, "Meester Hamblen, sell me a chub?" He got the chub.

At school after a few days everything went on all right. The trustees hired me to teach the fall term and increased the salary. I came back in September and taught. The school was large and advanced. Greek, Latin and French were taught as well as Geometry, Trigonometry and Surveying. There were no graduations in those days, each one went to school as long as he pleased and left when he felt disposed. Five pupils came from

Milo where I had taught, and two or three from Abbott. I enjoyed that school very much although I had to work very hard. There was a high moral tone in the school. Two of the boys became deacons, one a lawyer, one a doctor, one a clergyman, one a financier and one a librarian. While teaching here I "made up" my college work and found myself rather tired at the end of the year. My next term was at Monson. In this school several war veterans became prominent factors. The old poets of Greece and Rome invariably associated Mars and Venus in every prominent act in the drama of social life. They must have been right for ever since they have been inseparable. "The bravest are the tenderest, the daring are the loving." Those war scarred veterans divided their attention between grammar and the doorsteps leading to the many attractive parlors of that town noted for pretty girls. In two weeks Lord could conjugate *amo* like an ancient Roman. He always gave the active voice, said he had no use for the passive voice. The *progressive* form was just suited to his nature.

Cruel war had deprived Ricker of one arm, but he made the best use of the remaining limb in embracing every opportunity for an education and some other things. His geographical knowledge was defective as he discovered one rainy lyceum night when he offered to gallant a young lady home who lived somewhere near Moosehead lake. Carver's hearing had been injured in a big battle to that extent that he could never hear the clock strike one A. M. Douglas was more conservative. He never had but two girls at one time. The boys studied well and made good progress in their studies considering how many nights they stood guard pacing the deserted streets and guarding the commissary and outflanking the other fellows. Instinctively they formed themselves in foraging parties, and turnip field and corn patches and cucumber yards suffered. A local poet reminisces about those days as follows:

A careful review of the last forty years,
In spite of all croaking and carping and jeers,

Shows many bright spots, many labors well done,
Some storm, some sunshine, some tears and some
   fun.
But 'tis hard to believe that the gray-headed men
Were boys and girls at the Academy then.
I cannot imagine that staid Deacon John
Ever rang a church bell or tooted a horn
On the 4th of July, put on the gloves or handled
   a bat,
Or talked with the girls at recess and all that,
Ever smiled upon Emma or Clara or Nell,
Ever wrote little notes and received them as well,
Ever flirted or courted, Deacon John, O no!
His children take after the mother you know.
And Carol whose wisdom the wisest enjoy
Can you even imagine he was ever a boy?
There's a story, made up of fiction and truth
That Chapin, the banker, was at one time a youth
That the Parson, so learned in Biblical lore
Stood many a night on the steps of the door.
Did Nelson attend with the girls and the boys,
That silent, still lad never making a noise?
Can it be that these walls did ever resound
To the voice of Bailey, so deep and profound?
No prophet was needed the future to scan,
A boy with the heart and brain of a man.
And the records proclaim that a long, stately form
Whose head rose far above clouds and the storm
Sat in the back seat with his hair standing straight
Where now there appears a polished white pate.
Twas Carver the soldier, Carver the flirt,
Companion of Lord and Loring and Bert.
Did Reetus sing then? Ask the rocks and the hills,
That echoed his quavers, repeated his trills.
Old Orpheus so sang that the rocks jumped around
And the trees promenaded all over the ground
But Rectus could stop the wild comet's career
And Aurora oft stopped her horses to hear.
And once when his tones outrivaled the lark
She forgot all about the light and the dark
And left the old Sun down under the water
Till the school bell struck at eight and a quarter.

And the world never knew the terrible fix
Old Sol was then in at half past six.
O singers, beware, take warning I pray
Don't frighten old Phaethon's horses away.
Don't deafen the lark when he's up in the sky
He flies you know a mile or two high.
A myth has come down from the 60's or so,
If false or if true I'm sure I don't know,
Of a boy possessing such marvelous brain
That the skull couldn't stand the terrible strain
When it worked together, so each part took a turn
And what would come out you could never discern.
When his eyes were fixed on his reader or grammar
A whirl of the brain now 'twas Jennie or Anna.
The preaching brain next and then speculation
And he tried every one without hesitation.
No girl and no boy will ever forget
Burb Loring the joker with hair black as jet,
And lots more boys whom *fama obscura*
Has hidden from sight, *et femina pura*
And some tell of a girl from the shores of Moosehead
Whose weight was 300 or more it is said
Lord walked with her home one moonshiny night,
When the weather was calm and the stars twinkled bright
Till he came to the door he never once knew
That Chapin had walked on the other side too.
Who pulled up the beans? Was it Chapin or Lord?
Or Leonard, or Francis, or mischievous "Thod?"
Who raided the hen-roost and foraged the corn,
And courted the girls till the break of the dawn?
I shall not tell. Those gray-headed chaps
Quite have forgotton those frolics, perhaps
Are now warning a daughter or son,
Never to do the things they had done.

Loring was there too. Shall I attempt to describe him? No, the task is too great. Future historians must do this or he will "die unsung."

There was a boy who attempted to study Greek. He never got beyond that paragraph in the Anabasis which declared that "To Darius and Parissatis were born two sons." But he was a genius and became a famous financier and promoter in busi ness circles in more states than one. He is now engaged in con verting Martha's Vineyard into a crockery shop.

Not one of the trustees of the Academy of those days is alive at the present time. Aretus Chapin was the President and did all he could to make the school profitable. Mr. Chapin was one of the old settlers, and always held some town office. He was later a member of the House at Augusta. His well known temperance principles produced a marked influence upon public opinion in Monson. He is ably represented at the present time by his son, Hon. A. W. Chapin. Mr. Chapin does a large busi ness in town and is active in every movement for public improvement or in educational lines. "Bert" was a soldier, and one of the boys before mentioned in connection with the school, but he was always one of the *inside* guard.

Dr. Sumner Patten was also a trustee. He was a fine speaker and somewhat of a politician. He was State Senator later. He sent to school one of the sweetest girls I ever had the pleasure of teaching. She is now Mrs. Walter Pullen of Wash ington. I also have the kindliest remembrance of Walter. He was a fine scholar and a gentleman and has made a very success ful business man. Charles Pullen, an older brother, I remember with pleasure. He married a favorite pupil of mine, Miss Celeste Knight, and holds a responsible position in the business world in Brooklyn.

Among the bright-eyed young ladies was a Miss Celeste Robinson of Greenville. She was never idle a moment, or still many, during the day, and had a musical laugh that would dis arm a cynic, and a smile that brushed away every frown that her mischief caused. She is now Mrs. Sanders of Greenville, occu pies a very prominent position in the social world and is uni versally admired.

From the forest bound shores of Moosehead Lake came a young lady, Miss Masterman, apt to learn, with retentive mem ory, bringing with her all the modesty and shyness of her sylvan home. She was a lovable girl, tall and graceful, and made rapid progress in her studies. She now lives in the West.

Miss Arvilla Serepta Burdict labored under the most euphonic name of any one. Miss Ellen Carr Flanders' name did not quite suit me, so I persuaded her after five years of assiduous attention to change it to Ellen Flanders Knowlton. Whether or not that change has been beneficial to her the recording angel only knows, but it was the most fortunate undertaking that ever engrossed my attention.

CHAPTER XIII.

EXETER AND DEXTER.

In 1863 I taught some weeks at Exeter. A young man commenced the school, but some difficulty arose which terminated his stay in town. The school, on the whole, was pleasant, but there were disagreeable features in it. Many of the pupils had caught a theatrical fever—which ran very high. There was a young man among the pupils by the name of J. M. Hill who was the leader in the "craze." Every morning, noon, and night theatricals were discussed, and much of the time appropriate for study was wasted. The condition was something like the modern status of interest in education.

Not long ago I stepped into a hotel in a town noted for its schools. In a few moments several students came in, and for a half-hour those boys conversed together. Football, basketball, and baseball were fully discussed; the last prize fight received due consideration, but not a word about a single mental exercise, the graduation class, books, rank, college expectations; all these things would have interested me, but in silence I endured the most senseless gabble of those boys, feeling quite sure that somebody was wrong; either I or the boys, or the teachers of the boys.

I propose to make no raid upon athletics; it would be foolish to do so. The fever is on; let it have its run; there is no such thing as "breaking up a fever." Only quacks ever claim such power. When the poison has worked itself out of the system the time will be ripe for teaching healthful athletics, mental discipline, moral principles.

Well, I let the theatrical fever at Exeter have its run—when I thought the fever ought to "turn" I just "turned it." All communication in school hours ceased. No more rehearsals at recess or noon, all books or plays were seized as contraband; study was required, perfect lessons demanded; and, in fine, a complete change of program was insisted upon. There was rebellion at first, but this soon subsided and some good work was done by the pupils.

Many of the pupils belonged to families well known in the State. There was a young lady in school who did not behave very well and one day I was discussing the matter with her father when he said: "Take a birch and give her a h——l of a licking." Not fully understanding Exeter's interpretation of the amount of punishment permitted by the expression, I concluded to adopt another method.

F. M. Hill became, in after years, the famous theatrical manager of New York and Boston. There was a very pretty boy in the school, about nine years old. His name was Arthur Barker. He was the son of David Barker, Maine's most celebrated poet. Arthur was a sweet-looking boy, with rather a girlish face, a bright scholar but rather mischievous. When he was born, David Barker sent to the New York Evening Post the following exquisite stanzas:

"One night, as old St. Peter slept,
    He left the gate of Heaven ajar,
When forth a little angel crept,
    And came down on a falling star."

"One Summer, as the blessed beams
Of morn approached, my blushing bride
Awakened from some pleasing dreams,
    And found that angel by her side."

"God grant but this, I ask no more,
    That when he leaves this world of sin,
He'll wing his way to that blest shore,
    And find the gate of Heaven again."

I have spoken of Barker as Maine's greatest poet. In real genius I thing he would rank above any poet who wrote in Maine. N. P. Willis, Longfellow, and others, we can hardly claim. Barker was a strange man. Much of his poetry was of a low order, but when a real inspiraton seized him, the truly artistic showed itself.

In "The Covered Bridge" there is real poetic merit; also in "The Lion and the Skunk," "The Beveled Grindstone" and others. I feel sure that a more judicious editor would have added to the volume some poems discarded, and would have discarded some that were published. Only the best of any man's writings should ever be published.

There was a very pretty little girl in school, about seven or eight years old. Every hair was firmly laid in just the right spot, and every act and word was always just right. I was very fond of that little girl. In after years she became the "First Lady of the State," and no Governor's wife ever graced the position with sweeter dignity than did Mable Hill Plaistead.

One girl wore number five boots, I remember, and one boy was six feet and three inches tall. George S. Hill was a merchant at the Corner, doing an extensive business. I became very well acquainted with him and enjoyed many pleasant chats in that store; a few years after, Mr. Hill became an Episcopal clergyman and was engaged to preach at Presque Isle, and superintend the services of the St. John's School. I was to be the Principal of the school. Mr. Hill was thrown from a mowing machine and killed. No other man could be found for the place, so I lost my position at Presque Isle and went to Caribou, which was a fortunate move as my salary was largely increased.

I taught one term of school in Dexter, in 1865, a summer term and boarded with my cousin, Mrs. H. C. Parsons. At the same time I studied law in the office of the Hon. Josiah Crosby. Mr. Crosby was at this time in the zenith of his career. Very few men understood the technicalities of the law as well as he. He was the most painstaking man I ever knew. Although remarkably well posted in law, he never prepared papers without consulting the Revised Statutes, and never gave advice without doing the same. He had fine literary taste and read many good books. I enjoyed his society very much and heard of his death with regret. Two of his daughters attended school. They were bright, intelligent young ladies. One is now the wife of a wealthy railroad president in Minneapolis. The other lives in Washington. One lawyer came from that school, Edgar Russ of Dexter. The schoolhouse stood on Zion's Hill, so called on account of the pronounced piety of some of the neighbors. The schoolroom was in the second story. One day a fifteen year old girl fainted and I carried her down stairs to the wagon that had come to take her home. She weighed one hundred and fifty pounds. I was not able to teach the next day. One day a young man in reading Latin translated these words, *Jacet ingens litore truncus caput avulsum humeris,'*—"They put his head in a big trunk on the shore." The same young man translating that passage in Virgil that describes how the Greeks came out of the wooden horse, read,—"They came out through his ears." He was probably thinking of some men he had seen. I remember a Miss Mary Thompson in that school with pleasure, who was a fine Latin scholar. I enjoyed the school and think they liked me. I made many pleasant acquaintances in Dexter who showed me great kindness. Mr. Parsons and I played backgammon every night until twelve o'clock, then we would agree at what hour we would have breakfast and that devoted wife of his would call us at the stated hour. Would every wife have done that?

Dexter is a picturesque town. A small stream runs through the middle of the village, propelling the machinery of several factories. The town is built upon the hills arising on either side. The roads are "Tommetized" on the upper side. This process consists in placing in the inclined bank alternate rows of grass sods and small rocks. The grass grows up and holds the rocks in place, so that a bank thus "tommetized" is never affected by rain or frost. Thomas Bicknell first built the wall in Dexter, and immortalized his name by green banks and good sidewalks. "Tommie" was not a great man, but he did a good work and his monument will grow greener and fresher as time rolls on. The world is full of histories of men like Thomas Bicknell. They were humble actors in the great drama of public life, but left to the world a legacy rich in practical value. The patent office shows that but a very small proportion of the inventions patented is ever available. By the way, why do politicians always send patent office reports to constituents of no especial influence? The book is not very entertaining to a reader of literary or poetic nature. The professional inventor rarely succeeds. The marvelous specimens of machinery now operating in this country are the combined results of the thought of many minds, each adding something to the efficiency of a machine then in use. This teaches the fraternity of man, and ought to teach the moralist, who would make the world better, that he must not destroy all that has gone before but take whatever is good, add to it, make new appliances, devise new methods and await its results. This suggestion applies especially to teachers commencing a school in a new position. The first impression a teacher has, is the idea that his predecessors were deficient in some lines. The revelations of the first few days convince him that the other teacher did not thoroughly do his work. I used to think so until I began to succeed myself, then I began to understand that vacation makes sad havoc with the memory of boys and girls. Entirely new methods introduced the first week are disastrous, though every new method be in itself better. When a method of doing has been drilled into the every day thought of a young boy no new one will find lodgment until the old one has ceased to be an intuitive act of the mind. The better way is proved to be something like this: take the old method in form and add to it on one side, so to speak, and drop off something from the other side. This process repeated daily will in a little while present an entirely new way of conducting that exercise.

In matters of order a little more strenuous method may be necessary. The first day should show the school that there must be a predominating spirit in that schoolroom, and that factor is the teacher. This should be done quietly but firmly. These ideas are further treated and discussed in a lecture recorded in another place in this book.

As before remarked, the streets of Dexter are nearly all up-hill one way and down-hill the other. This daily exercise gives the people great strength of muscle in the leg. All the boys are good football players. I noticed that the trousers of most of the men bagged at the knees, caused by the constant right-angle action of the knee in daily climbing. Josh Billings said Dexter was named from the famous trotting horse Dexter, and that it was three thousand miles west of London. It is an enterprising town full of active business men. Political opinions are always freely expressed, as are religious ideas. I remember one politician who declared with a string of oaths that would have astonished a river-driver, that he would not vote for a man that did not believe in religion! They were not an excitable people in those days. I remember an old man hung himself before breakfast. The rope was cut and the man carried into the house and the doctor sent for. He came, examined the subject a moment or two and said, "I guess he isn't dead· after breakfast I will see what I can do for him." After his matutinal meal, the phlegmatic doctor "brought him to."

Dr. Fitzgerald lived in Dexter at that time. His stable was a marvel. The stalls for his horses were trimmed with ebony. The doctor, I remember, effected a remarkable cure one day when a quarrelsome fellow called him a liar. As the said fellow lay on his back gazing up at the sun, he must have formed a new resolution, for he was never known to want to fight afterward.

I was well acquainted with Mr. Barron, whose tragic death caused so much discussion later. Dexter is at the present time a very prosperous village.

CHAPTER XIV.

FOXCROFT ACADEMY. TEACHER.

In 1864, I became Assistant Teacher of Foxcroft Academy. S. T. Pullen was the Principal, and, as there was sickness in his family during most of the year, I acted as Principal a part of the time. I became Principal the next year, and enjoyed the school very much.

There were about one hundred pupils, most of them well advanced in their studies. There were some I especially remember for some peculiar characteristics. I can hear, today, the stentorian tones of A. W. Gilman, as he frightened the timid country lasses, while expounding the mysteries of Algebra, or parsing Milton's 'Paradise Lost." I called upon him one day to read that clause which commences as follows: "He called so loud that all the hollow deep of hell resounded." I never knew how loud that was before.

I remember with pleasure Eugene Wade, a lovable young man with great ability, and that sweet sister, Augusta, whose portrait might have been painted for the face of a Madonna. Near by her sat Eliza Mayo, an excellent girl, and as kind and conscientious as a young lady could be. I remember her with much pleasure. I roomed just across the way from Mr. Mayo's when a boy at the Academy. Mrs. Mayo was very kind to me then, and I have always rejoiced at the prosperity that has fol lowed the family. The Mayo family is, perhaps, the wealthiest and most prominent one in the county.

I very distinctly remember the sweet face of Sally Crocker, and she was as sweet as she looked. There was something very

attractive about that little Miss.   She is now a famous painter.
I remember that the handsome, stately Miss Susie Brown used
to recite extraordinary lessons in Virgil; and that there was a
stately dignity connected with the movements of Henry B.
Flint, which has been a safe-guard against nervous prostration
ever since.

I had the pleasure of teaching E. P. Sampson Latin and
Greek for a year or two.   No student was more faithful in his
work.   Mr. Sampson graduated from Bates and taught in Foxcroft Academy very acceptably.   He has been teacher of Thorn-
ton Academy at Saco, Maine for a long period of time.
Mr. Sampson has become eminent in his profession.   Few
teachers have been as successful and none surpass him in zeal,
devotion and tact.   His Alma Mater would honor itself by
bestowing upon him a well-merited LL. D.

Dr. Putnam was a studious boy.   He is now in the West.
One boy I remember who had a rather swelly way of doing
things.   Years after I met him and remarked that he had
changed somewhat.   He replied: "Good Heavens! I ought to
change.   I have been in seven states."   A nice, quiet, studious
little girl sat over in one corner of the room, who always looked
very much relieved when the lesson was over   She was a
fine singer, and Mrs. Henry Hudson still sings finely, and is a
lady much beloved.   There were three young ladies from one
family by the name of Merrill.   They were very nice and attentive.   Lizzie still lives in the old homestead.   I should do violence to my own soul not to mention David Dinsmore.   That
smile of his cheered me in many a gloomy hour.

Dr. C. C. Hall was a very diligent student and made his
studies go as he has everything since.   He not only has occupied a high position in his profession, but has held the office of
County Treasurer and was Representative at Augusta last
winter.

A very bright young lady, Miss Gilman, I remember always
had her lessons nicely learned.

I can see the bright eyes of Miss Wyman today. How they used to sparkle when she laughed! And pretty Rowena Woodbury sat near the post, and Miss Macomber and Miss Robinson just across the aisle. Those two Misses were bright and interesting. I liked them exceedingly well, but used to wish, sometimes, that Latin was a more serious study, causing less smiles.

I recollect a very quiet, nice little Miss who sat up very straight in her seat, and was always studying. When she did any work on the board, every figure was just right and in place, as was every hair on the head of Annie Whittier.

Miss Clara Getchell I well recollect as a very lively young lady of good ability. She is now the wife of L. P. Evans, editor of the well known "Piscataquis Observer."

A. M. Robinson was President of the board of trustees when I taught at Foxcroft Academy. I became very well acquainted with him, and knew him in his last days. He was by nature a grand man. He possessed great analytical ability. He could dissect a proposition with such nicety that every part appeared in prominent positions easy to inspect. When he had thoroughly inspected every part and searched for the weak places, he attacked these with vigor and persistency. He always massed his arguments upon a few points and continued to enforce them by illustrations, figures of speech, logic—and repetitions. I write of him as he appeared to me, a boy, listening to a very succesful lawyer. There was an air of sincerity about him when speaking, that gave me the impression that he must be right, and the jury apparently thought the same. He gained many cases. He was never what is called "eloquent," but was an excellent debator, persuasive pleader, and held his audience till the end.

His choice of words was noticeable. Not a word was used that did not drive home the argument. His thought seemed to be,—one link broken, the whole chain was useless. I particularly noticed that he used more purely Anglo-Saxon words than any other man at the bar.

Mr. Robinson's friendship once secured, he was a friend for life. He was a man of few prejudices, and judged every man and principle on its merits. Honest and kindly in all his relations in life he was honored among men, and loved by his friends and associates.

CHAPTER XV.

BRIMFIELD.

In 1866 I went West and came back in August. Learning that a teacher was needed at Brimfield, Mass., I went to that town and interviewed the trustees, and secured the position; and, a fortnight later, commenced the school. It was a very enjoyable set of pupils. The atmosphere of the schoolroom and of the town was conducive to easy teaching.

Brimfield is a typical Massachusetts town. There is an indefinable something about Massachusetts people that is distinctive and characteristic. An inherited taste is always superior to an acquired one. The people there, through a long line of descent, come naturally by a refinement of manners and thought, and language, which people newer in these matters cannot assume with the same ease, however much they may desire to thus attain. The hospitality of the people is remarkable, when once the doors are opened. It is not the best way, in Massachusetts, to slap a stranger on the back whom we wish to know, but when the proper advances are made and received, there can be no people more cordial and friendly and hospitable.

I loved that people and remember them with greatest pleasure. I sat on the piazza of the hotel, the first night there and enjoyed the view as the evening twilight settled down upon the landscape. In front of the hotel was a broad plain, covered with very green grass. Upon the right, at a little distance, could be seen, through the trees, the spire of the Congregationalist Church; on the left was the schoolhouse, a modest, rather pretty building; several pretty houses could be seen on

8

three or four streets. The fire-flies were flitting over the meadow, lighting their lamps, one by one, as the stars came out timidly to see if the sun had gone down. I remember now how fine it all appeared; how peaceful. The Committee had met me very cordially; the village pleased me; the salary offered was satisfactory; the evening was magnificent; I felt that Heaven was very kind, and I was happy.

A man came along, said "Good evening," and sat down beside me and inquired if I were the new teacher. Being informed that his supposition was true, he commenced an hour's talk by saying: "Well, I can tell you this; that you will be sorry you ever came." He then mentioned the Committee, one by one, and gave every one a character far from lovable, and totally different from the truth. That libeler then went right through the town and mentioned some sin or crime each had been guilty of. When that man left me that night, I was in a frantic state of dejeetion. Had there been a train out that night, I should have gone. Upon the next day I met many of the people, and found them ladies and gentlemen of a high and cultivated order. I never taught where I loved the people as at Brimfield.

Every town has a man like that one, but I never before met him the first day. If that man is in Heaven at this time, I would like to hear his description of the inhabitants of that place.

There were about seventy-five pupils, mostly from Brimfield. The adjoining towns sent about a dozen to the school. There were some very intellectual pupils and some very lovable ones. Taken together the intellectual status of the scholars was very high, as was the moral standing. It was a very easy school to govern.

Among the pupils was a young man of marked individuality. He was a fine declaimer and enjoyed practicing the art of public declamation. His laugh was refreshing. He was never dull in conversation, and had a very happy way of making the

teacher think he knew all about the lesson. He graduated at
Amherst College and became a lawyer in Boston. He is a very
prosperous politician; and holds the office of Street Commissioner of the city of Boston. All the old pupils will recognize
in the Hon. Salem D. Charles the sequel of the good-natured
Salem D. Charles of the Hitchcock Free School of Brimfield.

There was also a bright-eyed little miss who always had her
lessons well learned, but who had an irresistible impulse toward
restlessness. She could never be still a moment. There was
not a malicious thought in her soul, but the spirit of mischief
led her into all kinds of adventures that caused us to become
very well acquainted. The thankful manner in which she would
receive paternal advice from me was very touching, especially
when, by accident, I caught the twinkle in her down-cast eye.
Just as I expected, she has made a magnificent woman and holds
a very responsible position in an old and well-known institution
in the Bay State—Dean of Holyoke College.

As I write, the whole school comes up in array before me,
and I see them all as vividly as in sixty-six, seated in that pleasant school. I see the dignified Rebecca, reciting "The Cry of
the Human," the loving, impetuous Etta, one of the flowers that
grows between" the insatiable reaper gathered; the sweet, sad
face of Lizzie, whom the gods loved; the queenly Miss Chamberlain; laughing Belle Brown; Sarah Leombard, so quiet; and
Mary, her chum; Lizzie Monroe, never out of order; and Jennie, so positive; and Sarah, so shy and self-poised;—all these
and many more do I remember as though the long years had
never intervened between the last day at Brimfield and the present time.

I boarded at the Hotel kept by Mr. Monroe. No more
genial landlord ever managed a hotel. Mrs. Monroe became a
real mother to me. She had an especial pudding for each day in
this week. All those puddings had been christened by a theological name. I ate through the course, and decided that the
Baptist pudding was the best, and asked her if she was not a

Baptist. She replied she was; which accounted for the best one being thus named. I asked her to explain the meaning of the names. She did so, much to my amusement. The Unitarian pudding was "pudding" today, and became "cake" served up cold to-morrow. The Methodist pudding was what my mother called "Minute Pudding"—good while hot. The Orthodox pudding stood up very stiff and never lost form. Remember these are not *my* definitions, but the good lady's.

At the Hotel boarded a young man from Sturbridge whom I enjoyed very much. There was a lot of fun in him; but it was innocent fun. He was an industrious student. That young man is now a very successful physician at Leiscester. I had the pleasure of meeting him last year at Brimfield, and thoroughly enjoyed his company. We called upon the Doctor's old chum, Geo. Webster, and talked over old times.

Another boy at the Hotel was young Converse, a quiet, nice, boy. What lessons Miss Kenny used to accomplish! How pretty Lizzie Lombard was; and what fine pupils those were that came up from Sturbridge! How well I remember free and easy Miss Achart, Miss Ward with flaxen hair, and her prim sister; Miss Blashfield, always in earnest! I have not a list of the names of the pupils, and do not recall the names of all; but the pupils themselves, I recollect, every one.

One, I remember very well, wrote me, some years ago, about the old pupils. She lived two or three miles out of town. I can see just how she looked and how she recited; but her name I cannot recall.

I still recollect how finely Miss Parker used to recite, and what pretty black eyes she had. I wonder what has become of sweet little Miss Hubbard, and the Warren girls? The Brown boys I always liked. Fred Gates sat down by the door and was a good boy. William Potter, if I remember rightly, never intended to sweat. And Stone who divided twenty-two by two and obtained, as he told me, *"two ones,"* and the McDougal boy, who wrote "Penitentiary" ninety-nine times on the board before he got it right; shall I ever forget them?

Miss Orcutt still stands before me. Those nice Chamberlain girls and the blacksmith's daughter, all these are a part of my soul.

I visited Brimfield last year, and met a few of the old friends in the Hall; alas! how few! Only one of the trustees saw I there. The anxious eye sought, in vain, the kindly faces that used to welcome me with a smile; but I could not, did not, regard them as dead. I felt that they were there in the Hall, only the dull, cold eye of the earthly mortal could not see them. I know I felt the influence of my old friends upon my soul, that they too had a word of welcome for me.

In the evening, I stood alone upon the door-step and surveyed the stars; the seven stars forming that group were shining with unusual luster. I remembered that there were once eight stars shining in that group, and now only seven are seen; but the eight must be there still, exerting all the influence it ever did, only the finite eye of man cannot see it; so I felt that my old friend, Judge Brown, was giving me the same old, hearty handshake, and inquiring how the school was getting along. The never-forgotten smile of encouragement of Mr. Hubbard, driving away every home-sick feeling; the hearty laugh of Mr. Tarbell, and his cordial recognition still reached me, as if falling from the Empyrim above. They were all with me, though the eye saw them not. Such men can never die! They live in other lives, live in the influence they exerted; live in the institutions they founded; live in the unseen power they exert in the uplifting of humanity, the refining of society and the "hastening of the Confederation of the World." "Shall we know each other there?" Yes, I am sure, and we will find each other on some anniversary occasion in the same old dining hall where, as congenial friends, we met and held pleasant converse, while living on earth. So, I apprehend, will family reunions take place. When father and mother, brother and sister, never forgetting the old, familiar fire-place, will intuitively gather there and recognize each other, and hold sweet converse together. The thought is a pleasant one, and who shall gainsay the hope? Surely death can never destroy the deep emotions of the soul.

CHAPTER XVI.

MARRIAGE—HOME.

In 1867, I resigned at Brimfield and went to Monson and was married, the next day, to Ellen Carr Flanders by the Rev. D. P. Bailey. I was, at that time, twenty-eight years old, and had never seen a person married. I can recall now some of the emotions moving my soul at that time. I wondered if the young lady would be as dutiful as a wife as she had been as a pupil. One thing I fully realized; that I was about to enter into a relation which death only could terminate.

That relation has existed nearly forty years, and I have never regretted the words spoken that night.

My wife belonged to a good family. The Flanders family was a prominent one in New Hampshire; and is well-known there at the present time. The Carr family of Bradford, N. H., has, for many years, been well-known in financial and social life.

In my younger days I had resolved to live a single life. I had always had a great admiration for the girls in a general way, but had always thought of them as beings of entirely different order from myself. They seemed to be ethereal beings just lent to earth for a time, lifted far above the grosser things or thoughts of an earthly nature. They were to me objects of admiration,— a sort of abstract essence of the divine enlivening a form of clay most beautifully carved. That a being so sweet to look upon, so pure and so modest, so kind and affectionate, sympathetic and just, so witty and graceful, so self-sacrificing and tireless in all things good should ever be monopolized by one gross, rough, selfish man seemed to be an abuse of the most glorious gift of Heaven to man.

But later in life some of those illusions vanished. I dis covered that a young lady could not only be beautiful, but useful. That her mission while on earth was not only to beautify, but to make all things better. She was to become not an idol to worship, but a being to love, cherish and even to listen to. I discovered by observation that she was a necessity to man's highest moral elevation, and that her influence was the best when she held the responsible position of wife. All these things led me to change my mind and marry.

I am convinced that man ought to marry. There are many reasons to confirm this statement. The Creator evidently intended that man should marry since there is implanted within the soul of man an intense desire to enter into that condition, and certainly observation teaches us that there seems to be some-thing lacking in the makeup of a man that never marries. Such people never have a home. How many writers have attempted to define that one word home. No one has succeeded fully. Home implies a wife and a house, and many things in it. There must be something more there than just what is needed. There must be something there like the Lares of the ancient Roman; something more precious than any other thing; something call-ing forth an emotion akin to worship. These household gods may be very commonplace things in themselves, but as precious as diamonds to the possessor,—an old clock that father used to wind up every night, a chair in which mother sat as she mended our tattered mittens, a little shoe that baby once wore, a book that the blushing girl gave before she became the wife,—many things associated with the struggles of the first years of mar-ried life; these things make home. There can be no home with-out them, but those are not all. Above all these there must be a wife in every home. By the word "wife" I do not mean just a woman who is legally bound to a man by the contract of mar-riage. I mean a wife who loves her husband, loves her children, her home; who has the happy faculty of inspiring every one around her with a love for everything good and noble; who patiently waits for the dawning in the darkest midnight hour and becomes a companion to her husband, a blessing to the community, a God-ordained constituent of a home. But the home is not yet complete. There must be a husband in that home. Not simply a citizen of the United States qualified to vote, but a man who loves his home and is willing to sacrifice all selfish things for its complete perfection,—a man who remembers that his wife paid him the highest compliment ever received when she showed her confidence in him by consenting to entrust more to him than to all the rest of the world,—a man who finds his highest ideals at home, who thanks God every day that there are dear ones for whom he can labor, to whom he can look in sunshine and storm for comfort and consolation. A log house may be a home; a palace, a barren shelter. Money can make a home glorious, but cannot make a palace a home where the essentials are wanting. Of course, the ideal home implies comfort, culture, music and those surroundings that wealth expended by an ideal man can furnish. But these are few. All cannot be rich, but there may be millions of homes that satisfy every longing. Many there are to whom the reality of the "Cotter's Saturday Night" is realized. From homes go forth children that make statesmen, good citizens. The more real homes there are the better will society be, the more prosperous our home-blessed land will be.

Unmarried men do not possess homes. Of course I am speaking in general terms,—there are exceptions to all rules. Unmarried women do often have real homes. They have their household gods, their pretty fancies and always someone to love. Every child is their friend, every suffering one has their sympathy, attention and care. Some of the noblest women I have ever known are of this class. Nor do they feel that they are martyrs wasting their sweetness on the desert air. They are loved, respected and never forgotten. Only a month ago an old lady, who had been a domestic for many years in the house of a wealthy citizen of Piscataquis, died in another town. Her body was carried to the rich man's house, where services were held in keeping with the position held by that honorable member of society. The church choir sang the same sweet songs that soothe the souls of the rich and refined, the parish clergyman was not a whit less eloquent and pathetic than if the wife of some distinguished citizen had crossed the river.

How many a dissipated young man has been brought to himself and led back to virtue when some day a vision of the old home flashes across his mind! Away from the scenes of childhood though one be for many years, that home is never forgotten. Unfortunate is that boy whose father has no fixed abode. All my young days were spent in one house, on one farm. Every tree around the house was dear to me, every hill and rock sacred. The barbary bush in the garden, the grapevine that bore no fruit, the butternut tree that was older than I, the Balm of Gilead that Uncle Joe had planted, the beaver dam where those wonderful animals had once lived, the orchard whose fruit was dearer to me than the apples of Hesperides, the mill-pond where I used to boat and fish, the brook along which for many days I had wandered,—all those and many more were, and are dear to me. There was a large pine stump standing on a high knoll in my childhood days, around which I had played for many hours. Returning to the old homestead a few years ago, I felt that something was wanting. The landscape was spoiled. That stump had been removed. The Balm of Gilead that had buffeted the wind for many years had at last fallen, and gone were the records of the early prowess of the boys of my childhood. No boy could be called a hero who had not climbed to a certain limb and carved his name there. *Eheu! fugaces labantur anni!* The tree is gone. The record is destroyed, and the boys are gray-haired and preparing to go. The grapevine still trails in negligent profusion over the trellis and the barbary bush looks old and feeble, but there are a thousand precious objects still dear to me at that old home. Not far from the house on a gently rising mound is "God's Acre," where my father and mother lie. When "Life's fitful fever" closes, God grant I may close my eyes in the room where I first opened them, and that the feeble engine through which my soul acted, may forever rest on that sunny hill-side, where I spent many hours in childhood days. I have never ceased to find a melancholy pleasure in wandering through the aisles of a cemetery. A feeling comes over one there unlike any other. The emotions are not wholly sad, they are subdued, refined, chastened. A kindlier feeling for humanity, a charity for human frailty, a forgetfulness of past resentments steals over one in that silent assembly that makes the man better who in meditative thought is listlessly contemplating the spot where he shall "lie down to pleasant dreams." Irving says, "Who contemplates the grave, even of an enemy, without a compunctious throb?" All are friends where the cypress weeps.

CHAPTER XVII.

MONSON. SUPERVISOR.

My teaching at Monson the second time was an unexpected event. I had engaged to teach at Cherryfield, but was persuaded to remain at Monson. The school had changed some what, but was enjoyable. I continued in the school until I was appointed supervisor of schools for the county; then I taught part of the time, and attended to the other duties the rest of the time. I enjoyed the work, on the whole, very much. The first experience was not very flattering. I was comparatively young, and thought I held a very important position. The first school visited was at Sebec village. I went to the door, rapped, and soon a fine looking teacher came to the door. I informed her what my name was, expecting to see great emotion show itself upon her face; but not a muscle moved. She simply stood there and looked at me in a sort of perplexed way. At length, I added the information that I was County Supervisor, and came to visit the school. She then asked me to come in. I went in and sat down. Finally she came to me with that same look on her face that I had often seen on the faces of pupils who did not know their lessons, and asked me what office I held. I then fully realized that she did not know that such an office existed.

That morning when I started from home, I thought I was a very important personage and held a very exalted position. As I sat in that chair, I felt that I would sell the whole business for a picayune. Finally she asked me if I would like to hear some of the classes recite. I said I would, when she had called them to order. At that very moment one boy was crawling out of the window; another was dragging a smaller boy out of his seat by the hair; and two or three girls were playing a game of "cat's cradle" with some strings. She looked a little surprised at my stupidity and said: "They are in order now." I think that was the noisiest school I ever visited. The schoolhouse was a good one, there were forty scholars, and the teacher was rather handsome, and finely dressed; but the cause of education languished.

The next school visited was taught by a Miss Robinson of Parkman. The very atmosphere of that schoolroom was refreshing. The teacher loved her work, and her pupils, and they loved the teacher, and enjoyed their work. I spent a day there, not to criticize but to admire and enjoy. It was an ideal school, and few teachers could be like Miss Robinson.

In the next school I found a teacher trying to hear thirty-two classes recite every day. There were twenty-five pupils in all. Of course her time was nearly wasted. In fact, the want of classification was the greatest defect in the schools.

In one school the class in Geography was reciting, and I asked a boy if he had ever seen the earth. He said he never had. That same boy, at that very moment, had a large portion of the earth on his hands and face.

The methods of punishment were sometimes unique. One teacher had some clothes pins on the lips of three of the pupils. They looked rather funny, sitting there with those patent clothes pins sticking out under the nose. These pupils had been caught whispering. In another school there was a boy with his mouth propped open by two cedar sticks. I told the teacher that there was danger of strabismus of the masseter muscle. In another school the teacher put cayenne pepper on the tongue to punish that troublesome member for lying.

In that little red schoolhouse, one day, a teacher told one of those restless, mischievous little fellows to fill the stove with fine wood. The boy did so. Then the teacher put in some paper, got some matches, and called the boy to the stove; she took off the cover and seated the boy on the stove, and lighted the match, and told him she was going to roast him. If ever those walls resounded with ear-piercing howls, they did at that time! Off from that stove the boy leaped, and, minus hat, coat and shoes, sprinted for home at a break-neck speed; screaming all the way, "I don't want to be roasted!"

Perhaps that boy's mother never studied rhetoric; but one thing I know; that she fulfilled Webster's definition of eloquence perfectly. He said eloquence consisted in action, action, action."

The jovial superintendent of one town told me that his method of grading his schools was very simple. There were two panels gone out of the schoolhouse door, making a small and a larger hole. Those that could crawl through the small hole went into the Primary School; those that went through the larger panel went into the Grammar School; and the rest went to the High School.

That County Supervisor law was a good one, and ought to have been continued. I admit that Mr. Johnson was unfortunate in some of his appointments, but many of the number were practical teachers. N. A. Luce was a man fully qualified to fill the position. W. J. Corthell was another member eminently qualified. Mr. Corthell has few superiors as an educator. An excellent public speaker, an acute logician, expert in rhetoric, with a mind unsurpassed in analysis, W. J. Corthell might have been one of Maine's best known public men, had his ambition run in that direction. But he loved teaching and has been determined to give all that is in him to that vocation, and has impressed himself upon many minds and built a monument, imperishable as the truths he taught.

Only three or four of the sixteen survive at the present time.

Stanley Plummer of Dexter was another Supervisor well qualified to act. He was a fine scholar and an excellent public speaker. Mr. Plummer later became a very successful politician and held a position at Washington. Mr. Plummer has been twice in the Legislature, and is at present practicing law in Dexter.

Mr. Eaton of Somerset was well qualified for his work.

Mr. Stetson was the personification of a Greek statue, speaking grave truths by a mechanical apparatus through marble lips. He was a man of great reasoning powers, but totally lacking in personal attraction. He died several years ago.

Dr. True was a man of great erudition and rather an interesting speaker for a limited time, but when the Doctor once got to going, his speech became "linked sweetness long drawn out." Dr. True did a good work in the educational field, and his name should be honored.

Mr. Robertson of Augusta was an enthusiastic worker and well skilled in methods. He died lately at Augusta.

The founder of the Little Blue School at Farmington made an excellent supervisor. Mr. Abbott was a very nervous man, and sometimes became a little rattled, but always recovered his composure.

N. A. Luce was fully qualified, both by acquirements and ability to occupy the position of supervisor. He had a superior literary ability and was somewhat of a poet. He occupied the position of State Superintendent for several years, with the full consent of the teachers of the State. I must quote a line from a poem of his written while in college. "Conservatism holds the reins, and progress plies the brush." Luce and myself once co-labored on a poem of four lines and produced a stanza that attracted the attention of one man at least. The Supervisor had a meeting at Augusta during the session of the Legislature. There was a member who called himself "the cat under the meal." He advocated the repeal of the law creating the office of supervisor. One day I wrote a couple of lines and passed it to Luce. He wrote two lines more and passed it around among the members. A reporter found it and sent it to the Portland Press. The next morning I strayed into the House. When I entered

Mr. C. was speaking with his voice raised to the dome, and wildly flourishing a paper around his head. He howled, "I will cane, I will beat him to the earth." He referred to the author of those innocent four lines. Mr. C's. partner, by the way, had been fined for selling liquor without a license. Those lines were these·

> "Have you heard of the cat that's under the meal,
> That honest old cat that never would steal
> Except from the government all on the sly
> By selling, unlicensed, a little Old Rye?"

But he did not cane us. Mr. Luce is still engaged in school and literary pursuits.

Mr. Sleeper of Aroostook was a very active man and could pop up and say a good thing and down again with great rapidity.

During the three years in which I served as County Supervisor, many very peculiar conditions came to my notice. In one town I held a public examination of teachers, and found one young lady totally unfit to teach anywhere. The Town Superintendent had engaged her to teach in one of the schools. I charged him not to allow that girl to attempt that school. He promised that she should be dismissed. When I came around to visit the schools, I found that young lady in that same school. I took dinner with a prominent citizen and at the dinner table I complained about the matter. Mr. A. said, "Don't say a word. B. is owing me for a cow, that girl is owing me for a cow. I told the Superintendent I would sue him if he did not give the girl a school. Don't say a word, it is all right." Two cows spoiled that school. Another school committee would hire no teacher who did not live in town. In some towns that rule works all right, but in others it is disastrous. The best teachers should be secured regardless of local habitation. I repeat that the county supervisor law was a good one. It would be well to revive it if the appointments could be disconnected from political machinery. The system now existing is good as far as the law is used but only a few towns act under the law. There are only two Superintendents in Piscataquis county, none in Aroostook and one or two in Penobscot. That the schools have improved under the supervision of Mr. Harvey B. Williams, the people of Dover and Foxcroft certify by repeatedly electing the same efficient officer.

That rigid school inspection is imperative, is apparent to every one qualified to judge in such matters. Even if the teacher is qualified and faithful, he can receive help from a visit of a man whose business is to inspect and suggest. But many candidates for positions are not qualified and should never be allowed to teach. It is positively a crime to put a teacher into a schoolroom to teach children, who is unfit. I repeat, a crime, because the school superintendent or committee make oath that they will faithfully perform their duty. It is their duty to discriminate. If they are not capable it is a sin for them to occupy the position. But it is urged that some towns are not the possessors of any one fully qualified. That may be a fact. Then that town should unite with some other town or towns, and unitedly employ some one who is qualified. "But," said one committeeman to me, "Mr. C. taught a good school if he was unqualfied, he was enthusiastic, kept good order and the scholars liked him." Well, suppose I hire a man to drive me around the country on business. He is enthusiastic and can handle the reins like Budd Doble, but he does not know the roads and lands me at last at the end of some cross road in a swamp. His very enthusiasm leads him further out of the way when he takes the wrong road, and the faster the horse goes the further from my destination I am carried. The less enthusiasm an incompetent teacher has the better for the pupil. An error projected into his mind with enthusiastic force penetrates deeply and irradicates with difficulty, if ever.

But there are teachers who do pass a good examination who do not know how to teach. Inspection shows this, and when this is once discovered, the teacher should be instructed

9

and if he fails to improve, let him be dismissed. A man may know every rule of navigation but he could not sail a ship if he cannot tell the helm from the anchor. A skillfully trained surveyor with wooden legs would make a poor land surveyor. A lack of ability to govern a school can only be discovered by inspection. If a teacher shows a natural deficiency in this direction, he should certainly cease to teach. No school can be profitable where there is disorder. I admit that there are schools where too much attention is given to obtain what is called a "still" school, where fussiness prevails. This is not well. There must be a certain amount of noise in every working school just as there must be noise in a machine shop, but no superintendent in such a shop will allow any unnecessary noise. Every adjustment must be so perfect that no friction can occur. The manager of a pile-driver will oil every gudgeon so no unnecessary noise will be heard.

But how shall good teachers be secured? And how good inspectors? There can be but one answer. The inspector should be trained to the business, and devote his whole time to that one occupation. Nepotism is the cause of more poor schools than all other causes. No business man can be a good superintendent. Insensibly his business interests warp his judgment. I am inclined to think that every school inspector should have authority to dismiss a teacher as well as to employ them. The school committee can delegate the power for hiring teachers, but cannot delegate the power to dismiss. I see no reason why an incompetent teacher should be allowed to remain in the schoolroom any more than an incompetent clerk should remain in the store, but of course, it must be shown clearly that the teacher is at fault. Sometimes through the incompetency of the Committee, it is impossible for the teacher to do good work. Text books are not furnished, proper wood is not in evidence, no proper classification has been attempted. Sometimes stupid inspectors become actual impediments barring every attempt at better methods and progress. In fact, few teachers are properly supplied with the externals needful for a good instruction.

CHAPTER XVIII.

GOING TO HOULTON.

My going to Houlton was a sudden movement. Dr. Ricker remarked to me, one day while out on the lake fishing, at Mon son, that perhaps I might receive a call to Houlton some day. One day in September, 1874, I received a telegram to go to Houlton. I started the next morning, went to Old Town, and, on the morrow, took the train to McAdam's Junction, where I commenced the most extraordinary railroad journey I ever experienced.

The Canada & New Brunswick Railroad, for the consid eration of five dollars, agreed to convey me to Houlton. The time required was not stated. The ticket was "good for this day only;" but the day was something like those mentioned in the first chapter of Genesis. The train from St. Andrews had not arrived, so I spent an hour at McAdam, viewing the scenery and trying to feel the full import of breathing the air which circulated over a land which was under the dominion of of a Queen.

I failed to realize any quickening of the pulse, and conclud ed to remain at ordinary size. But the landscape! There were rocks everywhere, and then some stones, then some ledges on which were boulders, surrounded by granite reefs. The earth was nowhere visible; nothing but rock and sky could be seen, except five or six stumps that were brought down with the drift when the glacier moved down from the North.

A hasty examination of the geological conditions convinced me that a huge glacier came down from the North, sweeping before it every rock it met in its irresistible course, till a mountain of rock, boulders and granite ledge was piled up. This mass became so heavy at McAdam Junction that the glacier struck solid rock and stopped. A change of climate melted the ice and scattered the rock round about and thus they lie today.

Before I had finished the survey, a Canadian Customs Officer examined my modest baggage with a pompous dignity that was amusing. I pitied that officer. His hat must have cost five dollars, the brass buttons on his coat were very brilliant and his badge was fear inspiring. That professional strut of his must have cost many hours' hard practice. The official tone he assumed when he, with stony stare over the top of my hat, said; "Open your baggage," would have made Wellington jump with alacrity. I hastened, with great speed to comply with his demand. I had simply a well-worn, old-fashioned valise as the sum total of my belongings. As I opened the delapidated jaws of that antiquated receptacle, and exhibited to that officer of the Queen a few handkerchiefs and articles of clothing, I pitied him.

His makeup fitted him to inspect a carload of diamonds, a cargo of silk or a puncheon of brandy. It seemed so undignified for him to simply rumple up a few articles of wearing apparel, without using a single key from that ponderous bunch hanging from his embroidered belt.

A black-haired girl, in one corner of the station, sold me a sandwich which was the first nourishment I ever received from a foreign potentate. I have been satisfied with Uncle Sam's cooks ever since.

At length the train arrived, not with the roar and dash of modern trains, but with all the dignity and deliberation of a conservative politician. I seated myself in a car and waited. The train was a mixed one and went up one day and came back the next,—sometimes.

After the conductor, a sad-looking, cadaverous man with reddish side whiskers, had shouted four or five times: "All aboard!" the train started. I was prepared for some rapid riding and began to catch my breath when they commenced to score as the jockeys do at the race-course. We would go up a quarter of a mile and suddenly stop. The erratic movement would precipitate me to the south end of the seat. The seats ran lengthwise of the cars and were covered with oilcloth. Then there would be a sudden retrograde motion back to the starting point, with the same unexpected halt, throwing the passengers back to "first mentioned bound," as they say in writing deeds.

This playful manner of entertaining the guests continued till they got the engine warmed up and a final "All aboard!" sent us off. What a rattling of brake chains, clanking of coupling links and pins and creaking and groaning of the body politic that delapidated array of moving vehicles made!

We arrived, at length, at Eel River, where we stopped an hour. On inquiring, it was discovered that the train was ahead of time, and must wait until the sun caught up with us. It seemed that it was usual to run off the track every trip, and so time was allowed for that performance, but, on that particular occasion, the cars kept the track; so we didn't need the extra hour.

Eel River was not a very picturesque hamlet. On three sides of the station was sawdust; and I noticed that they were burning sawdust on the fourth side. There is nothing very inspiring in a field of champed up timber, so the delay became tedious, and I even longed for some more toboggan slides on that slippery oilcloth. Eel River, a year or two afterwards, was the scene of a strange comradeship.

One day there was a meeting of a lodge of Orangemen, on the twelfth of July, and some of the boys of Houlton were there. There was also some fine, Protestant whiskey in evidence, and this had been rather freely circulated; Pat Murphy came along and, not knowing the peculiar mission of the convivial picnickers, accepted a half dozen drinks or so. Then they got Pat upon a barrel to make a speech which he did, in these words: "My friends, I'm wid ye, but not of ye." This expression has been, ever since, an explanation of conduct that is a little peculiar.

We only scored three times before starting from this place. The only delay was caused by stopping to let a few farmers off at cross-roads, and to take aboard a woman or two who had been berrying. At length, Debec was reached. Here Mother Earth was again seen. There was some green grass and a few trees. The conductor began to look cheerful, and, as the road to Houlton was down hill, the first attempt sent us off at a speed of ten miles an hour. In due time we arrived at Houlton and smiling Mike Welsh drove me to the Snell House.

I spent the first night in Houlton at the home of Deacon Barnes. On the following day I engaged the school and returned home. In a week I started for Houlton with a horse and wagon. The drive was a delightful one through the woods. The road was a reminder of the Aroostook War. When the outlook seemed to prophesy war between the United States and England, the government built a broad road, four rods wide, from Mattawamkeag to Houlton. The road was nearly straight and so well built that it was in good condition in eighteen hundred and seventy-five. Most of the way was through woods, with an occasional clearing breaking the monotony. Over this road had been conveyed all the supplies for Aroostook county before the railroad had been built. Over the same hundreds of teams had hauled the buckwheat, oats, and shingles that Aroostook sent to market.

There had been, consequently, hotels built at convenient distances along the whole route, for the accommodation of the traveler and the teamsters. Some of those hotels were very commodious and had done a large amount of business. One room they all had sure,—the bar-room, and I judged by the length of the counters, running completely across the room, that great accommodations were needed in that line. The hotels fell into disuse and decay after the railroad reached Houlton. Some were closed, some used for private dwellings, and a very few still remained public houses. Not one on the whole road looked very inviting. Somehow an old, delapidated hotel, with signboard still reeling in the wind, with windows broken and paint all gone. is the most desolate appearing of all ruins.

There is always something wierd about an old, deserted hotel. When a boy, driving a team to Bangor, I used to pass by a deserted house which once had been occupied as a public house. There was connected with the house the old story about the murdered peddler. I used to wonder how so many peddlers could be murdered, and still see peddlers going by every day. I never heard of a haunted house that had not a peddler hidden in some mysterious way, in the cellar. The house mentioned was undoubtedly tenanted by an uneasy ghost, since a reliable inhabitant assured me that strange noises were heard there nights.

It seems strange that a sedate, business-loving peddler while in life, should spend his spiritual existence in rattling chains, and pounding the ceiling. and making night hideous. It was a great relief when some tramps burned that old house.

I spent a night on my journey to Houlton in one of those old Inns. The landlord was an antiquated specimen of fossil that time had somehow preserved. With long, uncombed hair hanging down to his shoulders, with beard growing wild like bramble bushes, and eyes peering out from sockets nearly closed, he allowed I could stay in sepulchral tones that made a shiver pervade the entire lumbar region.

The ancient wife, with a black clay pipe in her mouth, gave a geneological history of her numerous family. The old man spent most of the evening bewailing the degenerate times the railroad had caused. It took him an hour longer to do this on account of the fearful amount of profanity used.

The chamber was a large one, with bare floor, in which were countless punctures made by the calks of the river-drivers' boots. The old lady informed me that room was the best room in the good old times, and bride and bridegroom had oftentimes occupied it. In the old days, when a couple was married in Aroostook, the bridal tour was a trip to Bangor by stage. If the happy couple came back still happy, future felicity was assured.

The road from Mattawamkeag ran seven miles through the woods, over a series of hills to Molunkus. Here was a small settlement, constantly growing smaller. From that place to Linneus there were few hills. Some parts of the drive were delightful. In one place tall elms, a century old, waved on both sides of the road, through the branches of which one could catch a glimpse of a small lake not far off. A long swamp with stunted trees disconsolately standing alone made a drive of an hour rather dreary, but soon "Happy Corner" made its appearance. I applied at a wretched looking house for lodging, but a tow-headed, shabby looking girl informed me that the woman was in jail for selling rum and the husband was on a spree.

I drove on to the next place where at Haynesville good accommodations were obtained. The weather was delightful. An occasional partridge would whirr across the road, frightening the horse and arousing me from a sleepy reverie; then a timid rabbit would, with bewildered uncertainty, scurry hither and thither out of the road; a few hawks screeched as they sailed by and squirrels laughed and quarreled as the mood came on them.

The time was conducive to reverie, to musing and reminiscences of the past. I pictured to myself that motley cavalcade of bold militia men as they unflinchingly plunged into that wild wilderness, determined to conquer, to return captains, colonels, nay, generals, or die on the banks of the winding Meduxnekeag. Caparisoned horses, champing the bit and tossing plumes in the air, drew those murderous six-pounders, flanked on each side by galloping cavalry and supported by unterrified infantry. I could fancy the echo of the hurried command, given in high falsetto, still reverberated from tree to tree and awakened a spirit of martial glory in every patriot's soul. A line of an old poem came to mind ; "I see them on their winding way ; About their ranks the moonbeams play." There was all the "Circumstance and pomp of glorious war." How different the return ! That was all summed up in a line of an old poem.

> " 'Run, Strickland, Run!
> Fire, Stover, Fire !'
> Were the last words of McIntyre."

I passed over that road years later with my daughter. We enjoyed the trip exceedingly most of the way, but when we came to the seven miles of unbroken forest, we found an exasperating condition of things. The State was repairing the road, and the commissioner had plowed the entire roadbed for more than three miles, and left it in furrows. It had rained the day after, and thus we found the highway ! There was no chance to walk by the roadside as it was flooded. That poor little horse, weighing eight hundred, had to pull us over that long stretch of road, carpeted with ten inches of mud.

When we were about half way over it, a man was seen walking before us. We noticed the peculiar way he used his feet. He lifted the right foot up very high, with a sort of spasmodic yerk, as a horse does who has the string-halt; then it went down like a pile-driver, scattering the muddy water in every direction. We finally overtook that man who, without stopping to say "Good-day," commenced to explode from his mouth the most extraordinary mixture of denunciation and profanity that those forests ever heard. If that commissioner had been within hearing, he would have learned his duty. We listened very sympathetically; barring the profanity, we agreed with him. When we had passed by, looking back, we saw that man walking along quietly, and stepping in ordinary manner. The dynamic force within had expended itself and the natural man asserted himself.

Not long after we met two cyclists on a pleasure trip. They had to tramp three miles through that sticky, clayey mud and push the machines. There is generally on the face of a pleasure-seeking cyclist a look that implies great satisfaction with himself, and a sort of ownership of the world. That look was not visible on the occasion mentioned. We thought the desire of the heart was that expressed by King Richard on that fatal field of battle.

On my trip to Houlton I wore a light suit with straw hat. After four day's riding over a dusty road, it seemed best to make a change of garments; so I stopped at Linneus and got some dinner, and changed the light suit for a dark one. There were several inquisitive girls at the house who were much interested in my movements. I learned afterwards they expressed the opinion that I was a horse thief, escaping into New Brunswick.

I arrived in Houlton in the afternoon on Saturday, and commenced to teach the following Monday; and continued that work for ten years. The family remained at Monson during that year.

CHAPTER XIX.

I found the school in a peculiar condition at Houlton. The former teacher was engaged to teach for another year, but, for some reason, did not; and, consequently, when the time came for opening the school, no teacher was apparent.

This school had been accepted by the trustees of Colby College as a "fitting school." The trustees agreed to endow the school and furnished teachers and all necessary means for prosecuting school work. The Academy was managed by a Board of Local Trustees, conjointly with a board nominated by the College Trustees. Dr. Shaw was the pastor of the Baptist church in Houlton and a member of the Board. Charles E. Williams, A. B., a recent graduate of Colby, had been engaged as assistant in the school by the trustees.

Dr. Shaw commenced the school as principal and managed it for a week. I then appeared and assumed control. The Dr. attempted to do but little teaching and less governing. Mr. Williams taught the Latin and Greek in the recitation room, as did Miss Madigan, the French. For a day or two chaos reigned, and I was simply an element in the confusion, but soon there was a calm; and within a week the machinery of the school was in running order. The "Faculty of Instruction" as the old catalogue has it, consisted of W. S. Knowlton, principal; C. E. Williams, A. B., teacher of Latin and Greek; Miss Fannie Madigan, teacher of French; James Archibald, assistant in mathematics.

The reader will notice that I spell that word catalogue the old way. I cannot endure the sight of the word, mutilated by the modern utilitarian idea. "Catalog!" Just look at the word. Don't it look like a big, shaggy dog with his tail cut off; or a Chinaman minus a cue, or a kite without a tail?

I have before me, as I wrote, many old catalogues, and a feeling of sadness inherently steals over me as I glance over the list of trustees and pupils. Every member of the board of local trustees is dead. One of the Colby Board survives, Deacon Moses Giddings of Bangor.

B. L. Staples was chairman of the Board, whom I shall never forget. He showed me much kindness and became my friend at once. Dr. Donald became my family physician and stanch supporter. With Mr. Cary I had much to do, as he was secretary of the board, and my friend. The office of the Hon. J. C. Madigan and his home became favorite resorts whenever I felt tired or discouraged.

There were one hundred and nine pupils the first term and no definite course of study. The work done by the instructors would appall a teacher of today.

I used to commence school at eight o'clock and teach till dark and often heard classes at my home, evenings; but I enjoyed the work. Nearly all the pupils were anxious to learn, were enthusiastic in the pursuit of knowledge. If pupils only knew how much more work they could get out of the teacher by doing extra work themselves, they would be more inclined to "give and take." I never knew when bed time came as long as a class was ready to recite.

The catalogue of the first year tells me many sad stories; many facts to rejoice at. Thirty-five of that number are sleeping the long sleep awaiting us all. How many hopes lie buried in those premature resting places! To me they are not dead. I stood by no bedside and saw no departure. They live in retrospection, and I can see them now, as they sat in that schoolroom, and remember the pleasant hours passed with them. Still is the influence of the sweet smile of Eveline Plummer lingering in my soul, which always greeted me when I entered the schoolroom. Laura, always so faithful, and Addie so full of life, will never be forgotton; and Ella, whose merry laugh was so inspiring; the kind heart of Etta, full of human sympathy and love, ceased to beat all too quick. Sweet, gentle Mary Hussey's ladylike ways I still recollect, and Winnie will never die as long as this heart beats. Georgie Davis and Frank Barker, Nutie Nye, all these were pupils whom it is easy to remember. Others have also passed away, not one of whom would I forget.

There were many in school that term who have become prominent men in the world, of whom mention will be made hereafter. The same teachers remained during the year, and were very effective co-laborers. Mr. Williams was a fine Greek and Latin scholar. He remained in the school four years, when he resigned and commenced the study of medicine. He graduated from a medical college in New York, and commenced practice in Houlton, where he built up a prosperous business, and is still in practice.

Miss Madigan had every requisite that could be combined in one woman, hence was a very valuable assistant. Mr. Archibald was simply James Archibald, Esq., thirty years younger. Mrs. Seamons also taught one term very profitably. Mrs. Seamons has since become a very effective public speaker in reform times. Father Pearley taught penmanship, but failed to make my chirography intelligible.

We had a peculiar way of hazing freshmen in those days, I used to write something on the board and ask the new scholars to read it, while the old ones looked on and grinned. I used to pity those bewildered seekers after truth.

Among the students at Houlton there were an unusual number endowed by nature with more than ordinary talent. Many of those have fulfilled the promise of youth, and are at the present time prominent actors in the affairs of life.

C. C. King, of Caribou, was one of the very brightest Latin scholars I ever instructed. He entered college at fifteen. Mr. King graduated from Colby and read law with his father. After being admitted to the bar, he practiced for a time, then went into business and has prospered. He represented Caribou for two terms in the Legislature, and was a candidate for the Speakership. He is president of a bank in Caribou at the present time.

Fred Perkins was a bright boy and very studious. Unassuming and modest he gained friends by his merit and had many. He entered college and remained for a time and was then appointed cadet at West Point and graduated from that institution with honor and became an officer in the U. S. army. He participated in the Spanish war and was promoted. He now holds the rank of captain and is stationed at a fort in New Jersey.

Frank Shaw was a fine looking and popular boy, and has made a brilliant lawyer out West. He was a very companionable young man and hence popular. His mind was analytical, vigorous and discriminating. He was ambitious and deserved to succeed.

James Archibald was one of the first boys who attracted my especial attention. He was an indefatigable worker and close reasoner. I made a sort of chum of him, but was always very careful how I put things when reasoning with him. He was what I call an incisive reasoner. He penetrated to the interior of every subject, and viewed all arguments from their relations to the heart of the subject. In fine, he was the James Archibald of today in embryo. Mr. Archibald has a fine legal practice, and is president of the Board of Trustees of Ricker Classical Institute. Mr. Archibald's wife was also a favorite pupil in the Academy. He asked me once whether it would be better to marry, or go to college. I told him to go to college. Since I have had the pleasure of meeting his wife and family at their home, I am sure I was very,

very wrong in my advice. Mr. Archibald and his admirable wife, talented son and sweet daughter, all know how to make people happy.

Ulie Withee commenced to fit for college, but poor health caused him to abandon the idea, and he became a dentist; but has not confined himself to that business. He has become a wealthy business man, and always was a good fellow.

H. D. Collins of Caribou sat in the back seat and was rather quiet. His mathematical skill showed itself at that early period. He is a prosperous business man now and highly honored by the people. He marks his vote in the second column and hence is not always in office. Mr. Collins is doing an extensive lumbering and milling business in Caribou. His honesty, kindness and interest in every good cause has endeared him to every citizen in the town.

Arthur Daigle commenced to laugh when three hours old and has not stopped yet.

Charles Weed was a bright student, and his early death caused much regret.

I have lost sight of smiling Byron Blethen. He was the gallant of the class and always recited with one eye on the girl that sat next to him.

I remember Howard Carpenter and Dell Mansur with pleasant recollection. They entered Bowdoin College, and I have lost sight of them.

Thomas P. Putnam graduated at Colby, read law and commenced practice at Houlton. Mr. Putnam is a lawyer of good ability, and just such a lawyer as every town needs. Put him into a town full of lawyers, as they go, he would find business. Mr. Putnam's mind, when he was a boy, was analytical. He always looked at a question from all points of view and drew his conclusions with due deliberation. Mr. Putnam has been first selectman of Houlton for several years, and this honor has been given without the least solicitation. Cincinnatus was called from the plow to serve the people, so has Thomas been repeatedly called from his law practice to serve the town.

F. M. Donnell, a *Bayard sans puer et sans reproche,* graduated from Colby and became a civil engineer after completing a course of study at Massachusetts Institute of Technology. A sweeter, cleaner young man never lived, and a long and useful life seemed opening before him, *sed aliter dis.* My heart went with the hearse that bore that dear boy to the tomb. Mr. Donnell was a young man of fine ability. He had an original way of arriving at results in mathematical demonstrations that was very remarkable. At the time his health began to fail a move was contemplated to place him in a professor's chair at a well-known school of science.

There was a very active young man from Linneus in the next class. He was a fine scholar and with the other boys entered college.

Byron was graduated from Colby and engaged in speculation. He is a very successful politician and has been Secretary of State for eight years.

Dr. Harry Putnam was also a Colby boy. He was a brilliant scholar at Houlton Academy, and ranked high at college. He taught for a time in Connecticut and found an excellent wife there. He has been very popular for several years as Superintendent of the schools of Houlton, and has been very successful in his chosen profession. Harry was in those days a keen reasoner and a genial, whole-souled boy. This success in life was guaranteed even in those early days.

Very few families in Maine can claim three college graduates. Mrs. Putnam sent her whole family to college—three boys, Thomas, Harry and Beecher, and results have shown that she made no mistake. Those young men have proved that a prophet can receive honor in his own country. They have always lived at Houlton and have come to be recognized as important factors in the town. All honor to that widowed mother who gave so much to the world. "Her children rise up and call her blessed."

C. E. F. Stetson showed a decided liking for mathematical studies, and has become eminent in his profession. I suppose Mr. Stetson has hardly a peer in the State in the line of engineering. He has been constantly employed for many years in the most intricate work, requiring great skill.

F. W. Knowlton, my nephew, was a good scholar and diligent in his work. He was the best declaimer in the school. He entered Colby and, after teaching for a time, studied law and commenced practice at Foxcroft. Later he received an appointment in the treasury department at Washington and was there several years and then resumed his law practice at Old Town, where he has extensive business relations. He is a fine public speaker and believes in Andrew Jackson.

From Blaine came A. J. Fulton. He was a fine scholar and improved every moment. I liked him personally very much and invited him home frequently and enjoyed his society. Dr. Fulton is a very successful physician, and leading citizen of the town. He represented his district in the last legislature with credit to himself and to the satisfaction of his constituents. I also had the pleasure of performing the marriage ceremony when he took to himself a wife. She was also a student very kindly remembered.

Parker L. Hardison has made his mark as a surveyor and business man. Mr. Hardison has been a candidate for office several times and every time run ahead of his ticket, but his party has always been in the minority and Parker failed to be elected. At Houlton Academy he excelled in mathematics. During the whole time he was there, he never failed in a mathematical lesson. Parker was rather shy of the young ladies in those days but improved as time went on and five years ago got married. May perpetual prosperity be his; he deserves it.

Herbert W. Trafton of Fort Fairfield was a faithful student and good scholar. He graduated from Colby and set-

tled at Fort Fairfield as a lawyer. He has built up a large practice and is held in great esteem by his townsmen. Mr. Trafton
also rejoices in the luxury of voting with the minority. Mr.
Trafton is one of those men whose very face reflects the honesty
of heart that prompts every action. He was just that kind of
a student at Houlton Academy. He looked at every proposition
from a moral point of view, and was ever ready to grasp opportunity to obtain knowledge and light. Though not devoid of
a keen sense of humor his energies were constantly devoted to
the performance of duty first and he had the fun at the proper
time. It is unfortunate for the country that Mr. Trafton votes
with the minority in the State of Maine. He has been a candidate for important offices, but the returns were unpropitious.
We need just such men as he in office.

F. G. Dunn was a quiet, studious young man who did not
especially enjoy declaiming. He graduated at Colby, read law
and settled at Ashland, where he is a sort of mayor, alderman,
chief justice and financier. Mr. Dunn is what everybody calls
a good fellow and has a lucrative practice. For some unac-
countable reasons he has never married. I am sure he is in
great danger every leap year.

J. K. Plummer was a diligent student, faithful in all his
work and a fine young man. He entered Colby and later studied
law and was admitted to the bar, but his extensive business
transactions preclude practice. He has lately returned from
a trip to Europe.

I recall with great pleasure a pleasant-faced young man
from Presque Isle. He stayed at our house his first night in
Houlton. He was very studious and quiet among the boys and
was salutatorian at graduation. G. Edward Wilkins is now a
member of the A. H. Fogg corporation. I expected him to go
to college, but he did better by selecting an excellent young
lady and securing an exceptionally fine wife. Mr. Wilkins is
today one of the most popular business men in the county, and
deserves thus to be. His social qualities are exquisite, his

business methods are unquestioned. Mr. Wilkins is par excellent—an ideal business man. I never could understand why a man need be disagreeable because he is smart or talented. Mr Wilkins would have made an efficient professional man had he willed.

John B. Madigan was at the Academy for a time and made a good record prognostic of the coming man. He was a young man of excellent judgment. He showed that in his choice of a wife. He has large business relation and extensive legal practice. A few years ago he was elected representative to Augusta though the district was opposed in politics. Mr. Madigan is a logical reasoner and carefully investigates as he proceeds in his argument. He has been a member of the school board for several years. He is also chairman of the Examining Board for admittance to the bar. Mr. Madigan is popular among the citizens of the town and state.

Cunard Miller was a studious boy: He did like to have some fun occasionally, but I liked the boy just the same and was sorry when he left the school to engage in mercantile affairs. He is now in business in Fredericton, N. B. Mr. Miller's name recalls the many pleasant visits I made to the family home of Cunard. Mr. and Mrs. Miller were very kind to me, and at no house did I enjoy more pleasure than in that pleasant home and with that companionable family, and have never thought a visit to Houlton complete without calling upon the Millers.

Beecher Putnam, the third boy in the Putnam family, after graduation, taught for a time, and then read law. He has always been much interested in politics, and is one of the pillars of the Republican party. He has twice been Senator from Aroostook. He was one of the committee for the revision of the Statutes of Maine. Mr. Putnam is a natural orator and a great lover of nature. While at the Academy, he was an extraordinary scholar, and a fluent speaker even at that early stage of life.

R. W. Shaw was another very active young man. He excelled in rhetoric and ethical studies. His reasoning powers were good. He first took a general survey of the subject and endeavored to find the weak spot in the adversary's defense and that spot he attacked. Mr. Shaw is a successful lawyer and politician. He was county attorney of Aroostook county for two terms and senator at Augusta. Mr. Shaw is an orator and has done considerable stumping in the past five years. R. W. can plead a case in court, prove the Republican party immaculate, sing a song and tell a good story with equal and exquisite grace.

Charles Carrel was an industrious student with a decided determination to "get there." He showed early in life that he would one day be a millionaire. Mr. C. graduated from college, read law, and opened an office at Houlton, where he has a lucrative practice. My impression is if the Democrat party ever, in the dim future, should be victorious Charles would be a very successful politician. His persuasive powers are invincible.

P. H. Gillen was a very enthusiastic student always ambitious, busy and painstaking. He showed in the Lyceum debates that public speaking would be his especial forte. Mr. Gillen read law with Judge Stearns and opened an office in Bangor. That city was at that time well supplied with eminent lawyers, and to me it seemed a rash adventure for an unknown young man to make. But talent told and in a very short time Mr. Gillen became recognized as an astute lawyer. His practice has increased year by year till at the present time it includes many cases in which thousands of dollars are involved. Mr. Gillen in the old days even when a boy reasoned from cause to effect in a most critical way and then showed that effects could have had no other cause than the one he had assigned. He never left a subject unfinished. Maine has few orators equal to Mr. Gillen. His rhetoric is never turgid and his eloquence never flags but rather captivates. A brilliant future awaits P. H. Gillen and he deserves it. A friend that never grows cold, a citizen always interested in public matters, tolerant in religion and conservative in politics P. H. can but have hosts of friends and innumerable admirers.

Monticello sent us a fine young man by the name of Guy C. Fletcher. He was very studious and smart. Could handle mathematics with perfect ease. I enjoyed his society and sought it frequently. Mr. Fletcher was postmaster under the administration of Grover, and is now a prosperous business man in Monticello and Bridgewater, and a first-class good fellow generally.

Later, Bertram L. Fletcher was a member of the school. He was a good classical scholar and attended strictly to business, with an occasional lapse *"pro bono calico."* He read law and is practicing in Bangor with profit.

From New Brunswick came the Bradstreet boys. They were studious and smart and have made good records for themselves. Fuller is a prosperous farmer in Bridgewater, and one of the School Board. Asa is a trader and Superintendent of Schools. Henry is a prosperous man in California.

Chas. Brown, now a prosperous man of affairs in California, I enjoyed very much. Charles was an excellent young man and would have been a clergyman had his health permitted. He had the qualifications to have made him eminent in that profession. Of Chas. Parker, the parson, I now know nothing but feel sure that he dresses well wherever he is.

Among the boys in those days was a young man who translated Latin elegantly. Walter Cary is a successful lawyer, but I feel sure that he would have made an eminent literary man, had he devoted himself to that pursuit. His knowledge of Latin was so pronounced in college that he became known as "Judy," a pet name of Colby's most famous teacher of Latin. Few men have as good vocabulary of English words, and very few know how to use them as well as Mr. Cary. I hope he will devote a portion of his time to literary pursuits.

From Linneus one day came a tall, rather shy looking young man whose name I learned was Ira G. Hersey. Mr. Hersey even in those days showed a predisposition toward that remarkable eloquence that captures juries and confounds political opponents at the present time. I voted for Mr. Hersey once for Congressman or Governor I have forgotten which, but my vote did not seem to turn the scale and he was not elected. Mr. Hersey was a great worker. If he could not solve a problem in one hour he took two, if he could not pronounce a word right the first time he kept at it till he and Noah Webster coincided. He was a young man of more than common ability and improved every hour in earnest study. Ability and industry have placed him in the "upper story" that Daniel Webster recommended.

Another family at Houlton contributed three boys to the school. The Hon. A. A. Burleigh sent his three sons to college, all of whom graduated. Everett, known as the deacon ; Preston, the mathematician ; and Parker, the ladies' man. Everett was much engrossed in the science of anatomy. His desk was always full of dry bones. One day I found therein the entire skeleton of a Frenchman's defunct "cheval." Everett would have made a second Darwin had he not gotten rich in land speculation.

Preston N. Burleigh was one of the keenest original mathematical thinkers I ever knew. Propositions in Geometry vanished before his glance like the mist of the morning. All he had to learn was the theorem. The solution evolved itself from his inner consciousness. I have always been sorry that Mr. Burleigh did not become a mathematical author. I am sure he would have succeeded. Mr. B. is a fine business man ; but though he becomes a millionaire, the world will have lost something.

Parker Burleigh was a good Latin and all-round scholar. He was the best natured boy in school, and had a smile for everybody. He read law after graduating, and practiced for a time. He is, at this time, extensively employed in lumber and mill matters.

H. T. Green of Hodgdon was a very polite young man and a good scholar. That such a fine looking young man should have escaped matrimony is surprising.

Prof. F. W. Watson was a studious young man with much literary ability. He was a good speaker and fine writer. Mr. Watson wrote poetry that deserved notice and received it. He graduated at Colby and became professor in a college in North Carolina, and has attracted much attention, in many states of the Union by his researches and lectures in the field of microscopic science. Mr. W. was a very pleasant man to meet. With him at the school was his sister Laura, a lovely young lady whom I remember with much pleasure. She is now the wife of a well known teacher in New Brunswick.

Aubrey White was the financier of the school and will probably die a multi-millionare. Mr. White is now in the West exploiting irrigation schemes and other financial ventures. Aubrey was always a good fellow and ready to help things along. He is the kind of a man that ought to get rich.

Chas. Dunn, Jr., last year at Portland executing righteous law in a secant way, was simply the grown up Charlie Dunn of the Houlton Academy. He was a young man of good ability and excellent purposes and one of the most companionable men I ever met. I have always thought Charles should have been a clergyman. That young man could no more have done a mean or doubtful act than fly. He wore his "heart upon his sleeve" as far as his moral sense went. His health has never been good but he has done a vast amount of work and is most highly respected for his works. His personality caused the Republican Governor of Maine to appoint him, a Democrat, sheriff of Cumberland Co. when Mr. Pearson died. I know no man more worthy of positions of trust than Chas. Dunn, Jr.

And Parker, the poet. Will his glory ever fade? No, not as long as his immortal poem adorns the book shelves of the old graduates of Houlton Academy and is preserved in the archives of that venerable institution. We quote in another place a few stanzas of that poem for the benefit of the boys who have unfortunately lost the copy purchased many years ago for a nickel.

I remember as yesterday the first time I saw David F. Smith. He came from Cary and was rather bashful. He was tall and not very graceful in gait but on the first day of his attendance at school I recognized the existence of a gigantic brain within the head of that young man. He would master the most extraordinary tasks with the greatest ease when once determined upon doing so. Mr. Smith has been district judge in Montana for several years and is one of the most popular men in the West and a polished gentleman. In his boyhood days Mr. Smith had a masterful way of analyzing a subject or problem. I used to state propositions to him purposely to observe his method of thought. He had somehow an intuitive way of getting at facts and when once a fact became indisputable he seemed to see at a glance every line of thought leading to that fact.

Walter Nickerson paid his whole attention to his books and made excellent progress. I always enjoyed the company of Mr. Nickerson. His kindly disposition and genial smile made many friends. He is now a man of affairs in Houlton. At the school at that time was a sweet-faced young lady that won her way to my heart at once. She was an excellent scholar and a lady. She later became Mrs. Walter A. Nickerson. She died last fall and I cannot write her name but with moistened eye, and while I remember my sweet mother, shall I remember Clara Tracy Nickerson.

And Dr. Nickerson was there too. He was just as fond of hunting as now, and, if I remember rightly, I had to hunt for him sometimes, but he always turned up smiling.

W. E. Parsons was a student at the Academy a short time. He is now a lawyer in Foxcroft with an extensive practice. He was senator from Piscataquis county a few years ago. Mr.

Parsons is regarded as a very eloquent speaker. He has been one of the leading politicians of the county for some years. Mr Parsons will undoubtedly be heard of hereafter in a broader field of politics.

Amos Putnam was never in a hurry, but he always had his lessons prepared. I always liked the boy. He was fitted for college but did not go. I think it was a mistake.

Arba Powers, the author, comedian, and the "and so forth" man, was what teachers sometimes call a "case." One day he, without the slightest warning, burst out in a hearty laugh. I asked him what the matter was and he replied, "I read a funny story, last night, and just saw the point."

I remember John Harrigan and his sister with pleasant reminiscences. They were both bright and industrious. She is now the wife of Mr. Benjamin Feeley, an officer in the custom house.

C. P. Barnes was a good student and excelled in Latin. I always like the boy for the talent he showed, and for the fun that he enjoyed, at times. Charles is a lawyer and is a success. He certainly had the ability to be. He is now county attorney of Oxford county.

William Braden, I remember as a ladies' man but he was faithful in his work and methodical in every particular. His examples were put on the blackboard with perfect precision. Mr. Braden, I understand, is still discussing the old question—to marry or not to marry.

E. E. Churchill known as "Foley" was the boy that on examination day, when he was explaining the affinity of the magnet, placed it upon my gold watch lying upon the table and said "It has no attraction for brass." Mr. Churchill has prospered in financial matters and is at present keeping a first-class hotel in Presque Isle.

No record of Houlton Academy would be complete without a recognition of Colonel F. M. Flemming of Missouri. The Colonel was a good scholar and has made his mark in the West as a Democratic politician. The Colonel is extensively employed in financial matters and civic problems in Kansas City. He **was** a candidate for senator last November, but he and Parker went down together in the political landslide. I remember **the** Colonel had a very pretty sister, now living in the West.

Poor Mark White, a very bright boy, he sleeps in an early grave. He spent an evening with us at Caribou. By chance there were present four or five of the old girls and boys. Do the best we could, there seemed to be a pall of sadness hanging over us that evening. Mark was very silent and sad. Within a week he was dead with the typhoid fever.

Teague, Cottle and Gorham were all good boys, and went to college after I left Houlton. Teague was a very busy boy and had good ability. He married an admirable young lady, also a student of Houlton Academy, and is now a prominent teacher.

Bradbury Cottle, after graduation, was admitted to the bar and practiced in Bangor with success, but soon ill health compelled him to retire, and soon after he joined the "silent majority." Mr. Cottle's name reminds me that I had more students from Deacon Cottle's family than from any other one family. George Cottle was one of my most esteemed pupils, and he is just the same man today he promised to be in those days. Six members of the family attended the Academy, all of whom I remember with pleasure.

George A. Gorham, Jr., is a lawyer in Houlton, and has extensive business relations. He was a fine declaimer and good Latin scholar. He was always a good fellow and merits the success that has come to him. We enjoyed many social chats at his father's house.

James Dougherty was a very industrious pupil and won his way into my soul the first term. He was a good scholar and popular among the pupils. Mr. Dougherty graduated from college and studied law, and is, at this time, a very successful practitioner in Springfield, Mass. He married Miss Hattie

Madigan, a most admirable young lady, for whom I had the highest regard.

Thomas, a brother of James, attended Houlton Academy a few terms, and is now a rising practitioner in law in Houlton.

W. T. Spear was a very active young man, and a firm believer in the unterrified Democracy. He is doing a good business at Fort Fairfield. The irrepressible George Welch still appears before my wondering eyes. From Fort Fairfield came George Cary. Mr. Cary was a lovable young man with great ability. He made rapid progress in his studies and was very popular with pupils and teachers. He has become an excellent man of business and has amassed a fortune. George always was one of the best fellows in the world.

Dr. Fred White was very quiet, always in order and a good scholar. He has built up a lucrative practice in the West.

T. C. White, also of Littleton, was a hard student and never neglected his studies. He has long been a prominent clergyman in the Methodist church and is now stationed at Newport. I very much enjoyed meeting him last summer and reviewing old times.

But the list would include the whole catalogue should I mention all the boys who have distinguished themselves. I feel that I am warranted in claiming that no school in Maine in ten years ever had so large a percentage of boys who became prominent in practical life. Nearly every one came from families comparatively poor and the boys had, to quite a degree, make their own way. The relationship existing between these young men and myself was peculiar. It was not that usually existing between teacher and scholar, but rather it was the brotherhood of men engaged in intellectual pursuits. The boys liked me and I loved them all and was interested in all that concerned them. The many family meetings we used to hold in the old Packard house on Court street kept me young and permitted me to use whatever influence I possessed to stimulate them to lofty ideals and useful lives. It may not be that a single one was made better by my ministrations, but it is pleasant to meet them now and receive the cordial greeting they ever accord to me. I love to feel that my life had been so intimately connected with so many men, and that I may be kindly remembered by them as a teacher and friend who lost no opportunity to prove that friendship by faithful work in their behalf.

I have only spoken of the young men, but what was said of their superiority can be as truthfully asserted of the young ladies. Most of them were young ladies of more than usual mental capacity, and many were superior in all those graces that made them lovely. There were some very fine singers among their number. The sweet voices of Lucia and Elloise never failed to awaken most pleasureable emotions, and their voices were but the index of character and soul. I shall never forget sweet May Alexander, stately Jennie Betts, smiling Lydia Clark. Patie Hussey was an exceedingly fine scholar in all branches. She was an excellent teacher later, and is now the wife of C. E. Williams, M. D., of Houlton.

Miss Carrie Miller was almost the first girl in the school that said kind words to the strange teacher. I have never forgotten those words, nor the speaker.

Etta Braden I always associate with that inevitable Caesar in her hand. I was very fond of her. She is now the wife of M. M. Clark, clerk of courts and the mother to two college boys. Jessie was pretty and bright and is married and lives in Philadelphia. I always liked Miss Lovejoy; she was so smart and sunny.

How all those young ladies come trooping back to my mind, as I renew the past, the early and the later ones, in sweet confusion. Before my mind, at this moment appears a very pretty girl, with pink cheeks that pinker grew whenever she blushed, with light hair, and pretty blue eyes. She was very nice and studied hard; but would sometimes give me a reproving look, when I kept her reciting too long. I was very fond of her, but used to like to tease her and make her blush.

The Madigan girls were among my finest pupils. They were fine scholars and ladies, and are remembered with greatest pleasure.

Miss Anna Barns attended the Academy for several terms, and was a much-loved pupil. She also assisted me in the school. I have always felt grateful to that young lady for her thoughtfulness. She helped and encouraged me infinitely more than she ever knew. She is now the efficient librarian of the Cary Library at Houlton.

Whenever I felt a little depressed and disheartened, one look at the cheerful, smiling face of Carrie Hone of Littleton, drove away every vestige of the blues.

I hope, if a large number of pupils never knew, on earth, how much good their very presence did to the worried, anxious teacher, they will know it in Heaven.

One of the young ladies that I always missed was Annie Estey. She was a bright scholar and a very pleasant young lady. One day, while I was absent from the room, Prof. Estes was walking to and fro across the room and Annie was following him with her eyes. He at length said: "Please do not look at me, Miss Estey, I am a very bashful young man." She smilingly replied: "I couldn't deprive myself of that pleasure for anything."

Aggie McClain-Tabor's cheerful smile and studious habits always pleased me. She was a good scholar, and a fast friend of myself and family. She now lives in Los Angeles, Cal.

Mrs. Sarah May-Packard boarded at our house and went to school. She became an excellent teacher and has the respect of all who know her. Alice Porter, Carrie Hogan and Miss Cassidy, I remember as girls whom I always enjoyed. I do not know why I always associate Luella Seeley and Abby Smith together in thought, unless it be that they were both very brilliant scholars. Sweet Nutie Nye, whose face I could paint today, left us in the very bloom of girlhood, promising so much; making all hearts sad.

With much pleasure do I recall the Putnam girls. They were all very bright and nice. I believe **Chrisie and** I used to have a *tete-a-tete* after school sometimes but I liked the girl. Cardie, I remember, assisted Father **Pearley** in his writing classes. She is now the wife of Albert L. Putnam, a very prominent citizen of Houlton, and the happy mother of three college boys and a young lady at a seminary. One of whom has recently been elected superintendent of schools. Hattie Bradford of Houlton was just as nice, good-natured and sweet as she is now.

Ada Staples lived nearby our house and I saw much of her. The more I knew her the more I esteemed her.

I remember, with great pleasure, Myra Seeley and her sister Mamie. Mrs. Seeley-Donald was very studious and orderly, and had an inspiring, musical laugh that still makes her attractive. Mamie was much at our home, a playmate of my daughter. Our home was made sad when the light went out in that young life.

Hattie Mayo and May Stetson were fine students from Hodgdon.

The Mulherrin girls were very fine scholars, and have made fine teachers. Hannah in the old days showed great enthusiasm in whatever she undertook. She has lost none of it.

Mattie Nye was a favorite with me. Miss Clara Stimpson was a fine mathematician and a very bright young lady in all respects.

Estella Newhouse was one of the very nice young ladies whom I especially liked. She has become very proficient in music, and spends much time in Boston.

I used to think, if the Creator should put a model young lady into a school, to show what a pupil may be, that her name would appear on the record book—Belle Lovejoy. I still think so. Every lesson was perfect, and every act that of a lady.

Five young men assisted me while teaching there. The first was C. E. Williams, of whom I have spoken. Mr. Libby was with me a short time, and was a fine young man and good teacher. He died some years ago. W. W. Mayo taught a year with success. Mr. Mayo is a fine mathematician. He has taught in several prominent schools since, and is now teaching at Hodgdon.

Frank Bullard was a fine scholar and very enthusiastic in his work. He went to Germany and studied medicine, and is now a physician of great note in Los Angeles, California. Mr. Bullard has invented several instruments for surgical purposes, which have come into general use. Mr. Bullard's wife is also a physician of extensive practice.

Dr. Estes assisted me one year. He afterwards attended John Hopkins University and is now a teacher in Erasmus Hall, Brooklyn.

These young men were all Colby graduates and excellent scholars. I have been very fortunate in the assistants who worked with me. I never had but one with whom I had the least disagreement.

Several young ladies assisted me in surbordinate positions during those ten years. Lucia Rose Madigan was always ready to hear a class on call. Miss Lucia was an excellent scholar and the best elocutionist in school. There was a charm in her voice never equalled by any I ever heard, and it still delights her many friends. I can never repay that lady for her kind ness to me. Elloise Bagley Ludwig was teacher of the primary department. Happy herself, and throwing sunbeams all around her, Elloise was very useful to me, and was duly appreciated. Her kindnesses then and oftimes since have planted roses in my pathway, whose perfume is a continuous delight.

Winnie Madigan taught French one term, as did Miss Emma Tenny. Both were very efficient teachers, and ladies.

Mrs. Annie Bradbury taught painting for a year or two and thoroughly understood her business. She was an educated and admirable lady. Her son James was an industrious student. Beecher Putnam assisted in mathematics one term very acceptably.

CHAPTER XX.

From Houlton I went to Presque Isle to teach in the St. John's school. This school was founded by Bishop Neely. It was a day and boarding school. There were about one hundred pupils. There was a head master and I was selected master. There were a classical and English course of study. It was my duty to teach Latin, Greek and the sciences. Another duty did not please me, I was obliged to sleep in a sort of attic, where small bedrooms had been partitioned off for the boys. There were seventeen boys and myself in that low, badly ventilated attic. There were many very interesting pupils in that school, some of whom have become quite prominent in the political and financial world.

At the middle of the winter term the head master resigned and I became head master. Mr. James Vroom of St. Stephens, N. B., was called to be my associate. Mr. Vroom was a cultured man, of great erudition, of keen inceptive powers and high moral conceptions. His coming was a great relief to me. The school session was opened each morning by the ceremonies of the Episcopal church. This was all new to me, the blunders I made would make a churchman writhe in agony. I remember one morning I asked the choir to sing a certain hymn com pletely through. The singers sang the whole hymn with a quiet smile lurking around the mouth. That hymn celebrated the glory of every saint in the calendar and one of the teachers asked me if I thought it was All Saints' day.

I was engaged to teach the next year but circumstances arose that made this impossible and I went to Caribou. The school through poor management and incompetent teachers rapidly declined and at last ceased to exist. The buildings are now occupied by a Normal school. "Of all sad words of lip or pen, the saddest are these; it might have been." I remember many pupils of that school with much pleasure. The pleasant smile of Miss Johnson, the music teacher, was refreshing; the methodical accuracy of Miss Noland, another teacher, was praiseworthy; the quiet after-hour talks with Mr. Vroom I shall never forget. Mr. Vroom occupies a prominent government position at the present time in the educational field of New Brunswick.

Can I ever forget Harry Haynes of Bangor? He was not a bad boy, but full of fun. One night he came in late and I brought him up next morning before the head master, who inquired in sharp tones, "Where were you last night?" "At the hotel," replied Haynes. "What were you doing there?" "Singing." "What did you sing?" was the last question. Haynes with childlike innocence beaming from every square inch of his chubby face replied with a drawl, "Oh we sang 'Where is my wandering boy to-night.'" Duty elsewhere immediately called me from the room. Harry is now a business man connected with a hardware firm in Bangor.

A. W. Dudley, another boy who had been a pupil at Houlton, the year before, was an excellent scholar, faithful and studious. He graduated from Harvard and is now a very successful practitioner in Cambridge.

Roy F. Bartlett of Caribou, was a very lovable boy, whom I came to know so well, and of whom mention will be made hereafter.

A. J. Taylor of Caribou, was a fine scholar and has become a very prosperous man of affairs.

Dr. Edgar Sincock of Caribou, was an excellent pupil,

11

never wasting any time, and is a very successful physician and business man of Caribou.

Newman Doyle also of Caribou, was a sort of chum of mine. He and I settled many political and theological questions that winter. He is one of the wealthy farmers of Aroostook.

Joel Beal, now an enterprising lawyer in Lewiston, always wore a smile of good nature, and Fred Whitney faithfully labored over the Anabasis. Fred now graces the legal fraternity.

I remember with much pleasure pretty Lou Pratt as the girl that gave such excellent translations of Virgil. Miss Pratt would have been a successful literary character had she devoted herself to it.

Miss Lottie Jenks was also a fine scholar in Latin. The tall, fun-loving How boys were fine mathematical scholars, as was Allie Herdison and Miss Cleaves.

W. B. Hall was a good scholar and singer as well. Mr. Hall is a successful lawyer at Caribou. Med Hayford I remember as the best natured boy in the school, and Charles Phair as the most dignified.

Philip Phair, a very studious boy, is now in Washington, D. C. Charles Rolfe is getting rich in Maysville, managing a large farm.

One can see by glancing at this list that few schools contain so many pupils who become prominent in after life, in so few years. Many of the young ladies became teachers and made a success of life in that line and are now happily married.

Presque Isle is a very pleasant town in which to reside. There are many educated and refined people there, whose friendship I much enjoyed. The Hon. T. H. Phair, the "Starch King," a gentleman and good fellow, showed me much kindness, as did Col. Allen and Amasa Howe and many others. There is a church in Presque Isle that stands upon a lot that was given to the society by a gentleman who inserted in the deed this proviso, "If ever hell-fire is preached in the church edifice, this deed shall be null and void."

In that school at Presque Isle there was a rule that forbade all intercourse between the sexes. No boy was allowed to speak to a girl anywhere on the school grounds or within the building. I remember one day Leon Howe sat in a seat with a young lady when the head master came in and said some very sharp words to him, closing with these words, "It is an insult to a young lady to sit down beside her." Leon replied, "Oh they like it all right.'

The question of co-education presented itself in a new light at Presque Isle. Both sexes were in the school, both recited in the same classes but at recess, noon and after school no one could even address another of the opposite sex. That certainly was a bad arrangement. It led to many clandestine meetings in doubtful places. When I became principal of the school, I allowed unrestrained intercourse between the young men and women in the schoolroom in my presence. The result was there were no more secret meetings. If there be a mixed school there must be a certain amount of social relations. There can be no objection to this if there be proper regulations. The result of observation proves quite conclusively that co-education is the best under certain conditions. Small boys and girls should go to school together. The boys need the little girls to check them in their rougher sports and treatment of each other. In my opinion, nothing but evil can come from collecting together a score or more of small boys and allowing them to direct their own sports and associations. They become rough, cruel and unruly. Girls are kind, gentle and lovable. With all these commendable traits they become jealous, nervous and fault-finding when collected in masses. Allow these boys and girls to associate together an hour a day, a great improvement will appear in both sexes in a few days. But there comes a time when these same boys and girls should be religiously separated in school life. There should be no mixed school when the pupils are from ten to sixteen years of age. The boy at this age has ceased to be a child and has not become a man. He is restless, noisy and don't know what to do with himself. He now for a time needs perhaps the rough and tumble experience that his fellows give him. He must run and jump, box and wrestle or he surely will get into mischief. He does not understand why the girl that two years ago would run races with him, climb trees and scuffle with him, will not do so now. He cannot assimilate himself to her prim ways. She no longer has any influence for good over him, and he is an injury to her. Of course, I am speaking of the real boy. That cyclone of human ity that will skate all day and half of the night and sleep till noon on the morrow, who can handle a gun like a veteran and fish till the brooks are dry, who never sees a new boy without desiring to wrestle with or fight him; that generous, tempestuous makeup, saucy and irreverent specimen of *genus homo* that can illy brook any authority or be influenced by gentle means. With hands in his pockets, hat on one side, with almost defiant mien he strides over mother earth with but one idea, to make all the noise he can and have some fun. His pleasures are almost wholly of the physical order. That's the boy that will one day stride into the governor's chair or gracefully sit behind the Senatorial desk.

"God bless the unspoiled boy of fourteen. Prince thou art, the grown up man only is republican."

There is but one really counteracting influence that can very much shape that young adventurer's career—the undying influence of a discreet mother. Father just now is not a factor. He has become the "old man" but at no time in his life does the boy love his mother as at the age mentioned. His older sisters don't want the awkard fellow near them at all. Father frets over his disastrous attempts to do any thing just right. His hands and feet are always in his own way, but mother takes him to her heart and excuses all blunders, lets him sleep mornings to his heart's content, and her he loves. Then let that boy receive his education in those years from the mother that bore him, from the attrition received from his boy associates, controlling discipline of a wise, conscientious, boy-loving teacher.

Of the effeminate boy I say nothing; the boy that never whoops and turns somersaults, who at twelve and thirteen wants to be a Beau Brummel, who would make a dudish gallant of himself, and begins to play the sweetheart, of that boy I have no hopes. Better dress him like Achilles in female attire and give him a female doll to caress.

At sixteen or seventeen the boys and girls should be brought together again at school. Manhood has settled down upon the erstwhile boy, not in full degree, but sufficient to change his whole nature. The mental, the ethical begin to displace physical pleasures. The young man now sees attractive qualities in his old associates. He seeks her society, but not in its old way. He wishes to appear at his best in her presence, he will sacrifice something for her benefit. He is pleased when she smiles upon him and unhappy when she frowns. Her nice, ladylike ways leads him to be gentle, courteous and well-man nered. In fine, the associations are altogether happy to him as long as the platonic relation exists. The young lady needs his influence as well. By conversing with him she enters a broader field of thought than girls are inclined to occupy. Through the association mentioned, she becomes more self-reliant. In teaching him by example, she becomes more confirmed in her rules of right and propriety. She learns that certain qualities must be exhibited to attract him and those she assumes. Thus, they help each other develop and educate the opposite sex.

The optimistic views of these last two gentlemen were a great help to me. If Mr. Howe should wake up some morning on a desert isle in the Arctic ocean, he would go to cutting ice before breakfast for some southern market.

I remember with gratitude the kindness of Deacon Wilkins, Harry Thayer, Mr. Pipes, Mr. Jenks and many others.

Of course I knew the Rev. Mr. Parks. Who didn't? He

is still alive or I should have written a long obituary in these papers. If I survive him I shall take occasion to do so.

Whatever Presque Isle starts in to do is done with impetuous vigor. While I was teaching there a bachelor one day seemed to have conceived the idea of taking to himself a wife. He proceeded to immediately interview a young lady about the matter. He evidently negotiated in the right quarter. For a month his place of business knew him but little, then they were married and "have lived happily ever since." That was business.

Presque Isle in the very beginning of its existence became very much interested in education, and very soon an academy was established there. The funds of the academy were, in 1885, turned over to the St. John's Classical School, with the arrangement that this school should serve the double purpose of academy and boarding school. The St. John's School ceased to satisfy the needs of the town after a few years, and the town built a fine High School building and have since maintained a High School of superior rank. Some four years ago those enterprising people decided to have a Normal School at Presque Isle. To determine was to do. The Legislature granted the charter and the school was started. Last winter a large sum was voted to build a dormitory. The school is in a very flourishing condition.

An incident occurred near Presque Isle some thirty or more years ago that was new to Maine. There was a man working around town who had become a public nuisance. He broke into David Dudley's store one night and stole some articles. The deputy sheriff, Granville Hayden, with a Boston commercial man went to a camp in Mapleton to arrest the burglar. They found him in a camp, arrested him and allowed him to sleep that night with them in the camp. In the night that brute arose, seized an axe, and killed the two men. A posse arrested him the next day and toward evening started for Presque Isle. On the way a crowd of people met the posse, took the man from the sleigh and hanged him to a limb of a tree. I visited his grave while in town, and could but feel that justice had been done if I did not quite agree with the method of procedure.

For a few months I was editor of a paper. I found the position required more labor and brains than I had thought. I liked the work and desired to continue in it, but circumstances were not favorable. I do feel that the editor of a country newspaper holds a very responsible position in the community, and can do a large amount of good—or evil. A paper placed every week in the hands of the young does to a large degree shape their thought. Many an editor, could he but know that his weekly utterances had done more than father or mother in moulding the character of the boy reader, would be more careful in his utterances.

CHAPTER XXI.

CARIBOU.

From Presque Isle I went to Caribou. The establishment of that school illustrates the energy and determination of the hustling citizens of that wide-awake town.

I received a letter one day from Caribou asking if I would go to that town to teach. I replied that they had no house, no funds, no organization. The next day Mr. Bartlett appeared with a paper signed by six responsible citizens guaranteeing me One Thousand Dollars for a year's work. I agreed to go. This was the first of August. Mr. Bartlett, C. B. Roberts, Mr. Taylor and others went to work to get things ready for a High School. They rented an unoccupied store, had some seats manufactured, black-boards made and all other necessary apparatus. Then a paper was circulated among the citizens who subscribed twenty-five dollars apiece for the support of a school. In this way two hundred and fifty dollars were raised; next a meeting of the voters of the district was called and the same amount was voted, which entitled the district to receive two hundred fifty dollars from the State. The remaining two hundred fifty was to be met by tuitions. All this was done within a month. On September first I appeared at Caribou and commenced the school. There were nearly a hundred scholars the first day. Among them were seven who had been pupils at Presque Isle. The task of classifying that heterogeneous mass into distinct classes was no light task. There was lots of hard work required in the first term. The room was too small, the ventilation very bad and the light insufficient. In one part of the room where molasses had been sold the floor was still sticky, and when the room was hot there was a tendency toward a fixedness of position that prevented rapid progression. In another corner of the room there still remained the unpleasant odor of kerosene. I sat the red-headed boy as far from that corner as possible. Over my table the plastering was loose and occasionally a piece would become detached and fall upon my head. That pleased the scholars but did not improve my good humor. The Grange would every week hold a session in the room above the schoolroom, which disturbed us not a little. The pupils were fine and well advanced in their studies. I taught Latin, Greek, French, Algebra, Trigonometry, Chemistry and many other branches. Among those pupils were many who have become prominent in educational and business lines. There were several from other towns. New Sweden sent the largest number. During the ten years stay in Caribou there were always some pupils from New Sweden in the school.

Among the students from New Sweden was John Hedman. This young man showed, at once, superior ability and an untiring industry. He made great progress in his studies, and soon conceived the idea of fitting for college. This he did and entered Colby, from which college he graduated at the head of the class. He was elected instructor, in the following year, and, upon the next year, was elected professor in the same institution, and given leave of absence for a year's study in Europe. Mr. Headman attended that famous school in Paris at which students from all the world attend.

In a class of six hundred, Mr. H. stood second in the class. Mr. Hedman has been invited to Harvard but feels it a duty to remain at Colby. Mr. Hedman has a brilliant future awaiting him. I know of no young man his superior in the department which he so acceptably fills. I esteem myself very fortunate in having been his instructor and friend in his younger days.

S. P. Hedman, John Learson, Washington Wiren, John

Nelson and John Oliembaum all went to college and were young men of real merit and fine scholarship. Mr. Wiren is superintendent of schools in a city in the Philippine Islands.

The history of New Sweden is an interesting one. In 1875, under the direction of Minister Thomas, a colony of Swedes came to Aroostook and were allotted a township of land belonging to the State. They were to pay for the land principally by building roads.

At first they built log houses and commenced to fell trees, and by patient labor at length became possessors of valuable farms. Then they replaced the log houses by frame ones and began to make the interior attractive. A person riding through that town today can hardly realize that ony a few years ago an unbroken forest stood where many elegant farm buildings now stand and where three church edifices invite religious worship. There is a large Lutheran church, an artistic commodious Baptist church and a very large Free church. These churches are filled Sundays with an intelligent audience. Almost every house has an organ or piano in it, and the town also boasts a brass band. I have never known a people more anxious to educate their children. The parents would hire a room or two at Caribou, bring sufficient furniture and house-keeping supplies and weekly bring out some food for the student. The boys would use this food and also cook potatoes, meat and coffee for themselves. Nearly all the pupils from that town were superior scholars.

The school at Caribou was supported the first year in the manner described. At the next town meeting the school was adopted by the district and one thousand dollars raised to support a High school. Tuition was paid by the scholars from other districts. As the number of the scholars increased it soon was found necessary to provide an assistant teacher. Miss Godwin, a Normal graduate was secured. The next two years Miss Grace E. Knowlton very ably assisted me in school work. In the meantime C. B. Roberts and myself bought a lot of land where the High School building now stands. This lot we sold to the district at the same price. A house was erected costing some fourteen thousand dollars. This house had the best ventilation of any school I ever occupied. When the law was enacted abolishing school districts, the town assumed the house and re-imbursed the district. I challenge the State to produce an instance where one school district ever equalled action like that. And the town, too, at the time it assumed that school house debt, was putting in water works, and building a twenty thousand dollar steel bridge. Caribou has always been an enterprising town. No misfortunes discourage the people, and no prosperity spoils them. When the last census was taken Caribou had about six thousand inhabitants. There are five churches, a Masonic Lodge, Odd Fellows Lodge, Grange and other societies. There are two banks and many stores finely arranged and fully stocked. Six or seven lawyers are flourishing on the sins of the inhabitants of the adjoining towns, and five doctors do miracles in the way of healing. There is but one undertaker and he is mostly supported by his farm.

I occupied the new house six years. Miss Webber was the next assistant, a fine teacher. In the meantime Miss Christie Miller and Miss Elva Roberts were sub-assistants. Finally Miss Roberts became the regular assistant. She remained in the school as long as I did. Miss Roberts graduated from the High School and went to Waterville and graduated from the Coburn Classical School. She was a fine scholar, apt to teach, tactful, faithful and a lady. No one could fill the position she graced better than she. Miss Roberts married C. F. Ross, one of the prominent business men of Caribou, and is now the mother of three most interesting children. She is the same lovely woman, diffusing sunshine wherever her presence is. Long may she and her good man enjoy their happy life.

That school became a part, a very large part of my life. There were very many most enjoyable pupils,—some very talented and very few disagreeable ones. We had an advanced course of study and regular graduations.

Among the earlier pupils was Herbert Hackett of Wood-
land,—a good boy who afterwards enlisted in the army during
the Cuban war and died in the service. Peace to his ashes.

W. S. Webb was one of the first pupils. He afterwards
graduated at Orono and taught for some years at Houlton, and
was later superintendent of schools at Caribou. Roy Bartlett,
A. J. Taylor, Allie Hardison, Newman Doyle, John S. Spaulding, and W. S. Webb were students of mine at Presque Isle
and the school consequently did not seem entirely like a strange
one. It was through their influence and their parents that I
received a "call" to Caribou. It has been my singular fortune
to teach but two or three schools for which I applied. All the
rest have applied to me. I have sought for positions, not many,
which I have not obtained, but to the schools where I have
taught I have been called.

When I first thought of teaching I suggested to another
boy a little older than I that we start out together to get a school.
So Frank Parsons and I started forth on a mission, that has not
yet terminated. We drove up to the town of Parkman and
interviewed each agent in regular order. Frank, as he was
older, had the first bid; his inexperience barred him out. It was
my turn next. I met my agent in the road. He was a large,
fat man and stuttered spasmodically. When I told him my age
he refused to engage my services, and raising himself upon tip-
toe and with mouth twisted into inconceivable shapes, with eyes
wildly rolling, with right hand frantically waving and left foot
digging holes in the roadbed, he stuttered "n-n-nooo, the-th-they
are ug-ug-lv as h-h-h—ll. I was afterward very glad that I
did not attempt that school. Some big girls attacked the teacher
the next term and drove him from the house minus hat and
coat. One never knows how many evils they narrowly escape.
A telegram took me to Houlton and the schools at Foxcroft and
Monson Academy were voluntarily offered me.

The first graduates from Caribou High School were Newman Doyle and W. E. Sincock, of whom I spoke in the Presque

Isle article. That was in 1887. The next year Roy F. Bart
lett, A. H. Hardison and W. S. Webb graduated. Mr. Har
dison is now a civil engineer in California.

The next class consisted of thirteen, two of whom now
sleep in the beautiful evergreen cemetery at Caribou,—sweet
Gertie Briggs and noble Vernon Hall. Miss Garden is teaching the Grammar School at Caribou very successfully, and
Alice Shaw is also a well-known teacher. The rest of the class
drew tickets in the matrimonial lottery, and were generally
fortunate I should judge.

Among the earlier pupils who did not graduate was John S.
Spaulding. John was a free-hearted, companionable boy, the
soul of the social life in town. Always ready to help and support everything that made the town better. His premature
death caused many tears to flow among all classes that knew
him.

Thomas C. Tooker was another boy who early showed superior ability in scholarship. He fitted for college, and graduated
with honor. Mr. Tooker won much praise also by his musical
ability. He is now a well-known teacher in southern Maine.

The Lafferty boys were good boys and studied well. Russ
attended strictly to business, and showed great good taste in
the selection of a wife later on. The Gammon girls were good
scholars and fine singers. Sampson was studious and good in
figures, and married pretty Gertie Campbell, a favorite pupil
of mine.

Eva Ross was always very nice, and smart, and Idella
Holmes never lost her good humor. The Briggs girls and boys
will never be forgotten by the teacher of that day. Josie was
sparkling and Grace Shaw would never get tired. Sweet Myrtie Small won her way to my heart the first hour; and Myrtie
Todd was near perfection.

W. H. Fisher was a very diligent pupil and rapidly
advanced. After leaving school he read law and commenced
to practice at Augusta. Mr. Fisher has been very successful in
the profession of law, and is now in Europe on a pleasure trip.

One day there appeared in school a bright eyed girl about 15 years old, who attracted my attention at once by the accurate manner in which she recited. She told me her name was Christine Miller. She attended school some four years, fitted for college and was a student at Colby two years. She was what I call an intuitive scholar. Her lessons seemed to evolve from her mind. She is at present one of the teachers in the Caribou High school, and deserves and receives great credit for her work.

I have alluded to Roy F. Bartlett. That young man attracted my attention at Presque Isle at once, and my interest in him increased the more I knew him. I saw much of him at Caribou and learned to love him. His whole soul was the ideal that young men might follow. His intellectual faculties were of a very high order. His reasoning powers were extraordinary. A keener sense of honor I never knew in any boy. When life seemed so glorious, when prospects so brilliant, when friends so hopeful—at that hour he faded from life, and left so many hearts sad, and caused a whole community to weep. Rare, lovable, brilliant Roy F. Bartlett, he will never lack a mourner while this hand can wield a pen or my heart beat.

The Hardison girls were always busy at something good, and have been very successful in their vocations in life. John Gordon, Richard Gardner, A. W. Spaulding were all good boys and are today prominent in business affairs and many others I might recall. Not one is forgotton. Louis Stearns was a fine looking boy and bright. He graduated at Colby and is now reading law. John and Sarah Roberts, Dana Therrieult went to college. They were all fine scholars. Mr. Spaulding has been on the Governor's staff. Mr. Therrieult is a promising lawyer. John Nelson is a good lawyer and first-class fellow every way. John Roberts and Louis Stearns I am sure will do honor to Caribou High in a successful professional career.

So many more I could mention with pleasure did space permit.

Madge Goud was a fine Latin scholar. She attended a Normal and Commercial School after graduating from Caribou and has had fine positions in the bank and business houses.

I remember, with pleasure, the sweet voice voice and cheery smile of Grace Stratton. Grace, somehow, seemed to me as my own daughter. She is still studying and learning, and always will be at something good and useful.

Hope Gardner, always bright and sparkling; Hannah, with her pretty eyes; Emma, the irrepressible; Ray, on whose brow was written success; Roy, the brilliant; Ethel, the thoughtful; all those, and many more, in memory's glass appear in all the freshness of the old days.

Poetic Bessie, and flirtatious Nellie, I would not forget. Nor the Powers boys, who used to personate each other to avoid declaiming. These boys had great dramatic ability.

The Gould boys were very popular and May Hitchings was smart.

The Thomas girls were very bright and I remember them with great pleasure.

During the years I taught at Caribou, three of the pupils who had become very dear to me, left me for other scenes and brighter skies. Brilliant, thoughtful, lovable Deasey Goud sickened and died just when she was showing a wonderful intellect, a heart full of love and purity, and grand aspirations. I loved that young girl as my own, and shall never cease to do so.

Gertie Irving, so sweet, so lady-like, so faithful in every duty; I followed the hearse with the deepest emotion, that bore her to her last resting place. I loved that little girl.

Ellen Anderson, a favorie with all, and beloved by the teacher, passed from us at the very beginning of a life of great promise.

> "All my fears are laid aside"
> "If I but remember only,"
> "Such as these have lived and died."

They were all so nice, and smart. It was a lovable lot of pupils. I also found many kind friends in Caribou. Many families showed my family and myself great kindness. The Getchells, the Bartletts, the Briggses, the Hardisons, and many others. Caribou is a very enterprising town, and, in the coming future will become a large commercial center of trade and manufactories.

Dr. Thomas and family, during my stay at Caribou, and since, have showed me great kindness and those favors will never be forgotten. The young ladies and Charles were always very kind to me.

CHAPTER XXII.

MONSON ACADEMY.

In 1895, I returned to Monson and taught ten years. Many of the pupils were the children of the old scholars. The school was much smaller than when I taught there before, for one especial reason. In the old days there were no High Schools, so I had pupils from several towns. Now there are High Schools in many towns, which fact must lessen the attendance at the Academies. I enjoyed the school, however, and had under my care some very bright scholars. Seven pupils entered Colby during the ten years, and two entered Medical Colleges. Mr. Larson graduated from the Medical School at Albany, and Mr. Sampson is at Brunswick. Both of these young men will, I am sure, make a success of life. They have the ability, and, what is more important, a desire to make something of themselves.

Miss Bessie Jones was the only young lady who went to college. Miss Jones is a fine scholar and a lovable young lady. The boys now in college are all young men of talent, and will doubtless graduate with honor.

My first assistant was Miss Agnes Powers. She had every quality requisite for a good teacher. Miss Powers resigned at the close of two years and attended a missionary school in Chicago. Later she married Rev. Mr. Bishop and is now happy in her work as a pastor's wife in Hodgdon. Miss Ethel W. Knowlton was assistant for a year. Her teaching was perfectly satisfactory. Miss Flora Gilbert was my last assistant.

During the twenty years I was teaching in Aroostook, Monson Academy sent two students to Bates College, neither of whom graduated. In the seven years I taught that Institution, eight entered Colby and Bowdoin.

I have always believed in a college education, provided certain things were true. An indispensable condition is a sufficient mental capacity. I would advise no student to enter college who has not a mental capacity to readily fit for college, and who does not exhibit to the teacher that capacity.

Secondly, no student should go who is not willing to sacrifice something to attain a college education. He must be willing, oftimes, to sacrifice the gratifications of many desires calling for money. He must be willing to use time he would like to devote to pleasure and friends. That one idea,—a college education,—should be the absorbing, all-controlling purpose of life. Of course, no one will understand that I would put that purpose above any moral duty. As I see it, the first great duty of every young person is to start on a Christian life. This course entered upon, will naturally enlarge the desire for usefulness, naturally suggesting a college course as the best means to prepare for that end.

During the ten years, we had two debates with other schools. The first debate was with Guilford High School.

The speakers on our side were John Humphrey, Harry Sampson, and Miss Stella Wheeler. These young people were well fitted for the position. Mr. Humphrey was a fine scholar and pleasant speaker. The logic of his argument was keen and incisive. Mr. Humphrey entered college a year later, and made a good record there until circumstances compelled him to withdraw.

Mr. Sampson is a very energetic young man of high ability. He is bound to succeed. He was a member of Bowdoin College two years, and is now on the last year's course in the Medical School.

Miss Wheeler is a very talented young lady, and a fine speaker.

On the part of Guilford, Hugh Montgomery, Frank Loring and Miss E. Rebecca Ellis were the speakers. I should certainly class these young people as far above the average in ability. Mr. Montgomery is, at present, reading law with J. S. Williams, at Guilford.

Mr. Loring, after graduating at Guilford, went to California. When he returned, he entered the University of Maine and pursued a course in that institution. He is at present in Parkman.

Miss Ellis showed in that debate that a brilliant future awaited her. I was particularly pleased with the originality of thought displayed, and the modest, lady-like appearance of Miss Ellis on the platform. Miss Ellis graduated from the High School and entered Wellesley College, in 1900. She held so high rank and showed such ability that she was elected instructor of the Sciences of Astronomy and Physics in that well-known institution and will be raised to a full professorship the coming year.

The victory was with us in the debate, but I should say that the Guilford pupils did not have a fair chance. The principal of that school resigned just before the debate, and the new principal, Mr. Snow, did not have proper time to attend to the matter.

The second debate was with Foxcroft Academy. Harry Sampson, John Humphrey, and Miss Lillie Piper were the debaters from Monson. Miss Piper won great praise, deservedly, on that occasion. She is a very intellectual young lady and a well-known teacher. Of the other two I have already spoken.

Lester B. Howard, H. W. Cass, and Robert E. Hall were the speakers for Foxcroft Academy. These young men showed themselves then and since, as superior in mental caliber and culture.

Mr. Howard is taking a course of instruction at the University of Maine. Mr. Cass, after spending two years at Bowdoin College, entered a law school at Boston. Mr. Hall entered Bowdoin and has always occupied a prominent position there. His executive ability has been recognized all through the course. He is a member of the Z. U. Fraternity; was Vice President of N. E. Inter-Collegiate Athletic Association; Associate Manager of 'Varsity Track Team; and many other positions he has held. All that know Mr. Hall predict for him a very successful career.

The contest was very close but the judges awarded us the victory, though I imagine some of the Foxcroft people did not coincide with the judges.

Such things are now out of date. Football has supplanted all such things. The intellectual has had its day; now muscle is at a premium. Perhaps the day will come when each will receive its due attention.

I should not be doing justice to my own feelings to close my reminiscences of my last sojourn in Monson without mentioning the Banigan family. Mr. Banigan is a New York lawyer of eminent ability. Overwork broke down his health somewhat and he came to Monson to rusticate. We became acquainted by a magic wand,—the fishing rod. I found him a most valuable acquaintance. His knowledge of the world was very extensive, his reading universal and his good nature was never ruffled. I never met a more perfect gentleman anywhere, and never enjoyed a fishing companion more. If I ever feel inclined to be critical in the choice of a companion it is in selecting a man to go fishing with. I could eat with, work with, sleep with a man that I would utterly refuse to fish with. One disagreeable fellow in a crowd of fishermen will spoil the whole day's sport. I enjoyed also the pleasant society and hospitality of Mrs. Banigan. Willie and Lou Banigan I most heartily enjoyed. I hope I shall see them again.

It has been my good fortune to have known some very pleasant fishermen. Clergymen, on the whole, are good men to go fishing with. The most of those with whom I have fished have been good fellows, and ready to do their part of the work. I suppose I was wicked when once I rebuked a clergyman for delay caused by a "season of prayer" after the boat was all ready. When I asked him why he prayed just then, he said he was praying that *he* might catch some fish. I thought he might have included me or taken some other opportunity to pray.

I went out, one day, with a lot of strange clergymen, on the lake, and among the number was a very sanctimonious minister who could not bait his own hook. There was also aboard the boat a professional fisherman. Just for fun, I addressed him as "Brother G." The minister thought he belonged to the "Cloth" and called him "Brother G." Brother T. lost his bait and wanted G. to put on another so he presented G. with hook and chub and said, "Brother G., will you adjust this chub to my hook?" Just then G. hooked a trout and lost him and, forgetting his surroundings, ejaculated very fervently: "D—— that trout!" I happened to be looking at Brother T. The dazed look that overspread his face was followed by one of astonishment and when the full import of that word came to him, the flash of indignation that came from his eyes fairly made the water sparkle. There he stood; chub in one hand, hook in the other, with both arms extended, for a full minute; then his spine assumed a very perpendicular direction and, swallowing a big lump in his throat, he said in a hard, dry tone: "Mr. G. will you hook this chub for me?" No more "Brother" for G. that day.

E. R. Haynes, of Monson, is the most enthusiastic fisherman I ever met with, and a very companionable man for a fishing trip. I think Mr. H. has a wheel-barrow load of fishing tackle.

The recent graduates from the school at Monson were all young people of good ability and are making a mark in the world. Miss Steward, Miss Jackson, Miss Sears and Miss Johnson are well known teachers. Of Miss Piper and Miss Wheeler, I have spoken in another place. Miss Grover taught for a time and entered a business college. Miss Phillips taught a year and entered a business college and is now in a printing office. Miss Phillips will be a success anywhere. Miss Wilkins is at Bangor in the training school and teaching. Miss Wilkins is a very fine teacher in the primary schools.

The Jones boys, Oscar Peterson, William Sherburne and Harvey Gilbert entered college. Ormon Steward was fitted for college but did not go. He is a young man of superior ability and an excellent teacher.

There were many bright scholars in the senior class when my connection with the school closed. One of the most promising scholars I ever taught is Harry Riddle of that class. He will enter college and some of the young ladies will go to Normal school.

Frank Phillips of Shirley is a fine mathematician and a first-class young man. I hope he will continue his course of study at some higher institution. I am sure he would be a success as an engineer. I received many kind favors from his family and himself, while teaching at Shirley.

CHAPTER XXIII.

SHIRLEY. BILL NYE.

One summer I desired to test some of the theories upon which were founded some of the new methods of teaching, so I engaged to teach a district school in the town of Shirley. Shirley is a small town, bounded on the east by Douty Hill, west by Squaw Mountain, north by Moosehead lake, and south by the illimitable Universe. The town has some very nice people in it, and I enjoyed the school very much. I drove up nine miles each morning, and back that night.

Attending that school was a beautiful girl fourteen years of age. She was a sweet and modest, lovable girl and I became very well acquainted with her, as she rode a mile a day to school with me. I taught her the names of the rocks and plants by the roadside and discussed books and lots of things. A year later, that lovely girl, her father and mother, were murdered by the most brutal assassin the State of Maine ever knew.

Sweet Carrie Allen! I can see her today, in all her modest loveliness, as she rode by my side and talked about the future, planning to get a good education and become a factor for good in the world. No crime has ever seemed so horrible to me as that one. All such things take a shading from our relation to the victim.

At Shirley Mills there is a house somewhat famous. It was the birthplace of Bill Nye. The house stands on the west side of the Main street and is what is called a story and a half house. It is in a good state of repair. Around the house some old-fashioned flowers grow, giving the premises a cozy and pleasant appearance.   In that house, in the west chamber, was born William Nye.   Mr. Nye was, for some years, recognized as an original humorist.   As long as Bill Nye wrote occasionally, his writings were very readable and oft-times first-class— but when he fell into the mistake that many others have made and began to write by the yard, he became dull and uninteresting.

But the man had real genius and many of his sayings and pieces will survive the wreck of time.   Perhaps no one of our humorists has been more maligned than Bill Nye.   For years the report has been current that his early death was the result of habits of intoxication.   Recent investigation has proved conclusively that he was not an inebriate, that he used liquors sparingly.   That in his ideal home in North Carolina, he was a model husband and father.

References are sometimes made to his last appearance on the stage at Patterson, when it was claimed he was intoxicated. A friend of his has recently publicly declared that he was perfectly sober that night.   The cause of his death was a shock brought on by overwork.

Maine has produced many writers, witty and humorous. Some of these will live in history; others will be unknown to another generation.   Seba Smith wrote some very bright things; but only a few people remember him today.   Seba Smith wrote some very sarcastic witticisms which showed real genius.

No one has ever written an adequate definition of wit, or humor.   S. S. Cox tried to do so, some years ago, in a magazine article; but even he must have recognized his failure to make the matter clear.   I shall only gossip a little about the matter, in a desultory way.

Wit is purely a mental affair.   It consists in the combination of thought in such a way as to produce surprise.   The combination is always unexpected.   The commonplace attracts no notice.   It is the extraordinary that causes surprise.   One may walk through a forest for an hour without noticing any especial tree, but a particularly crooked one, a remarkably tall one, in fact, any one differing from the mass, attracts the attention. Any unusual combination of trees of different kinds always receives notice. So, in mental matters, the unusual, the incongruous, the exceptional, the strange, effects the mind in a peculiar way.

The human mind is so constituted that such combination induces a pleasurable sensation, causing a visible play of the muscles of the face, and the audible exhibition of laughter. No one can tell why we laugh, except that we are made so. It seems a little strange that we do laugh sometimes. For instance, let a dignified gentleman come into an audience of refined and educated ladies and gentlemen and accidentally sit down upon his silk hat; every one will smile, but why? It was simply unexpected.

We are not universally a witty people. No nation has so high sense of humor as our own people,—and no one has ever produced more enjoyable humorists; but most of those cannot be called men of wit.

Artemus Ward was an admirable humorist, but no wit. Mark Twain combines in himself the triune qualities of humorist, satirist, and wit. I am inclined to think that the brightest specimens of American wit are found among what is sometimes called "the Common People." Wit must be spontaneous. It must come as an electric flash, called forth by a peculiar perception of the condition of things.

Our forefathers, back in Revolutionary days, must have possessed the quality to quite an eminent degree, according to tradition. When the Council in Connecticut passed an edict that a man should not kiss his own wife on Sunday, a young Benedict asked: "Why! Whose wife then shall I kiss?" Benjamin Franklin rather wittily obtained a grant from the Quaker Assembly of Pennsylvania for two thousand pounds of wheat, *and other grains*. He purchased one pound of wheat, and 1999 pounds of *powder*. Powder has grains, he explained later.

There have come down to us from those days but few printed specimens of wit, but reasoning from analogy, we should say that real wit was more abundant in those days than at the present time. The camp, the wood, and the stern realities of a strenuous life are conducive to the development of wit.—Ease, wealth, a happy condition of things, is conducive to humor.

Matthew Byles was known in Boston as a witty man in Revolutionary days. He was, at one time, anxious to marry a beautiful woman; but she married Josiah Quincy. When he next met her he remarked, "Well, it seems you preferred Quinsy to Byles." (Boils) There is a bit of a pun in the remark, I admit, but right here I have a kindly word to say about the pun. I know, of late, the pun has been somewhat under ban, but it is coming back into favor again, and properly too.

Some of the brightest scintillations of wit I have ever heard or read have been clothed in the garments of the pun.—To illustrate—when the poet said that, in tracing out the family line, "Many an aristocratic family found it waxed at the other end," and a very deaf old lady bought a trumpet, and, "The very next day heard from her husband at Botany Bay." There are the garments of the pun, but there is wit, nevertheless.

Just after the Revolution two eminent gentlemen were walking by Old South Church, which, at one time, was used as a hospital. One of these men was a Unitarian clergyman. He had formerly been an orthodox. The other gentleman remarked, as they passed by; "I was vaccinated in that church." The other said: "I was baptized there." "Yes," the first replied, "and it took in neither case."

The only production of Revolutionary days I have ever read which claimed to be witty was written by the author of "The Battle of the Keags," Francis Hopkinson. There are flashes of wit in spots, at considerable intervals.

In the tragic days preceding the Civil War, when the prophetic soul could almost hear the mutterings of the contending forces that later shook our national fabric to its foundations, James Russel Lowell wrote pages of satire, from which flash occasionally pure wit. "The Courtin" is full of wit.

> "Zekle's heart went pit-a-pat"
> "And hern went pity Zekle."

Our own John Neal wrote a few very witty things. Bob Burdette is the prince of good fellows and humorists, but he is occasionally witty. There is a man in New York, a Mr. Landon (Eli Perkins) who thinks himself a wit, but I never read him or hear him without thinking of a little verse I learned when I was a child—

> "Says Bill: "I really think I'll set up for a wit."
> "Says Jim: "The best thing you can do is down again to sit."

Dr. Holmes wrote some very witty poetry, and said many witty things in his lectures. John G. Saxe, of Vermont, was a witty man, though mostly in the way of puns. When he said the fisherman, being a landsman, "couldn't keep the log" and so fell into the water, he surprises us, and hence was witty.

During the Civil War, Patroleum V. Nasby wrote some very local witty things. Josh Billings was witty. Mark Twain has said many very witty sayings. When he found his friend in Palestine, one hot day in July, watching a mud turtle very carefully for an hour, and discovered that he was waiting to hear him *sing*, relying upon the text of Scripture which says: "The voice of the turtle shall be heard in the land," we laugh, for we know that the turtle dove is meant. When Mark wept over the tomb of Adam because he was a relative; "distant to be sure, but none the less a relative," he was witty.

There have been brighter exhibitions of wit in the bar, the pulpit and in Congress, than in any professedly witty publications. I heard a clergyman, at a camp-meeting at Charlestown, pray for a young man who had made himself obnoxious; and he closed his prayer thus: "Now, Lord, we pray that thou wilt, in the mightiness of thy power, take that young man and make his heart as free from sin as his head is from sense!" I think he prayed for complete holiness.

That unmarried female preacher who asked the bachelor bishop if St. Paul's exhortation: "Let the bishop be the husband of one wife," wasn't mandatory, expressed a sort of heartfelt wit.

John P. Hale, of New Hampshire, was one of the wittiest men ever in Congress. It was said that he was the only man that the duelist, Foote of Mississippi, was afraid of. It was his wit, and not his pistol, that awed him. When Hale was told, one day, by Foote, that a donkey passing in the street, was one of his constituents, he replied: "O, yes, going down South to teach school." Tom Carwin of Ohio, was a very witty man. S. S. Cox of New York, was a buffoon generally, but occasionally a wit. Tom Reed said a very witty but rather cruel thing when he made that famous reply to a brother member. The member said: "I had rather be right than be President." Reed said: "You will never be either."

Wit is almost naturally cruel, but yet some of the brightest flashes exhibit the kindliest heart. It seems unfortunate, at first glance, that the great mass of witty sayings are lost. They are never written, they flash forth in unexpected places, and at all times, with no scribe to commemorate. Wit can never be forced, can never be cultivated, except in kind. Cultivation refines wit, but does not produce it. Wit has made a few men famous, and has written the early epitaph of many an aspiring politician.

Had James G. Blaine never called Conklin "a strutting turkey-cock," he would have been president of the United States. The New York senator's reply was equally fatal, when asked to speak for Blaine. He said he had gone out of criminal prac-tice. He could never be president after that speech. Zack Chandler threw away his last chance for the Presidency when he said that the Republican party, in stealing the Presidency for Hayes, was only guilty of "petit larceny." And many other witty, but fatal, sayings might be quoted which have had an undying influence upon private and public life. This has been true in all nations and at all times. The Archbishop who preached the Coronation Sermon before Queen Elizabeth pre-destinated his fate, when he took for his text: "A live dog is better than a dead lion."

I have treated this subject, perhaps, at too great length; but have been impelled to by a native keen sense of appreciation of wit and humor. I never boasted of possessing either, per-sonally, but do enjoy a good thing in that line, coming from others.

Perhaps I might have had a bit of something of that sort about me, had not my budding genius in that direction been cruelly frozen in the May Day of its existence. I never aimed to be witty or funny but, somehow, I always fired too high or two low, and failed to bring down the bird and sometimes wounded the game-keeper.

I tried, two or three times, to say pretty things to the ladies, but always failed and had to give it up. When my readers have perused the following lines, I am sure they will say it was the best to resign. One day, while playing Logomachy, I select-ed the letters that formed the word "Columbia" and neglected to put in the letter "u," and gave them to Miss P., a maiden lady whom Dr. Holmes would not have called a "spring chicken." After a time, she said: "Why! it is Columbia, the gem of the ocean, but the "u" is not in it! I replied: "My dear Miss P., Columbia would not be the gem of the ocean without you ("u") in it." That lady did not speak to me for a month.

On another occasion a nice looking assistant of mine by the name of Miss Fields came to school dressed completely in green and when I suggested that she reminded me of a line from Dr. Watt's Hymn Book,—"Sweet Fields, arrayed in living green," I received a box on the ear which thoroughly cured me of that sort of thing.

I never attempted to be a punster but once. One day I was cutting down a dogwood tree when a man came along and said "Woodsman, spare that tree!" I replied:—"Touch not a single bow-wow." It took him five minutes to see the point. I have ever since confined myself to categorical statements of facts.

CHAPTER XXIV.

FUNNY PEOPLE.

Observation and personal experience teaches that all classes of people are inclined to be funny sometimes and at other times to blunder. They are funny when they do peculiar things as when a man with a chubby face wears side whiskers or when a woman of fifty dresses like a girl of sixteen or when a young man of twenty talks too much or when a young lady is sure that fate and not her personality has prevented a good match.

People blunder when through thoughtlessness or excitement they do or say what they did not intend to, or when they misconceived the conditions. That office-seeker who said after his nomination, "For this nomination I congratulate you," simply blundered. The Irishman that thought his ox did not girth six feet because he could not get a six foot chain around him, blundered from a lack of knowledge. Even clergymen sometimes blunder.

A student from Andover was in Concord last year and was asked to speak to the convicts. He did so, and most earnestly urged them to believe in infant baptism. A candidate once came to the coast of Maine to preach where three-fourths of the audience were fishermen. His subject was "Humility." In the course of his remarks he said· "Be humble. Your Master deigned to associate with fishermen, the most degraded, ignorant and wicked people on the face of the earth."

I knew a clergyman who, in a fit of absent-mindedness, suggested that the choir sing the fortieth hymn to close a revival meeting. The opening line of that funeral hymn read: "Sister, thou wert mild **and** lovely." **The** chorister thought he **was** thinking of his old girl.

An amusing scene once occurred in a church in the town where I was teaching. The clergyman knew nothing of music but he could sing just one hymn,—Ariel. One Sunday he noticed that some of the choir was absent, so to help them out, he thought he would have them sing this, his only tune. He read a long-meter hymn and, looking across the church to the choir in the gallery at the farther end of the house, he said: "Sing *Ariel*" as he pronounced it. The chorister did not understand him and asked the soprano what he said. She replied: "He said, 'Sing or I will.'" That chorister was wroth. He arose to his feet, which were two yards from the top of his bald head, and, with indignation written in every line of his face and fire flashing from his eyes, replied: "Sing yourself then!" Just imagine the effect upon the minister and the audience!

There is something peculiar about a chorister. The man is usually a distinct character. His whole soul is so absorbed in rhythm and harmony and the execution of sound, that he often-times becomes oblivious to other things. I once spoke in the Methodist church at Houlton. The chorister was allowed to select his tunes and hymns. I glanced over a list he gave me and looked up the hymns in the book. The hymn he had selected to sing just before the sermon commenced thus:

"We lay our bodies down to rest,"
"Lord, guard us while we sleep."

I thought it was bad enough to have the people sleep during my speaking, without asking the Lord's blessing upon it, and so changed the hymn.

The first chorister I can remember was an oldish man, and very spare and tall. There was no organ in the church. When the time came to sing, he would arise, take his tuning fork from his left-hand vest pocket, give each lip of his mouth an outward curl, give the fork a sharp nip with his teeth, which were very long, then, with a sort of parabolic curve through the air, he would place the fork to his ear, close his eyes, and hum "Dome" with a nasal twang. The whole choir would "take the key" and "sound" and sing the hymn.

In the old days the choir always sang the whole hymn through. I once heard the choir sing one of those old hymns in this way. The clergyman told the choir to omit the second stanza; so they sang the first and third without an interlude, and the audience was somewhat amused by the sequence of thought. The last line of the first stanza read "Shall I among them (the ransomed) stand?" The first line of the third stanza read: "Forbid it, Lord, that this should be."

I remember being once at a funeral of a citizen not particularly noted for his morals when the amateur chorister started his improvised choir off with "We all, O Lord, have gone astray."

We have all heard of the clergyman who married a couple in church and then gave out the hymn commencing "Mistaken souls who dream of bliss."

When a lady told me that they had the church walls painted a dull yellow because the pastor's moustache was of that shade, I thought it savored of Oscar Wilde.

I heard an old lady once say, on returning from her husband's funeral, "Everything went off tip-top." The phraseology was a little unfortunate.

If I had recorded all the blunders my students made they would have filled a volume. Many of these were very funny, especially when the personality of the boy or girl was in evidence. That small boy with molasses and bread crumbs plastered over half his face, with hair uncombed and hands fresh from the embrace of mother earth, with a squint in one eye and a voice pitched on high C, had just the *toute ensemble* to spell "hupping koff" in that artistic way. I give a few of these blunders without the settings.

13

A boy in Atkinson astonished me by reading "Queen Mary often spent an hour in hemming pocket *jacknives*." A girl actually read, in my hearing, that oft-repeated line: "There was a great clam." This method of reading the Bible has led to some strange theology.

One day a young man was reciting in Physics and was giving the rule for computing the pressure on the bottom of a vessel; and rendered it thus: "To compute the pressure on the bottom of a ship multiply the area of the base by the height of the liquid, and this result by sixty-two and a half pounds." I suggested there was some mistake, but he said the book said so, that *"Ship"* was another name for *"vessel."*

A young lady, reciting the history of the Civil War, declared that they bombarded the fort with "cranberries and grapes;" a very mild substitute for cannister and grapeshot. The same girl said the *"corpse"* of Hooker was swept from the field. Being asked to explain, she said she supposed his body was carried off in an ambulance. A little further on she recited "Hooker re-formed his army." "Ah," I said, "how was that?" "I don't know," she replied, "unless he came to life."

A boy one day, reading the line

"Up, up, Maria,
"The lark is in the sky."

rendered it thus: "Double up Maria, The lark is in the sky." Another boy read "One by one they dropt down dead and died." A great, awkward boy, reading a line from "The Better Land,"—"Is it far away, in some region old?" gave it this way, "Is it far away in some ragged hole?" He got the metre all right but did some violence to the sentiment. Still another boy informed the audience that "Gradgrind iced his coffee in summer." Dickens wrote it "his office." The same boy gave this line, with fervid eloquence· "And his *bird* stood beside him and briny tears wept." "Bride" would have been more natural.

SOCIAL CHEMISTRY.

Address to the Students and Friends of Ricker Classical
Institute.

Scientific men tell us that this great world of ours, with all
its wonderful variety of forms and productions, is made up by
the multifarious combining and commingling of sixty-four distinct elements. These elements are rarely found alone but
almost always either mechanically or chemically combined,
sometimes with one but oftener with many others. Five or
more of these elements are gases; one a liquid metal, and eight
or ten metals, and the rest metaloids. Among the metals are
a few called royal metals on account of their scarcity, purity,
and incorruptibility. Nothing corrupts or tarnishes them.
Such are gold, silver and platinum.

But, although there are sixty-four elements in all, yet it
is true that the great mass of the earth and the living things
upon it are composed of only four distinct elements: Oxygen,
Hydrogen. Carbon, and Nitrogen. These are all gaseous; so
you see *gas* is the predominant feature in this peculiar world of
ours.

Now, as the physical world is composed of chemical elements, and governed by fixed chemical laws, so the social world,
in which human souls are the elements, were both created by
the same Almighty hand, hence there must be a similarity in
the process of development, and one must be closely allied to
the other. Then let us take the social world into our mental
laboratory and perform a few experiments and form some de-
ductions.

In physical Chemistry all we can do is to take combinations as we find them in nature, resolve them into the parts
that compose them, and, from what we learn by this process,
learn how to make new combinations.. So, in the social world,
we take society as we find it and endeavor to discover the elements or influences that produced the existing conditions.

Society is made up of combinations. There are many exhibitions of curious forms, ceremonies, and characters, but very little that is new. Almost every peculiar character on earth today is a reproduction of some actor in the past.

There are Adams and Eves in this twentieth Century who will never see Paradise again, men are trying to climb up to Heaven now as they did on Shinar's plain by stairways of their own constructing, with a resulting jargon of doctrine not unlike the Babel attempts of old. Lot's wife is looking over her shoulder tonight somewhere, while regretfully leaving scenes not conducive to her best being; Sampsons without number, with shorn locks, are doing their best work by dying. There are daughters of Jephtha everywhere, sacrificing heart and soul that some dear one may live; Jezebels still curse the earth.

Ruth and Naomi are still traveling, hand in hand, to find a Boaz; Mary still weeps, and Martha works; Judas is forever jingling his forty pieces of silver; and impetuous Peters will sometimes swear. Alexander reappeared in Napoleon Bonaparte and Caesar; and so on through history. All these are not the exact reproduction of the past, but as near as the time will admit.

As every rock of the field is the result of chemical combination, so men and women are what they are because of the spiritual chemistry of their make-up.

In the chemical world there is one great universal agency forever at work. Its power was mighty, even in the infancy of the earth. Oxygen, the grand central element around which all others center. It has the greatest affinity of all elements. It builds up and tears down, gives life and takes it; is never at rest and never found alone.

So there are oxygen men and women in society. They give life to everything around them. Every new enterprise, every bold endeavor, every combination of social or commercial forces, is the result of the energizing force of oxygen men. Those men are indispensable, but they must never act alone. They are too nervous, too headstrong, too much given to "frenzied finance." They would build a house with such impetuosity that friction itself would set the building on fire. Oxygen men are great joiners. They want to belong to every society and association, and this is all right.

They are not safe alone, but in combination are most excellent.

Nitrogen is a mysterious component of the natural world. It is past finding out. It constitutes four-fifths of the air we breathe yet it does nothing for us in this operation of breathing, gives no vigor, clarifies no blood, clears no brain, but simply dilutes the oxygen so we can breathe it. Nitrogen is needed, is useful in a way. So are nitrogenous men needed. And there are nitrogenous men.

They are useless for any great or important enterprises, but help fill up. Have no great mass of brain but enough to fill the space left vacant by nature. About so many men must die every year. Just think what a loss of vital force there would be if every man dying was a real oxygen man; again, if nothing but oxygen encircled the earth, it would set itself afire by the intensity of its own activity; so, if our Halls of Congress were filled with brainy, oxygen men only, we would see the Phoenix flame of genius bursting out through every crevice and cranny of our beautiful capitol and rising to the skies, encircle the whole heavens, like Phaethon of old. Don't be afraid! Our capitol is safe! There are plenty of nitrogenous men there. There will never be spontaneous combustion at Washington or Augusta. We need nitrogenous men everywhere. The world would get on too fast without them; and many places would be left void without them. Where, O, where! would we get our supply of bar-room philosophers and grocery-store politicians; where our rustic lawyers and senseless theologians if there were no nitrogenous men? Tell me, O thinking moralist! where shall husbands be found for that great mass of industrious, tired women who support themselves, family, husband and all, if all the men of straw are no longer in evidence to promise to protect and support? And what should we do in the social circle for amusement and entertainment if the grinning monkey in broadcloth, and the brainless golden calf should be annihilated? No, my beloved, we need them. Life would be too serious without them and probably right over across the way there is somebody of the gentler sex, softer she cannot be, who will be happy to lose her personal identity in a union highly beneficial to the party of the first part. And, indeed, nitrogenous men and women are sometimes needed as a sort of balancing force in the social world.

A highly charged, oxygen man should always form a union with a partner with a large percentage of nitrogen in her nervous constitution, so that when he becomes cross and irritable, faultfinding and restless, her calm demeanor, unexcitable nature, and non-combatable propensity will check the ungovernable impulses of the unreasoning enthusiast better than any argument or force. But let two positive parties unite, both surcharged with oxygen, if the divorce court does not raise up an adamantine wall between them, why then, my fellow teachers, never go there to board unless you are fond of pyrotechnics.

On the other hand, let two purely nitrogenous persons unite, one result will surely follow: Love in a cottage,—a small one at that—will be the highest attainment and posterity will languish. I have spoken of these two classes in this matrimonial way simply because parties thus connected are the most intimately related, but the same idea is true in every relationship. Two friends remain friends the longest when there is a diversity of temperament.

Now, my young friends, don't, I beg you, try to become nitrogenous because I have made this plea for the forceless man. Every institute boy and girl is expected to be an oxygen boy and girl, a young man and woman imparting life and energy through every vein, and artery, and capillary of the social world. Men do not have to try to become useless. Too many are born so, and grow up that way by a spontaneous accumulation of negatives. There will be dead-heads enough in the world without a single specimen from Ricker. Don't let inertia be your only active force.

Hydrogen is a notable element in nature. It is very light, spurns the bare earth, and is found soaring among the skies. It is made by the union of very common materials, but, like many men, seems to forget its parentage, looking down with disdain upon all things less ethereal than itself. In the social world there are many persons who may be called hydrogen men. They think themselves better than others, imagine their conceptions are as much higher than those of other men as the illimitable space is loftier than a cabbage patch. They carry their heads very high, impelled by a law of equilibrium. A rubber bag, filled with hydrogen will rise until it reaches an atmosphere as light as itself, and then rests.

The men I have mentioned, should the force of gravity be suspended, would leave the earth instantly, and go up, up, up,—how far? Philosophers believe there is a spot, infinitely far away where nothing is—an empty void—ah, there the equilibrium would be perfect, and there they would forever remain, hanging, like empty bladders, for the delectation of the man in the moon, if the old woman that sweeps the cobwebs from the sky did not disturb them.

And yet a spark of electricity will unite oxygen and hydro gen so perfectly that a drop of the purest liquid God ever made will trickle forth. So when an impetuous oxygen man becomes associated in business with the hydrogen man and a spark of ambition unites them in common sympathy, the wheels of progress will rapidly revolve impelled by an abundant water power.

Young man, young lady, if you have too much hydrogen in the cranium, take on twice as much oxygen even at the risk of dropsy on the brain.

Phosphorous is another element in the physical world totally antagonistic to nitrogen. Some one has rather wickedly said that it is a kind of Baptist element, as it has to be closely connected with water to keep it in a pure state. It is very erratic, liable to spontaneous combustion, will light the house, kindle a fire for breakfast, burn up the house, cook and all, the schoolhouse and the church; but, when properly combined, it becomes safe, useless, and almost indispensable. So there are phosphorus men, ready to strike fire at any moment, whenever the least friction occurs. They are very active but lack discretion. They fly into a whirlwind of passion on the slightest provocation and almost drown themselves in tears of repentance the next moment. Such men, such women should never live alone. Phosphorus has few affinities. It will only combine readily with sulpher and a piece of pine. Form this combination properly,—a first-class match is produced, a very useful article. So when a choleric, sometimes fiery tempered man takes for his affinity a sulphurous woman there is a match made that will burn with a steady glow after the first sulphurous smoke and splutterings are over.

Phosphorus in the physical world has another use. It is one of the constituents of the brain. It is that which gives the intense activity to the brain of the great men of action.

Now, my young friends, a large amount of this element in the laboratory of Ricker Classical School might be dangerous, but you can, with perfect impunity, lay up in the laboratory of your cranium enough to give you ten in every recitation, and make you a brilliant member of society later in life. Don't be afraid of spontaneous combustion, and don't expect your stomachs, stuffed with fish, to furnish the brain with phosphorus. The contents of books, meditation, discipline, great desires, and ready execution, is the food that keeps the phosphorus fires burning in the brain.

Young ladies, if, later in life, you would make a good match, keep those phosphorus fires ever burning. Young man, if a brilliant career is your ambition, let not fuel now be lacking.

Mercury is a cranky element in the physical world. It is a metal, but, unlike every other metal, persists in remaining liquid at anywhere above forty degrees below zero. It is sometimes used for a medicine but in the opinion of many it kills more than it cures. But it is good for one thing, at least. It is death on the itch. So you see there is use for the crank even in the social world. I have a certain respect for a man who cannot help being a crank. Some men are made so. They cannot help differing from the rest of humanity. But they are not entirely useless. The world can use them as the homeopath cures his patients; *"Similia similibus curantur"* is an old proverb. They may be used to kill off other cranks. But we do owe something to the crank of history. Occasionally some enthusiastic crank has made a great discovery, but it is usually an accidental one.

If the cranks, like the old alchemists, could be shut up in umbrageous log huts, or under-ground cloisters, and allowed to come out only when a real discovery had been made, then we would say with enthusiasm: "Let there be cranks!"

If every crank would confine himself to cranky notions and subjects, and let us poor common people alone, still would I say: "Salvate, O Cranks," without regard to race or sex. But there are many subjects which cranks should never meddle with. These interests are too interwoven into the weal or woe of common human humanity. All matters of public interest, of common morals, and beneficial laws should never be even discussed by men of one idea.

No, let the crank leave these subjects alone, and try to discover how to bottle up dynamic force, or make politicians honest, or find the accurate rule for squaring the circle,—or some method of converting a bore into a useful windmill. The religious crank is beyond endurance. He will fill a volume in describing the delicate structure of an insignificant gnat, while an array of camels go trooping down by without attracting the least notice. He will swallow a theological camel with a hump on his back as high as a church steeple and never strangle nor choke, while, with Sam Weller's extra double-acting microscope he is hunting for a schismatic gnat hidden in some brother's church creed. Religion is the most reasonable and common sense thing in the world. It should occupy the attention of every man, woman and child every day. God never designed it for the exclusive benefit of hermit, nun, or priest, but for all. He only who by actual association with man, has learned by the anxious heartbeats of the restless world, should attempt to interpret God's revealed will to man.

The educational crank is also a great nuisance. He wakes up some morning with the echo of a fevered dream still rever berating through his mind. He immediately, like Don Quix ote, starts out on a Rosinato received from some bankrupt advertizer and fights windmills with sycophantic Sancho Pan zas applauding and brings home Saratoga trunks full of rib bons and gew-gaws for the adornment of country school teach ers so they may be able to entertain the little folks and teach them. Had I the ability I should like to write a chapter on these trophies—the "exploded facts" that these dons have advocated. Better let them lay on the shelf labeled plainly with "vertical penmanship" till the proper writer rises.

Gold seems to be the old maid of the metal world. I have a great regard for old maids; so I have for gold, when it belongs to me. Gold does not attract by any self-reaching force. All admire it, long for it, somehow few can get it. It is pure, always worth something, and never becomes really tarnished. We need just such people in every community. What should we do without our old maids? They are the fostering patrons of the human race, stand by the sick-bed, close weary eyes in death and place the last flowers beside the cold form bedewed with tears. God bless the old maids of our land. The old maids are not the ineligibles. They are smart, mostly good-looking, and have every quality to make a first-class wife, but do not marry. Why? Simply because they are too good for any one man. Providence did not mean that their ministrations should be confined to one selfish man, but that many should be blessed by their love, care, assiduity and prayers.

Gold is the most precious of metals. It is good everywhere with the stamp and image of kings and queens upon it. Its value is universally acknowledged, but the veriest beggar could not make its value less by enstamping his image thereon. No corner of the earth would debar gold from its territory.

So there are gold men, gold women, golden boys and girls. No matter whether joy or sorrow impresses its stamp upon the brow, the heart is gold, unpolluted by base metals, always at par, never in liquidity.

There are many base imitations. Brass resembles gold in color, and often passes for it, but the most unsophisticated can soon detect the imposition. There are men of brass, but they do little harm, as it develops mostly upon the cheek and one blast of cold contempt exposes the base constituents.

There is another chemical compound resembling gold. It appears in beautiful cubes, shining with the luster of gold. It will, like the diamond, cut glass, reflect light and appears to be of great value. It resembles two or three precious stones in those respects. Tons of this compound have been quarried with the secret expectation of untold riches. It forever is holding out false hopes to a gullable world and often deceives. The chemist calls it iron pyrites, in the chemical world and we call the type among men a quack. Shun them all; all quack mines, quack friends, quack doctors, quack reformers, and appletree men, and quack schoolmasters.

We come back again to nitrogen. We said it was a mysterious element. In the air it is simply a passive, idle existence, but that same Nitrogen, mixed with certain other elements, becomes the symbol of intense activity. Combine it with glycerine and we have one of the most destructive, diabolical agents in nature. A thimbleful would destroy this hall in the twinkling of an eye.

We see now how it is in social life. A man out among men where the combination is just right, will be the very personification of good nature and smiles, but at home, where the wife happens to supply the glycerine,—something really good in itself,—he becomes a bottled-up earthquake, an already full grown cyclone, a smoking volcano, all ready to belch forth and fill the house with domestic smoke, cinders, and ashes. Sometimes the nitrogen is the mistress of the house. What then? The question is past solution, and I pass.

There are a few elements with a very limited range of affinity. They are good, useful and effective when acting alone, but seem always to prefer to thus act. It took forty years hard study to find anything that would unite with caoutchouc. At last it was discovered that when sulphur was united with it there was a perfect union, and a very valuable compound produced quite unlike either. So there are, in the social world, characters that seem to have no ready combining power; they fail to attract or be attracted. We call them old bachelors.

As woman was created last, she seems to have been supplied with every characteristic necessary to perform the duties of life. With man it was different. It was found that he lacked something; so a new creation was ordered to supply the deficiency. That new creation was woman; hence she becomes an actual necessity to round out the completeness of his existence. Hence the bachelor is incomplete without the chastening, refining, up-lifting, stimulating influence of women.

There must have been created for every bachelor at least one helpmate for him and if he ever finds her, what a change takes place. He is no more like his former self than the old-fashioned gum shoe is to the modern tony overshoe.

Another important fact we learn from the laboratory is that the elements that form sugar, alchohol, starch and vinegar, are the same combined in different proportions. Starch is rather unstable and passes readily into alcohol, sugar or vinegar, according to conditions. A little more Oxygen will develop the one, a little more Nitrogen another. Now the conditions must be carefully studied to procure the required result. Sugar is the basis of all these combinations, and from this alone the others may be evolved, with only slight modifications.

The statement was made, a few moments ago, that the most precious metals sank when the crust of the earth cooled. These were thrown up to the surface later by volcanic force. Nothing but a convulsion of the earth could bring them to the surface. So, in the social and political world, it takes great social and political upheavals to bring the best to the surface. As the present form of this beautiful world was accomplished by earthquakes and volcano, so civilization has been advanced by social and political commotions, each leaving the status of affairs in a better condition.

The Carboniferous Age covered the earth with a luxuriant growth of lofty trees, but they were of an inferior order. Something better the coming ages needed; and the far-off, prophetic age in which humanity would exist, would require fuel in abundance. So all those lofty, waving palms must be laid low and piled one upon another, to sleep the long ages through, till the tireless, inquisitive eye of man discovered coal, and his industrious hand conveyed it to fireside and furnace. So many a fair civilization must sleep that others may arise, more glorious, warmed and lightened by the imperishable relics of the past.

But great convulsions took place in nature, so they must in society. But progress always is made.

It takes a political earthquake oftimes to put the best men into office. I am aware that sometimes those commotions, at first, make very cheap men prominent, and elevate demagogues to the position of statesmen, just as iron pyrites are mistaken for gold, but such men are readily detected and laid aside as worthless. But the gold freed from the bare elements shines all the brighter and never loses its native characteristics.

And now, my dear ladies in the school, just a word to you. God has placed within your souls a combination of forces found in no other human hearts. Your father has it not, your mother does not now possess it; the Professor cannot claim it and the clergyman would pray for it in vain. If there is an image of an ideal God I could worship, it is the soul of a young girl, before the cares of life have sobered her, before the sorrow of disappointments has robbed her of her sublime faith, before she has ever discovered that it is possible to even tolerate the coarse, the low, or anything less than the purest, the truest and sweetest; before failure has robbed her of the fruition of her glorious dream; while she is yet a creature fresh from the hand of God, with the odors of Eden distilling around her.

Ah, how unlike the heartless coquette or the match-making anglers of later years sometimes. There is, my young friends, sweetness in your young souls. God gave it to you for a purpose. That sweetness you can preserve there and take to Heaven with you. Carefully guard it. Preserve your hearts. Be as careful of the heart of others as you are of the fragile butterfly that flits at your feet.

When sugar has been thoroughly refined it becomes the most imperishable substance in the world. Let the spirit of the peace-giving Christ be the refiner; then you will become the embodiment of all that can charm, elevate and enoble. But don't forget that unrefined sugar changes to vinegar tomorrow, or mayhap, into potential life-destroying alcohol, carrying within itself the seed of poison and death.

Let the fidelity of a Ruth immortalize you, the self-sacrifice of Esther glorify your life, the purity of Francis Willard sanctify you and let your own lives embalm your memory in the hearts of all associated with you.

But please remember that it is the lovely girl with all her glorious attributes that becomes the designing woman of the world when her heart has become the rallying place for wicked designs and unlovely desires. Mrs. Chadwick is said to have been a most fascinating, charming girl of fourteen. Remember gold is alloyed; base lead, never. The worst heart possible can only be made from a noble one. There are associations vou can form which heighten every lovely characteristic vou now possess, will stimulate every ambition and aspiration and beautify even beauty itself. When a famous Grecian sculptor had carved a statue of Minerva so perfectly that all Athens declared it perfect, beyond improvement, Pericles, with chisel and mallet, in a few hours wrought such a change that the statue became ever after the model of all that was beautiful and sublime in sculpture. That model every young lady may become.

Boys, young men, in your souls there ought to be much that exists in the young ladies', and more. Upon you should rest responsibilities that she ought not to assume, but there is no reason why you should not be as cultivated, refined and pure as she. This does not imply that you should ever become an effeminate or "carpet-knight." A young man becomes as lov able as the most accomplished young lady and all the time be fighting the battle of life with the most strenuous means. We need but few Adonises, but many Hercules.

There are, in your mental laboratory, many forces, given by God and inherited from parents. All you have to do is to make the proper combination with coming forces. The growth of a stalk of wheat straw illustrates, in the physical world how the young man should progress in the human world. That stalk grows very fast for a time, very tall and green (I have been a boy), anon a head appears, filled with some very valuable material but it isn't wheat yet, but will make wheat in due time.

The head now stands up very straight and is caught by every breeze. In a few days to the starch already there albumen is added, then an envelope of silica surrounds it all. Now we have a real kernel of wheat. The head is a little swelled, to be sure, but will subside in due time. Next the head begins to maturely gaze less to the stars, and more toward earth, and it is just here that nature comes in and sends up the stalk a large amount of silica. This is plastered all up and down the stock and forms a sort of back-bone so firm that, no matter how heavy the head becomes, it stands perpendicular.

With many young men there is a perfect development in all respects except the backbone part of it. A most essential omission. No matter what else he has he is useless without a stiff backbone so that, no matter what the temptation is, "No" is the easiest word to say. A backbone that will not wilt when ridicule assails, appetite urges, and friends persuade; a backbone that will not bend when principles are at stake; that will stand erect when endeavor begins to flag; when pleasant fields in the valley attract more than mountain height, when less than the first ideal seems to satisfy; when, in fact, you are being content to fall below any attainable heights.

The lack of silicious deposit is not confined to the young. The lack of it is felt every day in almost every community. It is noticed when righteous, though unpopular, laws are to be enforced, when improper candidates solicit votes, when duty requires action, and self-interest restrains.

Iodine shows a peculiar trait. It passes from a solid to a gaseous state without becoming liquid. So there are iodionic people in the world. Most people rise and fall by regular grades. The man, solid on some moral or political subjects, begins to melt a little, softens day by day, till at length every molecule of his conscience is in sliding condition. He is now what the text books call in unstable condition. He then easily passes into a gaseous condition.

The reverse process is sometimes true when a person decides to change for the better. But occasionally we see men and women unyeilding as Plymouth Rock converted into gaseous approval of some obnoxious idea by an almost instantaneous spiritual somersault; and return again to adamantine crystals before the ashes are cold that, a little while ago, caused the transformation.

Young men have sometimes discovered this sudden change in the affinity of yesterday, which today becomes actively repellant.

These iodine men are not very dangerous when well understood; but it is sometimes disagreeable to find a man solid one hour and gaseous the next in matters that concern us.

Iron is, perhaps, the most useful metal in the physical world. It remained on the surface when the other metals sank, affording an opportunity to men to obtain and use it. It is the most commonplace metal in existence, and has done more for civilization than all other metals combined. It makes railroads possible, steamships practicable and life enjoyable. It boasts not at all, but faithfully does its work, modestly and untiringly.

So, in this great, bustling, toiling, practical, social world of ours, the men of iron build the cities, railroads, and navies; carry forward every great reform, and are co-workers with the Almighty in pushing foward every good work.

Some metals are isomeric; that is, they appear under two forms, the brilliant, flashy diamond is simply carbon; so is the black, unsightly stick of graphite. The one is imperishable, valuable, a thing of beauty. The other wears itself away at every touch, and can be bought in every market at smallest price. One is crystalized, the other is not. So the same amount of facts in one cranium is always available, is brilliant; while in others there is simply a mass of undigested facts, easily rubbed out, soon gone forever. Every thought in the human mind is only valuable when fully crystalized. This process takes place in the mind, just as it does in the laboratory.

Conditions must be met to produce crystals in the chemical world. So thought will crystalize only under certain conditions. Facts put into the crucible of the mind, only crystalize when they are associated in such a way that like seeks like, and that they have the proper time to crystalize. No mental work can be done in a hurry. Facts must be accumulated in logical order, and time given for meditation before clear-cut results can be obtained.   We learn from chemistry that   most   useful things   have   many   constituents.   That   article   of   food that   produces   but   one   ingredient   in   the   body   is   regarded as a medicine rather than a food.   So is it with men.   That man who has but one attracting power will ever be lonely in a world   where   there   are   men   everywhere,   hungering   for   something that a brother man only can give.

Why is it, we may ask, that Mr. A. or Miss B. has such power among his associates?   Simply this; he has a soul full of vital forces, assimilating agencies, attractive powers; has something,   some   element,   every   other   man   can   assimilate.   It   is thought that albumen has 143 differing constituents.   Think of it!   143!   Now albumen is found in eggs, in wheat, in meat, and, in fact, in most living things.   It is the albuminous man that is the power in the world.   There is something in him that all men can appreciate; the wise seek to learn wisdom from him; the ignorant, knowledge; the weak, strength; the old man of seventy and the child of two are attracted to him because he thinks as they think, loves as they love, can solve the deep problem of science, or roll the hoop, ride a velocipede or rule the nation.

This spiritual affinity, operating in the hearts of the human race, is by far the most important factor used by the Creator for the intellectual and spiritual elevation of humanity.   Words may bring tears to the eyes; eloquence may excite the hearer to rapturous applause; heroic deeds light up the eye with a passionate enthusiasm, but all these, on the cold, calculating morrow, have lost their charm and power and the heart remains unmoved toward any assimilation; but when an undefined something, a love it may be, for some abstract virtue or art; a fellow-feeling for another's sorrow arises, when, in fine, one cannot tell why it is that he loves that friend so dearly, then the real, imperishable love, Heaven ordained, of the human soul begins to permeate heart, brain, eye and every fiber of one's being, and a new creature then appears.

The flint rock that defies the action of the strongest acids, laughs in definance at the drill of the artisan and the hammer of the geologist; bedewed with teardrops from the skies, and kissed by the smiling sunlight, yields up its stubborn spirit and becomes the productive soil of our alluvial fields. So are hearts softened, characters changed, and new ministering spirits made among men by the undefinable influence of a congenial soul.

The friendships among men are as mysterious as are many of the chemical unions in nature. But they do not just happen. Somewhere in the heart of one there is a susceptibility which something in the soul of the other causes to vibrate. There is need in the one, a supply in the other and as long as these conditions remain true, so long will they love and delight each other.

I said, a few minutes ago, that oxygen was the great central element around which all others center; that this element had a great influence on the character of the others. So, in the spiritual world, there must be a rallying point, a spiritual force toward which all naturally tend, the center, and are changed by that association.

Society could no more exist without this center than could the heavenly body revolve around empty space in the sky. The old Greek philosopher conceived that power was a triune one, and thought if he could but discover the true, the beautiful and the good, with never a false tint, and every line faultless, these he would defy and cause the whole social world, by centripetal force, to revolve around these, until man became the embodiment of truth; lover of nothing but the beautiful and the good. But he never found them. But the Magi of the East did when they discovered the Child of Bethlehem, and countless multitudes since have known that a power, not of men, is drawing all to one common center, that a heart beating for all created humanity, filled with attributes that attract every soul, glories with love for each and all, is binding restless humanity to a common center—the man Christ, the beloved.

CHAPTER XXV.

SCHOOL OFFICERS.

In my long connection with school officers I have had some peculiar experiences. On the whole, their treatment of me has been all that could be desired. Whenever the committee and superintendent have been educated and qualified for the position, there has been harmony and mutual good feeling. That a man knowing the least about a matter is the most censorious, is an old proverb. There can be no doubt that there are corporals in Oyama's army who criticised his movement northward. There isn't a street loafer in any town who cannot solve every question of finance that puzzles experienced statesmen.

Of all the contemptible little specimens of humanity whom, for purposes unknown, an inscrutable ruler of the universe allows to hold positions of authority, the most nauseating is a man who knows but little, but who, for personal spite, or self-interest, or just to exhibit a little show of authority, struts and swaggers, and swells in his puny world, and abuses those as superior to him as he is below the Hottentot. How much harm such men do sometimes!

There is another class of men who are great nuisances, but they are more excusable. These men are proficient in something, and, because they know how to build a chimney or hold a plow, think they can arrange a course of study for a school, or select proper text-books, and criticize the work done in a schoolroom. These men are honest as far as they can be, but have such an insurmountable bump of egotism that they can never be of any use outside of the one little thing they have learned.

There is another class who take many opportunities to learn how teachers of prominence conduct their exercises, and come back with a large amount of facts, but have not the skill to use these with any profit. Those they do use are so colored by their predisposed opinions that it is like new cloth on an old garment.

No one who does not know all about teaching, who is not a school teacher, who is not posted in modern methods, has any right to attempt to dictate to those who are by education, training, and experience fully fitted for the work. If the proper man cannot be found for Inspector, then let a man of common sense, a business man, be appointed, and let him select a teacher as he would an electrician, or an engineer, or a surveyor, by means of certificates from past fields of labor. Business men all over the country are conducting enterprizes of vast importance on just this line. They know nothing of the practical working of the vast machinery of their business, but men are chosen to preside over each, in whom the proprietor has confidence.

No teacher should be employed in a new position unless his fitness is unmistakably proved. If this is done to the satisfaction of the committee, surely there should be as little interference with his work as possible. If he is not doing good work, it will become apparent very soon to student and committee and community. When this is seen, let that teacher depart.

I have had considerable fun in observing the performances of some of my official visitors. Now I wish to repeat that the most of these persons have been qualified, kind, and impartial and I have worked in perfect harmony with them. But there were some striking exceptions.

When a certain man came in, I always reduced the noise of the school to the minimum, so as not to disturb his slumbers. He would sleep so placidly, with such a child-like expression on his face that I hadn't the heart to disturb him. I always dropped a stick of wood upon the floor to awaken him when the time for speech-making came. He always commended the good order. I gave another man, who pretended to know Greek, a German reader while the class read Homer, and he didn't know the difference. He said they translated admirably.

One man asked the pupils if they would all be ready to be examined the thirty-first day of September; and they said they thought not. He said that that day would convene him best, and urged them to be ready. The pupils were too polite to smile and so he passed out of the house, feeling sure he had carried a point, and had corrected Julius Caesar and all the Popes.

In one school eight weeks had elapsed, and there were four weeks remaining. The superintendent asked what fractional part of the term had passed. The class answered "Two-thirds." "No," said he, with a knowing look upon them and a disapproving scowl upon me, "You are wrong." "I will ask you again before I leave." Just as he stood in the door, when departing, he asked the same question again, and received the same answer. "You are wrong again" he said, "just eight-twelfths." And, smiling, he departed.

One examination day, the class in German put an exercise on the board, and one of the committee, who thought he knew German, in his speech congratulated the class upon the accuracy of the work; said he did not notice a mistake. I noticed that not a single sentence was just right, but it being examination day I held my peace; but that class got some hazing next term.

As I look over my old certificates, I see there is only one in which the name of the town was spelled without the assistance of a capital letter.

Many of my school officers were my best friends, and I have taught years under the same persons without the least friction. I claim no infalibility in matters of teaching, and think I have always been ready to be criticised whenever there was need, and that criticism was offered by a competent party, and in the right spirit. I am sure I have the highest regard, today, for the great majority of those men who employed me and superintended my work.

Some are dead. The memory of no man do I more cherish than that of Doctor Luce, and C. B. Roberts. Both these men assisted me in every way, and left a corner of the soul unsatisfied, when they died. Many others might be mentioned for whom I have the highest regard.

CHAPTER XXVI.

COLLEGE REQUIREMENTS.

A pamphlet of a hundred pages has recently been published, in which the opinions of several very distinguished educators are set forth in regard to a college education. Anyone reading that book would certainly be very much in the condition of a man standing near the ancient tower of Babel after the language had been confounded. The Harvard idea conflicts with the Princeton; and the Chicago with all others. Some advocate a three years' course, others more advanced preparation.

I propose to discuss the problem as it has presented itself to me through a long experience with young men fitting for college and a careful observation of undergraduates in college.

The college president is not fully qualified to discuss the question, as he only sees the boys after they have been subjected to influences which he knows but little about. Before one can fairly discuss the question about the age and requirements of the student entering college there should be determined clearly —what is the object of sending a boy to College, what does a college course do for a boy; and what should it do?

The obvious answer is that a systematic course of study trains and disciplines the mind, enlarges the mental capacities, and enables the student to comprehend more readily difficult mental problems. This is true; but by no means all. The same result would be attained with a private teacher. College should do more than this. The young man graduating from college should go forth from the college halls a cultured man, a person who had become by the attrition of associates, by the discipline of study, by the moulding of character through the inspiration inherent in a struggle to attain through self-sacrifice a distinctive individuality, "a perfect ashler," a polished image of the God that created him.

That college educaton is a failure that does not mould every conception of life; that does not ingraft itself into the formation of tastes, conceptions, and character. If this be true, then the conclusion naturally follows, that boys should be in college at the formative age of life, before their tastes, conceptions, and methods of reasoning are fixed. The boy should be studying the beauties of Greek conceptions, the artistic perfectness of Grecian architecture, both in language and in marble, while his own taste is being formed. Upon the mind of a young man of twenty, whose tastes and habits of thinking are to a great extent already formed, the eloquence of Demosthenes is lost. He may admire the sublime rhetoric and unanswerable logic of the great master; but the study of the "Oration on the Crown" does not mould his diction and unconsciously brighten his own rhetoric or sharpen his logic.

The boy of sixteen or seventeen, reading that oration, is stirred to the depths of his soul with patriotic sentiments, he is ready to die for his fatherland, becomes classical in taste and expression, and derives from the study of Greek that undefinable "culture" that college only can give.

The study of Latin literature should have its influence at the same formative period of life or it is partially lost. Of course, if a student goes to college for the simple purpose of rendering the intellect more acute, for the purpose of executing plans already formed, then the late college life is available; but he could obtain nearly the same discipline out among men in the active affairs of life.

Perhaps I have not made my meaning clear, but this idea I have endeavored to advocate; that the young man should be in college at that time of life when the books he studies, the associations formed, the impressions received, should all become a constituent part of himself; that they form his taste and conceptions, his loves and affinities; that material, so to speak, be taken into the makeup of the mental man so that the "polish" of college life be possible.

The conclusion we reach is that the student should enter college at an early age, and that the requirements should not be more than at present, but, indeed, less. That nothing less than a four-year course can do the work required. If the bustling young man of this uneasy age wants simply a practical education, a means whereby money can be obtained and means of livelihood, then let there be a course of study established in schools adapted to that purpose. But that is not culture; that is not receiving a college education.

It seems that the day of real scholarship is over in the minds of many engaged in the education of youth. The age is too practical for its own good. There is still need of scholarship even in these days. I admit that specialists are very prominent in science and business, but if no one is to succeed the all-round scholar and thinker of the past, there will soon be a lack of the means whereby the specialist may prosecute his especial calling. Those means come only through the profound researches of the man who knows more than one specific truth. No man can become a profound thinker who reasons only from one point of view. No one human interest can be detached from the general interest appertaining to all the interests of humanity. One of the sad results of simply specific research is seen in the cold, unfeeling, atheistic sentiments emanating from scientific men prominently before the world.

Parhassius tortured upon the rack a purchased captive that he might paint a face writhing with pain. Though that painter may have been the most famous of all painters, he never should have painted a picture that human eye should see. Every painting of the old masters extant today shows, somehow, in the prospective or background, a recognition of the common claims of humanity. Even the angels are painted with human forms, and faces lighted up with human emotions.

But referring again to the formative age, we meet the objection that young boys are subjected to great temptations at college. I know whereof I speak when I assert that the temptations surrounding the boys in most schools where they are prepared for college are far more alluring and fatal than in college. Of course there are especial fitting schools where the students are especially cared for; but more schools there are where this is impossible, and the unrestrained association of students and town boys is pernicious to an eminent degree. The boy forms tastes and habits that could never be possible in college.

In the fitting schools there are coarse, uncultivated students, who are only there for a time, but whose influence can be felt; these become, per necessity, associates. A young man rarely changes his secret tastes and desires after he is eighteen. Then put him into college young in life, where the refining influence of the seniors, the all inspiring dignity of the junior, and, if need be, the discretionary care of the sophomores, may all combinedly chisel out of the plastic marble a prefected, classical, all-round man whom the world needs, and God loves.

Of course, there must be recognized the moral, refining, enthusing influence of the college faculty. This will, or ought to be, all-powerful for the accomplishing of the objects before mentioned. A college professor never knows what a power for good often lies dormant in his opportunity. No one can so model, uplift and lead out a human being as can that professor who feels that God has commissioned him to be a fellow worker with Himself in fashioning men.

PREPARATION FOR TEACHING.

How should teachers prepare themselves for work? They should first get a good academic education. Then, if convenient, attend a normal school. But I insist that they should be thoroughly prepared to teach, as far as requirements are concerned, before they go to the normal school.

This is evident for many reasons. It is easy to see that no student has time or ability to accomplish the double work of learning a science and, at the same time, discovering how to teach that science. Whatever teaching "per se" is done in a normal school should be review work. Then the student can have his whole time and energy to perfect his knowledge of that science, and learn how to teach it.

I certainly recommend young ladies and gentlemen to attend a normal school. We have some fine schools in Maine. I am personally acquainted with Prof. Corthell, of Gorham, who is one of the finest scholars, deepest thinkers, and systematic teachers in Maine. I also know Prof. Richardson, of Castine, and know him to be a scholar, a fine instructor, and a gentleman.

Teachers should also visit schools where well-known teach ers are employed, and observe how these teachers make use of the knowledge they have. Many graduates from the normal schools fail to be able to apply the knowledge they possess. They cannot apply the perfect model to the misshapen form presented them to fit. The funniest thing I ever saw in the schoolroom, was to see a new graduate, who had never taught, try to run a model school of observation in an old schoolhouse, with twenty ill-assorted, unclassified, uncultured boys and girls. She tried all those side-lights recommended; put on a new ribbon every day, and did up her hair in forty different ways; tried to execute all the stilted maneuvers sometimes enjoined; thought she could induce those uncultivated youngsters to become so in love with books that no mischief would be thought of; spent half an hour the first day in showing why one and one make two; and thus on through the day while "Confusion grew more confounded."

It would be a fine idea to transport a normal school around on wheels one month a year, and let the professor and pupils see our schools as they really are in some rural districts.

I close these remarks, as I began, by advising all who intend to teach to attend a Normal School.

Further, no teacher should be allowed to remain in a school, who does not every day read something fitted to enlarge the mind, refine the taste, and give information. Of course, the teacher ought to constantly read books bearing upon his profession, but by no means should he stop here. He should read poetry, essays, history, politics, library books in general. I am inclined to think that no teacher should receive a certificate who had not read "The Vicar of Wakefield," "Pilgrims Progress," "The Scarlet Letter," Longfellow's poems, "Ivanhoe," and who could not tell whether Ruth or Esther gleaned in the field, or what was the matter with Simon Peter's wife's mother.

I care not what the scholastic acquirements of a person may be; if they know nothing but text-books he is not fit to teach boys and girls. Another thought is this; no man or woman should enter a school as teacher who has an interest outside of the schoolhouse tantamount to the work therein. The work there must be all-absorbing all engrossing. No teacher can do his duty in the schoolroom who lives there only six hours, and only in bodily form at that. While county supervisor, how often I saw teachers go through the routine of work like an automatic drilling machine. Their look, mind, interest, soul, were not there, but centered upon something interesting them more than did those exercises.

I taught school one day, expecting to hear of the death of a dear friend every moment, and realized that night that I had robbed those pupils of six hours' service. I wish every pupil of mine who proposes to teach would go into the first school with the determination that he would never ask for another school. Then they would so work, so devote themselves to the work, that they would make the school such a success that the committee would be compelled to employ them. They would offer such teachers positions, unsolicited. I know a lady who has never solicited a position, since her first school. All may not be able to do this, especially where nepotism prevails, and the superintendent has a large circle of relations; but the experiment is worth trying.

A young man went, last fall, from Piscataquis county to Aroostook to teach. He made this resolve before he commenced school; I will compel the committee to employ me another year. Any position in that town was placed at his disposal at the close of the term.

Finally, that man or woman who would make teaching a life work must resolve to become, to a certain extent, a martyr; but not a John Rogers. His enemies burned him. No teacher should allow disobedient pupils, unreasonable parents, or cranky inspectors to make him a martyr. I used to lie awake nights, made wretched and sleepless by the misbehavior of some vicious pupil; but I soon learned that it was far better for him to lie awake than for me. When the conditions are of such a nature that the teacher must act on the defensive or offensive, he should not hesitate a moment. A defensive army is always at its worst. So is the teacher.

TEACHING THAT PRODUCES POWER.

(Delivered before Teachers' Association at Monson.)

Power is that property of material or spiritual things which is capable of manifesting itself upon other material or spiritual things so as to bring forth results. Thus we say the dynamic power of nitroglycerine is 1000; of powder 75. A cord of wood has so much of caloric power. A flume of water has a certain amount of speed power when properly applied for mechanical purposes. And this energy is always the same under like conditions.

The same is true in the mental world. A thought has power in it when said thought has within itself, inherent in its nature, the capability of manifesting an influence upon other thought or mental conditions. That thought has power when it will do, in the mental world, what dynamite or steam will do in the physical world. Given a certain amount of dynamite, a mountain range of granite, an adequate, intelligent direction in application,—and the result is sure—a tunnel through the mountain. Given the mental capability of the human mind, a proper amount of power-producing thought, and a logical adaptation of the latter from the former, and the result is no less sure.

Teaching that produces power. To produce is not to create. The Almighty alone creates, but nevertheless, the majority of things in nature are the product of God's hand in the manipulation of his few creations.

To produce is to combine given forms and influences so as to bring forth conceptions; to so combine what is that new developments shall appear. To teach is to draw out what is within,—to assist in the combinations mentioned above; to suggest to another the proper combination of facts and conceptions, so that a given result shall appear.

In the material world power produced by humanity is the resultant of many forces, generally. A billiard ball is made by a skilful player, to execute a certain amount of work; for instance, to strike two other balls, driving them in different directions, and going, itself, in a third direction. But to do this the player must estimate how hard he must strike the ball with the cue—just where the impact must be, he must carefully estimate the distance between the other balls, and how far his own is from each; so that momentum, velocity, space, force, are all acting in and are all used by an all-directing intelligence, acting through the human brain, and the mechanical power of the arm. Let there be miscalculation in any one particular, the usual result is not obtained. There will be a result, be sure, but not the best.

The man who would make a master stroke on a billiard table, must be master of all the conditions, and could only teach another to make the same stroke when the learner has some knowledge of reflected motion, momentum and space. Mental conclusions are never the offspring of only one mental force, acting on one objective point. To induce another to accept our theory of a certain condition necessitates discovering the exact condition of the mind upon which we propose trying our power of conviction.

The politician, the sharper, and the omnipresent book agent understands this, and trims his sails to suit the breeze under which he finds each one sailing.

I shall assume that the word "power" in the same text means power for good, a power that renders boys and girls proper agents for doing God's will in the world. This is the only power that ought to be developed, but not always the one that is in evidence in the moral world. Sometimes this power for evil is the result of misdirected efforts of unskilled workmen in the intellectual and moral field.

The child presents himself to the teacher, not with an unmarked mental black-board upon which the teacher is to make certain lines and figures, but he comes with lines already written, crooked lines, zigzag lines, crossed and intermingled. There are many figures there but none that Wentworth himself could use to demonstrate the simplest theorem. The child has many facts, more fictions, real knowledge and imaginary illusions and illogical conclusions, all in blissful confusion, piled up in his mental storehouse which very much resembles the contents of his pockets, where top, gum, jackknife, gum-drops and matches are jostling each other in dangerous prox imity.

In addition to this he has a moral nature in which generally antagonistic forces are seething like contents of an alchemist's crucible; and all these mental and spiritual forces are housed in a physical dormitory and are acting upon the world outside through physical appliances.

Now, in order that a boy shall take his place as an active force in the world and become a power which will add one iota to the individual, intellectual, financial, moral influence that is consistent with the nineteenth century, he must be so taught that there shall be a perfect conservation of the mental capacities of his brain, a full development of his moral conceptions, and a development of his physical sufficient to allow the most perfect mental activity.

No one of these three can be neglected without deformity. If the mental alone be developed the boy may become an Aaron Burr, but never a Lincoln; if the moral alone be matured, he becomes like the latent force of a subterranean stream, or gold hid in the mountain, a Hamlet, knowing his duty, but lacking force to execute it. And that teaching which unduly develops the physical at the expense of the other two reminds us of the man who plated his balance wheel and cylinder of his engine with gold, and took little care to have his steam box tight and in order, and his fires brightly burning.

I have assumed the Platonic axiom in this paper—that the child has in his nature all the faculties he ever can possess— that all the teacher has to do is to help develop, combine and draw out those. There are, in the mental laboratory of the pupil many elements more than in the physical world. There is ambition, imagination, memory, logical deduction, curiosity, mischief, laziness, willfulness, cruelty, kindness, conscience, etc. Hence the *regime* of good teaching is that of good mental chemical analysis.

The teacher must play the same part in the work that Mn_2 does in the development of oxygen from potassium chlorate. The very presence of the manganese seems to energize the other compounds; but the manganese comes out from the crucible unchanged.

Hence the teacher must first discover what there is in the pupil. He cannot teach him otherwise. It would be useless to dig for gold in our slate quarries. It would be foolish to attempt to precipitate silver from a solution in which no silver was contained. Teaching is oftentimes useless because it assimilates itself to nothing within the mind of the child. It is not always easy to discover just what is there,—a casual glimpse will not reveal it.

15

The other night, just after sunset, I stood by the bank of a lake. I noticed the crescent moon in the sky sailing majestically over the lake. I could only see a silver crescent there, shining in all its beauty. No human eye could see more of that moon, but anon the twilight, fading, fled across the lake, and the stars began to peep forth, one by one, and Lo! in the arms of the crescent the complete orb of the moon appeared! So must the student be studied, by daylight, by twilight, by search light, by the midnight lamp of meditation, and every known force in him be discovered and used, not crushed out, not covered up, but *used, used, used.*

His imagination, which naturally leads to untruthfulness and fish stories, should be combined with some dull factor that has no chemistry in its nature. I knew a student once that could never learn to decline a Greek adjective till imagining himself a Demosthenes he roared it, with a mouth full of pebbles, out on the barren sea-shore. It then became easy. The very pebbles seemed to fix the slippery endings.

The student's very sluggishness may be made a balance wheel, which once compelled to revolve, will produce constant force.

The teaching that produces power must be that method which will assist the student to make some use of every impulse, thought and capacity of the mind and to waste none of them. But just here, fellow teacher, there is need of caution. A proper charge of powder in a rifle sends the ball with the required force and right to the bull's-eye. If the quantity were trebled there would be a great waste of powder and no more dynamic force.

It is the all-round scholar we want to assist in forming; and when only one particular faculty is developed, by the neglect of others, there is a waste.

I know there is a tendency today toward specific training for one definite end. The idea seems to be to discover just what the student intends to become, and then bring every force to bear to perfect him in that one thing. The idea is detri mental to all good mental training and to a successful attain ment of the object in view. Teachers discovering some remark able development in one direction are too apt to pursue this to the great detriment of the weaker mental exhibitions.

The mistake that we make right here is the result of a misconception of the human mind. We speak of it as though it is made up of parts—each one acting along its own line of direction; when the fact is, the indivisible mind acts, with more or less energy, in all its lines of action.

The mind of the pupil, like the alchemist's crucible, contains many thoughts, emotions, and conceptions, as I before remarked. A crystal is the perfection of any element, and any element may by crystalized. So may any thought; and said thought is never a part of any education till it is crystalized.

Now the teacher has before him a human mind, a mental crucible in which a host of conditions exist, and if power be produced, he must assist in making the best combination possible. He must dissolve some, form others, and teach how the desired crystalization may be obtained. There is nothing in natural chemistry that cannot be made to combine; so, I claim, there is not a thought in the boy's soul that cannot be utilized by some combination. The teacher must often play the part of the Mno2,—but not always the same,—sometimes more explanation is needed, sometimes more patience obtains a new combination, oftentimes a smile, sometimes a frown. Love one day may be the talisman and severe discipline the next.

Crystals are generally imperishable. The diamond is almost indistructable. The graphite, composed of the same element as the diamond, shows its perishing nature on any line of written paper.

To sum up; that teaching produces power that assists the student to assimilate what is already in him to what he wishes to add thereto. Second; to show the laws and rules of crystallzation so that every thought shall be a crystal, pure, brilliant, recognized and imperishable.

Thought that is only half crystalized like the graphite easily passes away, or becomes absorbed by other thoughts, and is lost. No lesson, however trivial, should be pronounced aecomplished till perfectly crystalized. Thought is mental process when thus perfected like the diamond, will execute. The diamond cuts the hardest steel, makes its impress upon the flint rock, and never grows dim.

So the immortal thought of the human soul in its best state knows no defeat and writes its triumph upon the adamantine walls that would bar its progress.

CHAPTER XXVII.

PERSONAL.

I have been a member of several societies. I was made a Mason when twenty-three years old. I have always enjoyed the institution, and a year ago, became associated with the Eastern Star organization. This institution, I think is beautiful, helpful and inspiring. There is a wholeness to the idea embraced in a voluntary secret society exemplified in the Star Society that is very pleasing. The father, mother, daughter, can there all meet together and each receive all the benefits that the others do. After all, the family is the grand unit, heaven ordained and self-centered, around which all pleasure and profit centers.

It was inevitable that the Chapter of the Eastern Star should arise. The condition of social affairs in the twentieth century made it a necessity. Whenever any institution is born in the fulness of the times, it must flourish and never die as long as the conditions continue and the need remains.

The star came legitimately into existence, and will illuminate the Masonic horizon as long as the sun rises in the east. Its influence upon the sisters is wonderful in developing those interests so long dormant, and no man can spend an hour in the society of cultivated ladies without being made better; purer in thought, and better in manners. It is in a congregated capacity that the refining influence of woman best manifests itself. In private life this is less apparent because the little foibles incidental to the sex show themselves—but in public, never. Their better sense of propriety in public shields them even from these.

I joined the Odd Fellows in 1889, and was very much inter ested in the order while living where there was a lodge, but when I went away, I lost interest and fell out. I shall always have a good word to say of the order.

Two years ago, I joined the Grange. Mr. Gardner had suggested that a lawyer could not be admitted, but the Grange followed the advice of Deacon Jones and took me in. In a certain town there was a revival of religion, and a lawyer became converted and applied to the church for admission. The church hesitated a little, but Deacon Jones arose and said: "Brethren, I have already investigated the matter and have discovered that he is not lawyer enough to hurt him any." So they took him in.

The Grange seems to me a grand institution, and is doing a magnificent work. The work done by the Grange in the towns remote from centers is beyond computation. These towns have not churches nor other organizations. The Grange gathers the people together in orderly lines. All have an opportunity to became participants in the exercises of the meetings and become trained in methods of doing things properly. And more than this, much is learned beneficial to the interests of the farm-er. Still more, and most important, it has dignified the occupation, reconciled the young man who was getting uneasy, to stay on the farm and devote his best energies to own and beautify a farm of his own. The Grange has mended the broken fences, painted the houses, and adorned the front yard, and put newspapers and books upon the parlor table.

While teaching at Monson I was ordained to the ministry and was the acting pastor of the Baptist church. During those three years twenty-eight were added to the church, if I remember correctly, the bell was purchased and a new organ bought.

In my spare moments I occasionally read law. I wrestled with Blackstone for a year or two, and other law books, more for the sake of knowing about law than with the expectation of practicing it.

In 1869, on the motion of the Hon. A. G. Lebroke, I was admitted to the bar. I did not attempt to practice to any extent, as other matters absorbed nearly all my time. My first case was a divorce case. One of my old pupils was unfortunate in her choice of a husband, and she desired a divorce. I obtained it for her and received,—her thanks. I next defended a man who had struck another man on the head with a sled-stake. I got him off for one dollar and costs. I received a lantern and some promises for my services. The promises were never redeemed. Like Diogenes, I wore out the lantern looking for an honest client. I have sometimes regretted that I did not continue my legal studies and practice; but "quien sabe" perhaps it is just as well.

The chief reason why I did not was this; about that time I signed a sheriff's bond for several thousand dollars, and the party sued converted the property and went into bankruptcy, and I was called upon to pay his debts. I had an opportunity to earn more immediate money than I could at law, so continued to teach, but have never entirely abandoned the study of abstract law.

I have always been glad that I obtained what knowledge I did. What knowledge I had became very useful in the school-room in certain branches. I do not understand how a teacher can teach the Constitution of the United States without some knowledge of legal terms.

The lawyer's office has always been a favorite loafing place for me. I have been acquainted with quite a large number of lawyers and have found them, on the whole, a fine lot of men.

I wish here to acknowledge the many pleasant hours spent in the office of C. W. Hayes of Foxcroft, who has shown me much kindness and entertained me pleasantly in instructive conversation. I also thank Judge Smith of Dover for his kind assistance.

I used to call upon a young lawyer, twenty years ago, who was very studious.   But he did not confine his study to law books; he read good literature, poetry, all those books that refine the taste, correct the diction, and expand the mind.   That young man is now on the bench of the Supreme Court of Maine. Who knows how much the classical style, choice selection of words, admirable diction, has been shaped by that early reading! I do not think any professional man can afford to ever neglect reading good books.

The study of law is as good discipline as a person can have. There is a logical sequence of cause and effect brought out in the pursuit of the science that trains the mind finely.   The order in which the different branches are presented to the student is the result of much thought by the old masters.   If a friend of mine proposed to become a clergyman, I should suggest that the first year's study be a course laid out by a skilful lawyer.   The preacher who has studied law would never become as *ex parte* in his discourses as the purely theological student.

The lawyer is aware that every statement of his will be criticised.   Would not it be for the benefit of some clergymen if they were certain that their remarks would be as fully scrutinized?

I have never held any office of importance, except county supervisor.   I once "ran" for Representative, and came so near being elected that I had much difficulty in buying a hat big enough, for the next year or two.

I have voted the Republican ticket most of the time; but have been known as somewhat of a "kicker" and have cut the ticket whenever I felt inclined.

In 1881, Governor Plaisted nominated me for superintendent of schools, removing Hon. N. A. Luce.   The council, on purely political grounds, refused to confirm the removal and properly retained Mr. Luce.   I did not want N. A. to die, it would have been stupid for him to resign, but I did wish he might be chosen U. S. Senator.   I had the assurance, if there was a vacancy, that I should be confirmed. At that time the Houlton Times published the following:

"Superintendent of Common Schools:"

"We noticed the fact, last week, that Prof. W. S. Knowlton of this town, had been nominated Superintendent of Common Schools by the Governor. We regard this appointment as an excellent one. Mr. Knowlton was born in Sangerville, Piscataquis county. He fitted for college at Foxcroft Academy and entered Waterville College in 1860. After graduating he became principal of Monson Academy, the principal of Foxcroft Academy. In both of these schools he won an excellent reputation as a teacher. Mr. Knowlton next became principal of the Hitchcock Free High School in Brimfield, Mass., and remained there until he returned to Monson, to take charge of the Academy again. Under the supervisor law he became superintendent of Piscataquis county, and held the office until the law was repealed, and it is worthy of notice that Piscataquis county was almost the only one that voted solid for the law to the end.

Six years ago, he was selected by the committee to take charge of Houlton Academy. This institution had recently passed under the control of Colby University, and, under his direction, the school has become one of the most flourishing in the State. Teaching has been his life work and the uniform success which has, in the past, attended his labors we feel certain would follow him in the office to which he has been nominated.

Very few men, we believe, are so well fitted for the position of state superintendent of common schools. His knowl edge of teaching and of the wants of our school system is not merely theoretical, but practical. He would, therefore, bring to the position an amount of experience that would enable him to do much better work than could otherwise be possible. It is worthy of mention too, that he has a breadth of culture that few men possess, being a fine scholar, a first-class teacher and a good public speaker. We, therefore, sincerely hope that, for the sake of our schools, Mr. Knowlton may be confirmed in the position to which he has been nominated by the Governor."

BACCALAUREATE SERMON.

"Every man in his chamber of imagery."—Ezekiel 8; 23.

The prophet of the Lord was in spirit on the first day of the week when the spirit of the Lord led him away to the temple at Jerusalem and leading him to the wall commanded him to dig in the wall. He did so and discovered a hole in the wall. The angel commanded him to still continue to dig. Then a door appeared and the prophet went in and stood in a chamber hidden in the secret recesses of the temple. Then said the angel, "Oh son of man, seest thou what they do, every man in the chamber of his imagery;" The prophet looked, and behold, he saw the priests and elders, whose duty it was to offer incense to the God of Israel and worship the Almighty, every man with a censer in his hand offering incense to the idols he had set up and paying his adoration to them. Here were those men with door shut, every trace of secret entrance obliterated. There in the dark, though no eye saw and no ear heard; but the eye of the Lord penetrated that dark recess and revealed all the secret wickedness of that chamber. Those men had this chamber where they paid adoration to the secret idols of their selection. There they worshiped, there they loved and adored and became assimilated to the very gods they themselves had selected or created.

So has every man today a chamber of imagery, where in secret he goes and communes with that secret chamber of the soul. From that chamber he comes and mingles with men, with the incense of that secret chamber still pervading every act and thought. When do men enter this chamber? At all hours and in all places. Sometimes in the crowded congregation the vacant eye shows that one hearer, at least, is no longer conscious of his present surroundings, but has floated away to his ideal world, and is dwelling upon scenes the clergyman knows not of. At the evening hour, when alone, almost before he is aware, he stands in his chamber with censer in hand and is worshiping some idol that he loves. Everyone, I repeat, has this chamber, and there are formed the deepest loves of the heart. It is there that temptation first allures and captivates; it is there that the great resolves are formed that lead to noble and holy lives. There ideal associates are cherished whose counterfeits we seek in practical life. Every young man especially spends some moments each day as he stands in his chamber of imagery. Into that chamber he goes, shuts the door and fancies the world will never know to what god he sacrifices. Perhaps he ought to be elsewhere, should be in the holy temple of Jeho vah, ought to be doing some duty for humanity, filling some position assigned by virtue of his condition, but all these he neglects or ignores and flees away in soul to his secret chamber and worships.

Into that secret chamber of the soul come the silent influ ences that operate upon the heart and paint upon the walls the scenes, beauties and inducements that each advocates. Ambition, remorseless ambition, that spirit that led the Israelites to ask for a king, that led Napoleon Bonaparte to swim vast seas of slaughter that his insatiate thirst for power might in some degree be satiated, that leads men today to seek power, position, wealth, regardless of the rights of others,—ambition comes and paints upon the walls in gorgeous coloring, the gloriou triumphs and magnificent victories the daring may achieve.

The dead and dying are not represented, the broken hearts are not seen, the dying groans not heard, only the peans of victory swell out upon the air. The young man sits in his cham ber of imagery and gazes upon these lurid pictures. He is at first, perhaps, shocked at the delineation upon the wall. Conscience reproves, mercy pleads and justice cries in sternest accents, but yet ambition in bright lines, more glorious scenes portray, weaker and weaker grows the reproval of conscience and the voice is drowned in the shouts of victory till at last the surrender is won, and the man stands in his chamber of imagery with his censer in his hands, worshiping the ideal pictures upon the walls. There in that secret chamber, the resolves are formed which are executed in practical life. Into that chamber comes an inordinate love of wealth, beautiful houses with brown stone fronts, horses and carriages, bank stock and bonds are painted upon the walls, and how alluring are they! All the refinements of life that wealth can bring, luxury can furnish, every aesthetic taste fully satisfied, beautiful scenes of earth visited,—all these pictures are thrown upon the screen where mellowed light softly falls. What young man is not allured by such magnificent promises? The sleepless nights of anxiety, the clouds that so often darken the horizon are not painted in the picture. The manhood lost that wealth may be gained, a soul bartered for dollars; conscience violated that desire may prevail,—all these are in the background overshadowed by the halo from the inviting. The censer stands before the longing eyes of the young man, pondering, hesitating he stands, desiring the results, but lamenting the sacrifice. At length when the heart is ready, the hand grasps the censer and adoration is paid to the ideal, and out among men, disregarding every moral obligation, burying manhood under stocks and bonds, he starts on a course of "frenzied finance" which, has he the ability and fortune favors, will carry him to the boulevard that leads to castles and chateaux and secures the stocks and bonds.

There are many haunted houses in this land of ours. Stalking through the halls and corridors are the ghosts of happiness that die when the first dishonest dollar was obtained, the apparition of peace that passed out when unholy desire entered.

Into that chamber hypocrisy slinks with smiling, smirking face and paints her fancies there. The front view is fascinating in the extreme. The front is only shown. Like many an imposing structure standing upon streets, the front facade but hides the insignificant house in the rear. Strange as it may seem so many stand before that wall with censer in hand and pay their heart's devotion to the false, the hollow, the wicked, and so in fancy's flights they build whited sepulchers and call them mansions fair. Among men these idolators live and act according to their ideals, and leave the world worse when life's course is over, with halting steps and paints her pictures upon the wall, Sloth comes, couches for repose, chairs of ease and shady lanes are the pictures offered. Why tire the muscles and weary the brain and climb mountains when sunny plains stretch invitingly from horizon to horizon? In dulcet tones she sighs, "A little more sleep, a little more folding of the hands in sleep." Why toil and agonize for riches that have wings and fly away? Why weary the brain with fatiguing thought? Why recognize persistent duty demanding labor? Why listen to that voice within calling to lofty thought and glorious deeds? And the indolent suggard with half filled censer wearily pays his devotion to idleness and sleep. Among men he becomes the reality he desires to be in his chamber of thought.

Sensual pleasure pictures upon the wall scenes upon which the novice gazes at first with a blush of shame inherited from the mother's soul, but anon those scenes seem less hideous and at length attract, allure and fascinate.

> "Vice is a monster of so frightful mein,
> As to be hated needs but to be seen.
> But seen too oft, familiar with his face,
> We first endure, then pity, then embrace."

Here it is in the secret chamber of desire that the reckless, dissolute youth commences the life of dissipation and disgrace. Bright, glowing pictures allure and captivate in the meditation hour. At this quiet hour when no human eye can see, no ear can hear, the young man sits and thinks over the scenes of the day. He recalls the glowing accounts given by his companions of the good times they have indulged in, reviews the scenes they have pictured over, and feasts his soul upon the ideal engagements he has conjured up before himself. He sees but one side of it all, calls not up before his vision, health ruined, reputation gone, friends in despair, life wasted. He only sees what he wants to see, and when he becomes in love with these he goes out into the world and plunges into the actual with all the disastrous results following. And thus the whole catalogue of human passions array themselves in that chamber of imagery.

But these are not the only visitors to that chamber. The better elements of the human soul present themselves and plead for recognition. True ambition, a desire to excel comes to the young in his meditation hour and paints on the walls names of men and women whose fame will never die. These are written high on the walls, enveloped in glory true and undying. As he gazes upon these, a desire arises to write his name along beside them, to so live that all coming ages will remember the name made famous, and which will brighter grow as time passes on. When these illustrations have stimulated the soul to earnest desire, then begins a course in life whose consummation is the highest possible attainment. Then every hindrance is laid aside, weak indulgences he no longer regards, trivial considerations receive no attention, all small desires lie grovelling in the dust, one grand, over-mastering purpose animates the soul,—to make life something grand, something honorable, something that will compel all coming time to recognize and weave into precepts and copy as models.

Purity dressed in garments of snow with modest mein and downcast eye, with brow serene and step made firm by self-consciousness, paints on the wall the lovely chaste portraits that so resemble the pictures of the Madonna, and she whispers, These, and these alone, you must worship, O young man, these, and these alone, O dear young lady, you must dare even think about." No gaudy colors plant there their brazen effrontery about the pictures that Purity paints upon the canvas. But they are not attractive. There is inherent in the heart an appreciation of all that is pure and beautiful and good before the taste becomes violated and the desires depraved. If only the young could learn to love the pure with an actual emotion while the

God given appreciation is active, if he pays his adoration at that altar, if he burns in his censer the purest spices and the frankincense of an unpolluted heart, he will never fail amid the most fascinating temptations; but that love must be as strong, real and active as a desire for gross things can be. Oftimes a toleration is mistaken for a love. A half-hearted approval never leads to forcible acts.

On that wall are painted portraits of men and women who have laid aside every selfish thought and desire, and worked together with God for the uplifting of society, the amelioration of suffering.

Into the chamber of silent thought comes the "still, small voice," pleading for a better life, higher motives, purer thought. Away from the noise of the busy world, separated from influences that have drowned that voice, its power is most potent.

In the heart can be heard the familiar tones of a mother's prayer, falling, as it seems, from her home above, pleading with her prodigal boy. Gently knocking at that door ever stands the Christ, and asks to come in, pleads to come in. When allowed that to do, what glorious pictures are painted on the walls! The cross is there to be sure, but a halo of glory illuminates it. Jesus of Nazareth hung upon that cross. Through the cross, life and salvation came to the world; by means of the cross, humanity dies to sin, and receives "life more abundantly." By the crosses of life, character is perfected; the heart enlarged and life made worth living.

But other pictures are there: A glorious life spent in the service of God, spent in doing good among men, a life in which every motive, thought and desire are prompted by the spirit of God. Other scenes are portrayed. Ambition robbed of all selfishness finds its highest conception realized in full development, emblazoned with undying deeds that Heaven can bless, a Christianized intellect, every fond hope and purpose purified and made clean.

All these things are on the wall, and more than that, "A home in Heaven," the house of many mansions, the golden streets and pearly gates; a life with God, where the immortal soul, with its almost infinite longings, shall have opportunity to study, investigate, to know; a home where all is pure, beautiful and incorruptible; where friend shall see the heart of friend; where partings can never be, where all that an infinite God can do for the perfection of human happiness is done.

As the young man gazes upon these scenes, and listens to that pleading voice, he can but feel an impulse to accept at once; but there are other pictures upon that wall, other voices call, the voice of the Siren, in dulcet tones, is heard, calling to other scenes. He hesitates, thinks, meditates, stands with censer in hand, almost distracted; but right there, in that secret chamber, the decision will be made; a decision that nor time nor eternity will be able to change. In this secret retreat are the issues of life and death.

O young man, young woman, as you sit alone in your chamber, and fashion for yourself an ideal life; as you review the pleasures of the day, and contemplate the duties of life, as you appreciate the temptations that surround you, fix your eye on the Christ on the cross, and open the heart to the pleading voice calling to better things. Close the eye to every scene not approved of Christ, not embraced within the landscape of his portraiture.

CONTRIBUTED FOR ALBUMS.

Several of the students have sent me a contribution from albums in which I had written. I ought to state that two or three of these contributions were written when I was a young man.

Found in many albums.
"You'll not forget, when this you see,
That this is my chirography."

To Alice.

Alice, in your eyes I see,
Love supreme, and coquetry,
Give to me the first and best,
Let the world take all the rest.

To Lucia Rose.

Be a white rose, pure and neat,
Be a red rose, blushing sweet,
Every path in life adorn,
Be a rose without a thorn.

To Miss Elloise Bagley.

Elloise,
Busy bees
Honey find in flower or trees.
Thus may you
Ever do,
Find in all things something true.

On receiving a box of grapes as a philopena present from
Miss Ada Staples:

Accept my thanks, Miss Ada S.
Payment in full I now confess.
The sweetness of the grapes, methought,
Was borrowed from the hand that brought.

To Mary.

Of kind words be never chary,
Let your smiles be frequent, very;
When you're sad or when you're merry,
Be perfection, then be Mary.

A PRAYER TO PROF. OSLER.

Dr. Osler said that a man at sixty ought to be chloroformed.

My dear Professor, if you can,
Please lengthen out our earthly span.

We've passed the sixty milestone by,
With step still firm and undimmed eye.

Can swing the scythe like long ago,
Can handle axe, or plow, or hoe.

Can measure mountains, moon, or star,
Can solve the tough hyperbola.

Of steak or pie can eat our fill,
With Edwards reason on "Free Will."

Can Plato read and Socrates,
And "square the circle," at our ease.

We still would stem the heat and storm,
We do not want your "chloroform."

We think it hard to leave the track
Because that stupid almanac,

Says we were born in thirty-nine,
And must with gloomy Pluto dine.

We have a nag that's twenty-four,
We want to drive that nag some more.

No man of twenty, none but us,
Can drive that fierce Bucephalus.

Our mooley cow, though gaunt and lean,
Makes butter still, at "sweet sixteen."

No "kid" of forty ever born
Can milk that cow with "crumpled horn."

And our old dog, though blind of eye,
Still wags his tail, as we pass by.

Shall we lie silent in the vale,
While that old dog still wags his tail?

We have a wife, less old than we,
Shall she a youthful widow be,

And soon her sable plumage burn,
While we lie senseless in the urn,

And grace the home of some young host,
That only forty years can boast?

My dear Professor, don't you feel,
The world sometimes gets tired of "veal,"

And, like St. Paul, "for stomach's sake,"
Wants, now and then, a slice of steak,

Where age and sweetness nicely join,
Or juicy roast of tenderloin?

Go east, Professor, o'er the wave,
And shed a tear at Gladstone's grave.

Go east, Professor, far away,
And let me live my little day.

When "mal de mer" your stomach's on,
Then take your dose of "chloroform."

AN IDYL.

THE KISS AT PALMER.

I stood, one day, on the depot steps
  With lawyer, priest and farmer,
And my heart was stirred to its lowest depths,
  In the beautiful town of *Palmer*.

Close by my side stood a bright-eyed Miss,
  No statue of Juno was calmer;
And the cruel engine began to hiss
  Farewell to that girl at *Palmer*.

Her eyes were bright as Venus at night,
  And her heart, through their lashes, bewildered with flashes,
And her sunshiny smile would a Cato beguile;
  With voice soft and fine as the breeze in the pine.

We'd loved, in a sort of Platonic way,
  I and my exquisite charmer,
But part we must, forever and aye,
  In that terrible town of Palmer.

My tongue was tied by a nameless spell;
  I prayed that nothing would harm her;
And I gave my hand, in a silent farewell,
  In that hopeless town of Palmer.

She pressed my hand, O, joy! O, bliss!
    The very air grew balm'er,
And with sweetest lips gave me a kiss
    In the glorified town of Palmer.

The world seemed changed in a moment's time,
    The Millenium Dawn seemed nigher;
That engine, grim with soot and rime,
    Elijah's chariot of fire.

I felt like the Peri, when freed from sin,
    She saw the gates of Aiden
Open wide to let her in,
    With that precious tear-drop laden.

That gloomy station, rough and brown,
    Became a mansion, fair.
And the Poor House over in Monson Town,
    Grand castles in the air.

Every pebble seemed a precious gem,
    To the eyes of the Holy Palmer,
As he walked the streets of Jerusalem;
    And I the streets of Palmer.

I'm a grandsire now, with a child by my side,
    And the passions of life have grown calmer;
But I'll never forget till eveningtide,
    That girl and that kiss, at Palmer!

THE PARSON'S EXCHANGE.

One evening Cupid took a stroll,
    And brought his bow along;
He lighted on a grassy knoll
    And hummed a little song.
"The parson is writing his sermon," said he
"What do you think his text can be?
I'll sit me down on the window sill
And watch the flight of his gray goose quill.
Some musty old thought on the duty of man,
How Eden was lost and the terrible ban—
O! pshaw! parson, now I'll give you a line
That serves as a text for all sermons of mine."

And the mind of the parson was thrilled through and through,
And his duty he saw in a light that was new,
And he heard his heart beat in ecstatic surprise
As a text flashed forth as if from the skies.
" 'Love ye one another,' " he repeated o'er and o'er.
" 'Love ye one another.' That I do, and more."
But the sermon still lingered, his forehead grew hot,
No spiritual light, no answering thought,
But the odors of Eden seemed filling the room.
He Paradise saw with lilies in bloom,
And angels with garlands of flowers
Seemed beckoning on to perennial bowers.
The parson grew frantic. "I'll write it," he cried,
"Or die the dire death that the martyrs have died.
What power can it be that is thrilling me so?"
He then heard the twang of the bright silver bow,
And the arrow sped straight his corselet between,
And a sweet voice whispered "Charlene, Charlene."
A blush of surprise on the parson's face broke;
He thought his own heart its secret had spoke,
And visions he saw more precious. I ween,
Than ever before by mortals were seen,
Except by a lover—well you and I know
Just how it was, in the sweet long ago.
But the sermon stopped there, it couldn't be done,
And Cupid sat smiling, enjoying the fun.
He wrestled, like Jacob, with angels unseen,
But the angel that conquered was the charming Charlene.
"It's of no use," he cried, "My thoughts they will range.
It cannot be done. I'll have an exchange."
Though the highway was rough and the wintry air keen,
He flew like a dove to the home of Charlene.
'Twas the same old story, it never will change;
Heart spoke unto heart, they made an exchange.

Influenced by the imperative demand of former pupils of
Houlton Academy, I take great pleasure in immortalizing this
book by presenting to my readers W. H. Parker's Byronic poem
published in those happy days.

POETRY.

Come, friends, I pray, and listen
　　While to you I do relate
A few words concerning one
　　With whom we often meet.

'Tis of a brave and gallant youth,
　　Well known unto us all,
His stature 'tis not great,
　　And some might call him small.

His name is a familiar one,
　　But if you cannot guess,
I may as well tell it,
　　His name is W. J. Betts.

He is studious and industrious
　　As ever was a bee,
And when he leaves our school he's going
　　At travelling with apple trees.

He's very fond of the ladies,
　　As it's natural for to be;
And when he has one by his side
　　He seems so full of glee.

But for one he has a special love,
　　As often is the case;
She's tall and young and sprightly,
　　But has a freckled face.

This young Miss is very tall,
　　As before I did relate;
In order for to see her face
　　He has to look up straight.

And now I'm drawing to a close,
　　I must bid my friends adieu,
And all the rest of his worthy acts
　　I will simply leave with you.

But his loved one's conduct toward him
　　The hardest heart might touch;
She cares so little for him,
　　While he loves her so much.

But I must leave the gloomy scene
And another course pursue,
So I will quietly drop my pen
And bid you all "adieu."

W. H. Parker.

A PAPER ON ORDER.

More teachers fail on account of an inability to govern a school than by any other means. They do not understand that there is science in the governing of a school. One fact must be admitted at once; that some are "born to command." But even those have a system by which they work. The very first principle to learn in governing a room-full of scholars is strategy. The teacher must so plan that the least amount of force possible be called into action. To explain; every class must sit on the recitation seat in the order in which they come from their seats in the schoolroom. No class should ever, in the smallest school, come into the floor except in regular order, one pupil following another; then, when all are before the recitation seat, they should all be seated at once, by the tap of the bell. Every scholar should always occupy the same position in the same recitation, through the term.

The class should be dismissed in the way they are seated, by a tap of the bell calling them up, another tap sends them to their seats, where they stand till the bell seats them.

No communication should be allowed in the class, and nearly all text books should be left at the seats. No geographies should be carried into the class. The teacher should carefully notice those in the class who are inattentive, and without directly telling them the reason, call upon them the most frequently to recite. They will see the point very soon. Every teacher should tell the pupils, at the beginning of the term, that he will seat the pupils where he thinks it best for all concerned, and should make such changes as he thinks best.

The school should march out at recess and, when they come in, stand by the seat till seated. They must, by all means, be required to come in immediately when the bell rings and that bell should only ring a stroke or two. I advise every teacher to strictly enforce this suggestion. Do not ring the bell five minutes, or one minute, but strike it so it can be heard and insist that all, large and small, shall come in at once. If this is required at the beginning of the term rigidly, it will save very much trouble and assist in other matters of discipline.

When I was county supervisor of schools, in a certain town was a schoolhouse so located that the pupils could run around it. One day I drove along by the house and saw half a dozen scholars sprinting around that house with the teacher behind them. I thought they were in sport and stopped to watch the fun, but soon I noticed that, one by one, the pupils dodged into the schoolhouse and, at last, all went in, followed by the teacher. I learned that was the usual program every recess. It was good exercise for the legs, but not a brain developing exercise.

The water pail is a great source of disturbance in the school room and I am inclined to think it ought to be excluded, but perhaps it is not wise to do so, as so many think that children need to drink every half hour. It is an unhealthy and pernicious habit, and ought to be abolished. Water that has stood an hour in the schoolroom is unfit to drink at all. If the teacher must have the water pail, let the scholars "be watered" at regular intervals, in perfect order, and suspend all other exercises.

All punishment should follow the offence, as a rule. A pupil caught in the act of disobedience recognizes that he is wrong, and deserves punishment. If he receives it then and there, a reformation usually follows. But if that pupil is told at ten o'clock that at the close of school he is to receive punishment, he thinks the matter over during the day, talks about it with the pupils, and by night comes to the conclusion that the offence does not justify punishment. So, when it is administered, it leads, not to repentance, but to stubbornness.

Of course, there may be instances where it may be better to defer.

That teacher who publicly proclaims that he never punishes, had better change his business. My rule is—punish if I must,— but show by example that the minimum quantity only is needed. I have never whipped a pupil or used a ferule. I have shown a few that this world revolves very rapidly sometimes; I have deprived them of privileges, and subjected them to mortifications; but I always informed the superintendent and pupils that I should whip them, if I thought best, and they deserved it.

Whispering is the source of most of the disorder in a school room. I suppose there never was a school where there was not some, but it should be reduced to the smallest degree possible. It is often said, "Gain the love of the pupils, and there will be no trouble." A moment's thought will show that this alone will not maintain good order. Johnnie loves his mother better than he can his teacher, yet he needs his mother's slipper quite often. The teacher should seek to gain the love of the pupil, but not by extraneous means. His work for the boy, his interest in his studies, will gain recognition, and love follows. Little and big folks very soon learn to care for those who sacrifice for them. It is very difficult to always decide just how familiar one can be with the pupil. My rule is: be friendly, pleasant, kindly, at recess, noon, and all times out of school hours, but never familiar. Never argue, dispute, nor allow them to criticize any act of yours done in the schoolroom. I never ask much of them out of school hours. I would ask a boy to get a pail of water in school hours; but would get it myself at noon.

I always say "please" to everyone in ordinary intercourse, in school hours, which serves as a request; when that "please" is not used, the request becomes a demand. A private talk is very effective with many pupils, useless with others; nay, harmful. One experiment will determine.

Should a pupil ever be expelled? Certainly. When it is for the well-being of the great whole that one pupil should no longer absorb three times as much of the time and energy of the teacher as he deserves, and shows, on his part, no disposition to reform, let him depart, for the benefit of the rest.

The best way to manage those restless, idle, nervous little folks is to keep them busy about something the teacher suggests, and not what they choose. They must learn that their wills must, for the time being, be subjected to the teacher's.

The most vexatious pupil of all is that contemptible coward who, every day, will stop just short of punishment. At last, the teacher can stand it no longer, and punishes the pupil, not for the overt act, but for the misdemeanors of the whole week. The boy goes home and reports the punishment as given for the last act of his. His parents and the school committee think the sin was trivial and the punishment too severe. They do not know the many hours of care and perplexity that same boy has caused that long-suffering teacher.

Some teachers think it brutal to punish a pupil. If punishment be administered in a proper spirit, there is nothing brutal about it. The teacher administers that punishment, impelled by duty, not by a love of it, and no one is made worse by doing duty. The pupil who is made to obey and be decent is certainly less of a brute than before. But, of course, the highest ambition of the teacher should be to so interest the pupils in their studies, and in him, that an interest will arise which will predestinate good order and good work. This may be done, in most cases.

To superintendents I make an earnest appeal. In all the primary schools, let more time be given to reading, spelling, and writing. The Almighty fixed the time in which the mind of a child can best do certain things. No human decree can change that order. Children can learn to memorize readily, and should be taught to do so. They don't stop to consider *why* a thing is so; then take advantage of that fact and teach spelling and reading at that unreasoning age. The spelling and pronunciation of English is, for the most part, devoid of all reasoning process. All pupils less than ten years old should read four times every day, and spell as many. They should write every day. "But," vou say, "there is not time." Take time. Let the child learn the addition and multiplication tables. He can do it, and should do so, both for profit and mental discipline; and let his time-absorbing "number-work" be in abeyance till his reasoning faculties are developed somewhat. Language lessons are all right at the proper time, but should not, at an early age, absorb too much time. Many an hour is wasted on children in that exercise, because they are too young to appreciate what is taught. When the child is ten years old, he should be taught simple grammar, both orally, and from a book. Then should commence his real mathematical education.

In three or four years the boy will learn all the arithmetic he needs. He will learn more at seventeen in one year, than in two at twelve or thirteen. I have taught men of thirty arithmetic easily; but I could not teach them grammar or reading or spelling.

Another point interests me very much, the matter of promotion. In every school of fifty, there are, at least, five or six who have no especial mathematical ability. These pupils, at the end of the year, fail to pass and hence are retained another year in the same grade. Many of these drop out of school, and those that remain are idle half of the time and become mischievous. In my opinion, such pupils should be allowed to go on, and a course should be adopted, fitted to their conditions. This may lay some additional burdens on the teacher, but the effort is worth the while. Some of the really brightest boys and girls I ever knew, have been pupils of the kind mentioned. The world would lose much should they drop out of school at an early age. They could have some new study assigned, or be required to do extra work in the prescribed course and leave out the mathematics.

Suppose the pupil be thirteen, and cannot pass in arithmetic. That pupil may go on in algebra all right, and, when he is older, he very likely will accomplish the arithmetic readily.

A word about supplementary reading. I believe in practicing a class in reading all that is possible, but the book should be a drill book. There should be a variety in it, and not simply a continuous story. No pupils become good readers without drill in all forms of reading.

Let the bad boy suffer, and not the teacher. The same remarks apply to the other parties mentioned.

But the teacher must, nevertheless, sacrifice something. This sacrifice must be a voluntary one. There are pleasures and social enjoyments which are his by right; but these should never so absorb his interest as to diminish faithful work in the school room. There cannot be a divided love and interest when that love is intensely active. When the love is cold and dormant one could teach in a listless way, and spend half the night in pleasure; but when pleasure becomes a passion, the whole stream of emotions runs in that direction, and the teaching will be totally insipid.

CHAPTER XXVIII.

"I create new heavens and new earth." Isaiah, 65 ; 17.

In the beginning God created. The heavens were created and the earth was put into form. That form was not a fixed one. Doubtless this earth of ours once consisted of a mass of gases held by affinity in a common mass and by centripetal force moulded into a spherical form. In that gaseous world were included every element that now forms a constituent part of the earth as it exists today. The gases parting with a certain amount of heat became liquid ; then the earth became a new one in appearance though not a new atom had been created. The liquid, under the influence of fixed law, transformed itself into a solid and a new earth appeared, the same in elements, but new in form. But the earth was not yet ready for human occupancy. Countless ages must be consumed before God's transforming work was done. At length amid the beauties of Paradise, God's crowning creation looked out upon a new earth, fitted for the high development of man.

For many ages, doubtless, man saw no changes in the natural world around him save that which the seasons bring. Certain phenomena were noticed year after year but were little understood. In course of time the laws appertaining to the physical world began to be understood, then a new earth appeared ; the same in reality, but better understood. Old in form but new in force ; old in elements but new in combination. In fine, the earth is never just the same in form and appearance every day, sun, heat and storm, chemical affinity and external forces are forever producing new forms and combinations hitherto unknown, and still it is the same earth that God created in the beginning.

As man came to use the forces of nature he discovered some were easily understood and others past finding out. He could use these forces but could not fathom the deep mysteries of their existence.

Man discovered also that there were many phenom ena which he could not use. Every day he was aware that natural laws were operating around him that were as far beyond his comprehension as was the divine Author of those laws. One by one these laws have been understood and subjected to the use of man. The force of gravity, the expansive power of water, the terrible explosive force of nitrogenous combinations and many others have changed the social relations of humanity and made civilization possible. A new earth has appeared infinitely superior to the one the prophets saw and understood. Mother earth then seemed surcharged with forces that rent her in twain by earthquake shocks engulfing puny man in hopeless ruin. The sky seemed but the depository of hail and snow and the hiding place of the terrible thunder bolt, whose voice alone caused the face to blanch with fear. Today she is Mother earth indeed, holding in her bosom the precious metals and gems that delight humanity, concealing but lightly the fuel for our warmth, force for our machinery and a thousand gifts heretofore unknown. The very poisons by whose fiat man once died now give health and vigor; and that awe inspiring voice from the sky, once so terrible, now becoming translatable, is simply the concentrated echo of the trolley car and dynamo. It is all the same in God's sight, but to us a new earth.

"I create new heavens." Perhaps some violence is done to the text in the way the word "heavens" will be used in this discourse, but yet we think it may fairly be used to designate our conception of the future abode of man. The earth is his present abode. By the term "heaven" we designate in general his abode after his disappearance as a living, acting being on earth.

God made the earth man's present habitation. God made heaven man's future abode. God's creative power stopped when the elements composing the earth were finished, so heaven was finished when God made it. The earth we see and study,— heaven we believe in and see by faith, and as the Holy Book says, I, God, create new earth, so I, God, create for man new conceptions of heaven. The heaven of our fathers is not today our heaven, though in God's sight the same forever, and as man's conception of heaven changes, it follows that our ideas change in regard to what is requisite for that heaven. But it may be urged man cannot change these things, God only can. True, but it is God who makes all these changes, using man sometimes as an agent or co-worker. The theme led directly to a discussion of a somewhat difficult subject,—progressive theology. Difficult, because erroneous premises were assumed and hence wrong conclusions reached. All things in God's world are progressive, his creation was first the living plant, at length the giant oak and lofty pine,—at first the uncouth monster of the early ages, those were superceded by the graceful, athletic animals of later days. Each were necessary in his time and condition. The immur millions of ants were necessary, so were the ant-eaters, equally so the carnivorous anmals to destroy the same. So in teaching man and leading him up to his real life, God works in progressive ways and gradually leads from higher to higher till the summit is reached. Now understand me here. God never changes, not a natural law is ever changed or annulled. Abstract right as God sees it never changes. But our conception of right may change. The application of moral law may change; expediency may change. What was once right may become decidedly wrong. The applications of prohibitions may be right in one age and wrong in another. Now what our conceptions of the future state are must have a bearing upon our moral conduct and religious life here. In fact one can write a history of civilization and of culture by simply consulting the recorded conceptions man has of the future. In Homeric days the poets conceived that the heroes passed to the Plutonian regions with all their scars, human resentments, their horses and dogs. The wicked were punished by physical tortures and bodily pain.

That conception plainly showed the ethical condition existing among men. It was all physical; the spiritual hardly existed in their conception. In Virgil, the heroes still had these scars, but they were scars impressed upon a spiritual body. The people now began to recognize a spiritual existence here on earth. In Dante there was pictured a heaven from which all baser things are banished, but all the loves, resentments, jealousies of earth were reproduced. A great advance has been made in civilization and spiritual pleasures and sorrows displaced the love and hate of the physical life which had prevailed in former days. In Milton's "Paradise Lost," we have a pen picture of a purely spiritual heaven. All the earth is left entombed with the physical body—all human affection, every earthly hope and ambition were gone. Man's only employment, joy, desire, was to praise God for the great boon of salvation. The conception of Milton fairly illustrated the puritanical thought of the day. Butler, a hundred years later, voiced modern thought in conceiving heaven as a spiritual existence where all the surrounding influence, atmosphere, the Divine presence brings all into harmony, where nothing but purity can exist, where God's will will be man's desire, where those immortal longings that rob the eyelids of sleep while vainly seeking satiety here on earth, will have opportunity to study, admire and in humble reverence glorify the all-glorious Jehovah, who spoke and it was done. In truth the Christ had made salvation possible.

In this ethical age the spiritual, the ethical is the only recognized part of man worthy of consideration. The body is but a temple in which the man lives. Our conception now is that not a noble attribute of the soul can die. A love for the beautiful here on earth will make the pure life all the more enjoyable where all things must be charming. A love for humanity here on earth will find eternal joy in realizing the felicity of the innumerable multitude in the many mansions. A love for par ents or child, that made all those places of life sublime, must find its fulfillment where that love can render perfection. That hungering after knowledge that wearies the brain in unsatisfying researchings must be satisfied where God has prepared a perfect habitation. Of course the first, the great, the all-absorbing emotion of the soul will be to give glory and honor and adoration to God the Father for his unnumbered blessings, mercy and love, and thanksgiving and praise to the Christ who hath made heaven ours.

We have no very definite description of Heaven in the Bible, but are told that God is there, God the Almighty, the pure, the holy, the just, our Father. Christ told the world that there were mansions prepared for those who are pure in heart and love God, Christ will be there.

John saw the Holy City with its streets pure as gold, its gates as imperishable as precious gems, and heard the uncounted millions sing songs of praise to God the Almighty and to the Lamb who hath redeemed us. But why did not Christ coming from that blessed abode fully describe it to an anxious world? Evidently for the very reason already hinted. Heaven must forever remain to us while on earth as a conception inherited from our Father in Heaven. That conception must change as man changes, as civilization advances.

Now civilization can only become possible where Christian ity prevails, hence the conception of Heaven that man enter tains is the direct result of the same Christianity. Granted this proposition,—the conclusion naturally follows that our concep-

17

tion of Heaven must become grander as the state of society becomes more elevated.   At some periods in the history of the church, piety consisted chiefly in faithfully adhering to the dogmas of the church.   When that idea prevailed the conception of Heaven must have been a place where the man of prayer, the martyr and the faithful defender of the faith would receive his reward.

Today all is changed.   There is one great theme absorbing the soul of the thinking world; who was Christ, and what did he do and teach?   The answer comes breathed forth from the soul of hungering humanity that he was the Incarnate Son of God; that he lived among men, loved humanity, healed the sick and taught men how to live and how to die.   Christianity today consists in being Christlike and obeying his commandments and following his example.   Christ recognized all as offsprings of the common Father.   To be Christlike is to realize that every man has an immortal soul for whom Christ died, and to feel a brother's love for every one needy, to weep with those that weep and rejoice with those that rejoice.   Heaven, to a man thus feeling, must seem but the perfect realization of what he has tried to realize on earth, and he knows that the more he understands God's laws written upon every leaf of nature's unsealed book the more he delves into the deep mines of human researches, the more he discourses truth and beauty in all created things, the more he understands God's moral laws.

If then a Christian life here on earth becomes broader, grander and more useful the wiser man becomes, it follows that a conceived heaven must present the opportunity for gratifying the undying thirst in the human soul to know, to study, to investigate and understand.   This is the new heaven only in our conception.   If the reverent being standing on some lofty mountain with soul surcharged with admiration while viewing the glorious scenery of nature, lifts up his heart and voice in praise to the Almighty God, who could so create, how much loftier must be that hymn of praise, when with spiritual body this same being, having listened to the "Song of Stars" as they go circling by, having seen with spiritual ken the unnumbered systems of worlds circling by other systems still more remote, will raise to the wonderful creator of worlds without number—to Him who has obtained mercy by being merciful, here on earth, the heaven awaiting him will be full of the recipients of mercy. He that has so loved on earth can but expect to love in Heaven. Nor do all these things one whit detract from a reverential belief in the Bible. That book must never lose its power in the human heart. But I repeat it was given for all time, and is to be interpreted by the light of each age. Nor does this in the least detract from its authority. Whether the narratives of Jonah be the statement of an actual occurence or an allegory, the moral is the same. A man fled from duty and God and fell into great distress. Repenting, he was rescued and became obedient. No one now claims that the world was created in six days,—similar to ours,—yet many once did. That was well in those days, it is well now as we understand it. The terror of the law did its work among lawless men, the Gospel was far better when the time was fitted for the coming of Christ. A miraculous conversion was necessary to turn a Paul from a persecutor to a believer. Great revivals were of immense value in Wesley's day. A stern creed of thirty-nine articles was a bulwark over which the infidel would not pass when unbelief was rampart.

But new days are upon us. New civilization blesses us. more sensitive spiritual fiber responds to gospel truth today. The still small voice does the work now that the thunder peal did on Sinai's mount. The child of tender years begins to realize for the first time that it once lay in Jesus' arms. Devoted Christians are zealously working in the church who describe the Kingdom of Heaven as Christ described it,—"First the blade, then the ear, then the full corn in the ear." The awe-inspiring priest with mitre, robe and censer were essential when men were moved mostly by physical exhibitions. The effective minister in the twentieth century is our friend and brother, more austere in his own morals but charitable toward ours. He is not less zealous, faithful and devoted than his ancient brother. He recognizes the needs of his flock with a heart full of sympathy, with a faith never flagging. He feels sure that Christ demands that his church in these better days shall be first in every movement, lifting humanity above the commonplace,—that the good Samaritan should be found at every street corner,—that love is the great spiritual lever that lifts men out of the slough of sin. By faith he foresees that coming day when "'Sin shall be banished, and death yield his prey and earth her nations Jehovah obey." Then, indeed, shall there be a "new earth," a new humanity, a new interpretation of God, a new heaven, a millenium of peace, love and holiness

EXTRACT FROM ADDRESS AT THE FUNERAL OF ROY F. BARTLETT.

Were I asked why Electra the Beautiful should have apparently fallen out of the glorious pleiades I could not tell; but this I know, there was harmony in the sky when eight stars shown. There is harmony now when but even seven shine down upon our mortal vision.

Though unseen by us, I know the "lost to sight" must still be shining upon more glorious shores than ours.

Why the beautiful flowers of summer must fade and die and lay their heads upon the sympathetic bosom of Mother Earth, I cannot fathom, but of this I am assured, the kind Father so orders it in his infinite love for the harmonious symmetry of all created things.

I do know there is harmony in all God's creations. When the "morning stars first sang together" all creation joined in the grand Diapason. The soughing of the gentle zephyrs, the thunder of the cataract, the deep voiced thunder, all blended with the timid note of the sweet songster of the heavens, in one universal harmonious hymn of praise.

Why the good Father should have covered this earth of ours with beautiful trees and flowers in the ages past, and then have swept them all away and hidden them in the ocean's depths for the future use of his created man, I cannot tell; but it was God's way of supplying man with needful things, and must be right. There was nothing lost. Angels must have wept o'er the scene of desolation, but out of it all comes light and joy to man.

God's love is manifested in it.

The harmony of his government was not impaired, and it is well.

Should you ask me why that divine teacher, sent by the beneficent Father to lead them into all truth, and interpret to them the mysteries of nature's laws, who came to feed the hungering multitude, to triumph over wave and wind, to heal the sick and raise the sleeping dead, who came to heal man from sin and call him back to his loving Father, should have lived but three years in his divine ministrations among men, I reply I cannot tell; but this I know, he declared, amid the quaking of the earth and the rending of the temple, "It is finished." It was God's way of accomplishing man's redemption, and must be well.

But is Christ dead? Nay, he rose from the grave, he promised his disciples to be with them. He said "I will not leave you comfortless." How many mourning souls today can testify to the truth of a realization of this promise?

Earth was too narrow, too earthly, for the sphere of Christ's physical influence longer. He came to earth, left his influence here and returned to the Father's House to accomplish, in a spiritual condition, the work he had to do.

So do our dear ones come to us. They enter into our souls, become a part of ourselves and can *never* die to us. We may lay the house they live in in the tomb; but they are not there, they are still in our hearts.

"There is no death! The stars go down
  To rise upon some fairer shore;
And bright in heaven's jewelled crown
  They shine forever more."

"There is no death! The dust we tread
  Shall change beneath the summer showers
To golden grain or mellowed fruit,
  Or rainbow-tinted flowers."

The granite rocks disorganize,
  And feed the hungry moss they bear;
The forest leaves drink daily life,
  From out the viewless air."

"There is no death! The leaves may fall,
  And flowers may fade and pass away;
They only wait, through wintry hours,
  The coming of the May."

"There is no death! An angel form
  Walks o'er the earth with silent tread;
He bears our best loved things away;
  And then we call them dead."

"He leaves our hearts all desolate,
  He plucks our fairest, sweetest flowers;
Transported into bliss, they now
  Adorn immortal bowers."

"The bird-like voice, whose joyous tones
  Made glad these scenes of sin and strife,
Sings now an everlasting song,
  Around the tree of life."

"Where'er he sees a smile too bright,
  Or heart too pure for taint or vice,
He bears it to that world of light,
  To dwell in Paradise."

"Born into that undying life,
  They leave us but to come again;
With joy we welcome them the same,
  Except their sin and pain."

"And ever near us, though unseen,
The dear, immortal spirits tread;
For all the boundless universe
Is life. *There are no dead.*"

Your son, my dear friends, is no less yours because he can no longer sit at your table and gladden your physical eyes. Is all the care and love bestowed upon him lost? By no means— all these things are immortal, because they are a part of the undying soul. Though you may feel like writing upon his tombstone, "'How many hopes lie buried here," yet remember, dear friends, though hopes may perish, possibilities on which hopes are built can never die. These live somewhere—are ours still by faith now, and by fruition hereafter.

Purity can never die. God takes the influence of every pure life and scatters it, like sweet incense, over the whole community.

Honesty can never die. The will of the Almighty immortalizes it. Nor can men die; but they pass over to other scenes in their active life, leaving their influence,—yea, *all* that they were, and thought, and planned as an immortal memorial among men. But the spirit has passed to its own natural condition—the spiritual.

"But the universal toll
Is the outward garb which the hand of God
Has flung around the soul."

Roy Bartlett can never die. "The "outer garb" lies before us but to the dear family, to those who loved the noble and the true, who admire manly character and lofty aspirations, he can never die.

He accomplished life's mission.

"That life is long that answers life's great end." Happy is he who can, in a brief period of years, accomplish what three-score years and ten can only do with many anxious souls.

He was a remarkable young man. Possessed of more than ordinary natural ability, endowed with an inherent love for the noble and the true, cherishing high aims and ambitions, he added a steadfastness oi purpose which would have led to a high position in the world.   Selfishness was no part of his nature, nothing low or base could appertain to his upright soul.

A devoted son, loving those who loved him so fervently with all his heart, a faithful student a friend that never failed, he has left to all a rich legacy of worth, worthy of tears and everlasting remembrance.

CHAPTER XXIX.

BRIDGEWATER.

My youngest and latest child is the High School at Bridgewater. I spend six hours a day with the boys and girls at the high school building, and the evening with the boys and girls of my younger days in my "Chamber of Imagery."

The school at Bridgewater is a very pleasant one. One of the committee and the superintendent were my scholars at Houlton. Their children are now my pupils. There are about forty scholars, among them several teachers. Bridgewater is a very pleasant town in which to teach. The people are cordial, and the school unusually bright, pleasant, and enjoyable.

My readers need remember, if this production is not very brilliant, that it was written in the night, after days of teaching. I wonder if in six weeks more I shall write at the close of my last school report—"Finis." I think not; provided health and strength and brain remain as at the present time. I have been so long with the girls and boys that no other association seems fitting. I seem to need the exhilarating influence exhaling from their hopeful, sunny, joyous hearts.

There is, at this period of my life, an interest in youth never felt fully at an earlier date. At sixty-five one can look back over the way and discover the glorious successes, and lamentable failures in the lives of former pupils. A retrospective view of this field causes the teacher of advanced age to feel all the deeper the possibilities wrapped up in the hidden future of those immortal souls committed to his care. Now he knows that some of those before him will become bright lights in the world, a power for good, a force injected into the mighty influence emanating from God, flowing down through the ages, washing away the follies of the darker days, and ushering in the Millennium Dawn.

He sees now that the quiet boy before his eyes may make a name that many thousands will honor; that another may so live that the only tears he will ever cause to flow, will fall on his bier, as the surviving multitudes pass by; still another may find ways and means to alleviate human suffering, help the needy and "rescue the fallen."

Looking out over those bright faces, that teacher can see a half century of time stretching out before him, a brighter day than he ever knew, a civilization more nearly ideal, a Christianity more Christ-like; a conception of the Father more in keeping with his will as revealed in nature; a recognition of a more universal love for the pure, the beautiful, and the good; a more general desire in human souls to rise above mediocre, a public conscience taking the Sermon on the Mount as the unchanging standard of right, spurning every unholy act in the political world; a toleration in religious matters that will make angels rejoice; a Good Samaritan at every street corner, and a Moses in every dark Egypt; a humanitarianism recognizing the divine rights of every man; a scientific world, conserving more of the forces of inexhaustible nature, an ethical condition in which the unsolved mysteries of this age shall be proclaimed from the house-tops;—all this and much more he sees, and knows that these will become factors in the "new earth" to be. And, alas! he also knows there may be some who,—God forbid,—may cause many hearts to bleed, may bring misery upon the world and close a life of sin in wretchedness and shame; that the bright, pure souls now so child-like, may become the rendezvous of all that is vile, debasing, Satan-tainted.

It is well that the teacher cannot fully realize the full responsibilities resting upon him as he stands before that school. He would be so appalled that he would hesitate to assume the position. He is aware he gives to those pupils just what he has, as Peter did to the lame man.

All that is in his soul becomes known to them whether he will or not. Nay, those plastic recipients will discover in his heart that which he himself knew not of.

But he should feel it to a degree, and carry to that school the brain that can instruct them; the love that will infold them; the heart whose secret thought will enoble their lives when infused into them. There does, every hour, come to me, at this time of life, as I look over the schoolroom, brighter visions of the possibilities awaiting that group of hopeful young souls. When I consider the undying influence of a truly good man or woman, how the good they do, in ever-widening circles, like the waves of the sea, goes on and on, till other spheres are blessed by the benign graciousness of a Christ-like deed,—I can see, in that studious boy; the deep thinker of the coming age, the philosopher to whom nature shall reveal mysteries so long sought for in vain.

Another stands before me as the prophetic statesman who sacrifices every personal desire that liberty, justice, and righteousness may prevail. That boy with thoughtful mien is a Wesley in embryo, or a Spurgeon. I can see the stores closed, the workshops idle, and tears falling like April showers, as a sorrowing people gather around the casket of a man the world loved, that man a boy now in school. The lawyer and judge, the doctor and clergyman, the painter and poet, the artisan and farmer, the teacher, the merchant, the soldier leading his country's army to victory; the admiral, making immortal the nation's arms, the martyr dying that others may live.

I can see in that timid, modest girl a woman, gracing a home where refinement reigns queen, where heaven almost seems to reflect itself, where Happiness and peace, looking in, declare: "This is Home!"

I see in another a Martha, standing beside the bed of pain, with hands filled and heart overflowing. Again I see, standing before assembled multitudes, a woman to whom God has especially spoken, leading men and women upward to higher and better lives. I see Mary sitting at the feet of the Great Master, qualifying herself for his service and to serve humanity.

These are but a few; but other visions arise, oh how different! To these I shut my eyes, and pray God that the realities may never come.

In reviewing life's work, I see much to regret, much I would fain forget. My life has been nothing like I had planned. Of financial ability I had but little. Of an ability to work I had a large amount; have been able to do hard mental work for twelve hours a day, for weeks; and I cannot discover any diminution of that ability. I have never pretended to be a genius, whatever I have accomplished is the result of work. I have always liked mental exercise, and have rarely become tired.

Whether I should have been a success as a lawyer, no one can tell. Think perhaps I may have been; my mind has a logical element in it necessary for a lawyer. I had ability to study, another requisite; but whether I had the faculty of combining theory and fact, of applying law to particular facts, is an unsolved problem.

I do not think I should have succeeded as a pastor. There was too much of the schoolmaster about me. There would have been, I am afraid, friction between pew and pulpit when the church became sluggish.

I am content if those with whom I have been connected recognize in me a man who has done aught to encourage, assist, guide and develop. If I have ever been a force awakening the dormant energies of any, an influence leading to a more useful life, an active quickening, undying impulse to attain something grand in the world, a moral power that has appealed to the soul, and led to better lives, and toward God; then I feel that life has not been wasted. God knows if these things have been true.

If I should write my own epitaph, I would, perhaps, write but one word upon the head-stone,—"Hamlet." A man who knew he had great duties to do, and recognized in some degree that he had the ability to accomplish them ; but, somehow, could never reach the plain on which those duties lie. The circum stances of life, the lack of courage, distrust of ability, an indefinable something, physical disability—all these have stood between many a man and the duty that follow him through life.

But I am content to let the boys and girls whom I have lived with, whom I have loved as my own, for whose welfare I have been so solicitous, whose lives and careers I have watched with almost parental care, write my epitaph.

I feel sure, if they could all stand around the "narrow house" when the bell shall be rung by other hands than mine, and school is dismissed, and the last good-bye is spoken, forgiving whatever was not pleasant in the by-gone days, letting time obliterate all but what is sweet to remember; they will not let me wholly die. *"Exegi monumentum aere perennium"* if I can but live in human souls, and could I arrange those services, no word should be spoken there, no song sung, no prayer offered except by those who knew me best, and whom I had taught and loved.

CPSIA information can be obtained at www.ICGtesting.com
Printed in the USA
BVOW10s1140190715

409416BV00013B/461/P